LA

WITHDRAWN

The Economics and the Ethics
of Constitutional Order

The Economics and the Ethics of Constitutional Order

James M. Buchanan

Ann Arbor

The University of Michigan Press

1994   1993   1992   1991   4   3   2   1

Library of Congress Cataloging-in-Publication Data

Buchanan, James M.
    The economics and the ethics of constitutional order / James M.
Buchanan.
        p.   cm.
    Includes bibliographical references.
    ISBN 0-472-10222-2 (alk. paper)
    1. Economics—Political aspects.   2. Economics—Moral and ethical
aspects.   3. Free enterprise.   4. Social contract.   I. Title.
HB73.B83   1991
330—dc20   90-26666
                                                                CIP

Preface

The initial subtitle of this volume was descriptive, "Post-Nobel Essays in Political Economy," and was designed to suggest that the separately written essays are temporally connected. Essentially all that I have written to date since the announcement of the Nobel Memorial Prize award in October, 1986, is included here. The exceptions are autobiographical essays that will ultimately be put together in another volume, a few policy-oriented pieces with no permanent shelf life, and, finally, occasional papers on aberrant themes (each of which involved a commitment mistake).

The temporal proximity alone would insure at least some integration. I would have found it difficult to shift my interest widely and for long within the three-year period during which these essays were written. The opposing danger lies, of course, in the prospect of redundancy and repetition. The essays were independently composed for specific purposes; they contain, I hope, a minimally necessary reiteration of my central themes and ideas. And there is a corollary benefit that stems from the fact that each essay can be read separately.

Eighteen of the twenty essays were prepared expressly in response to post-Nobel invitations to present lectures or to offer papers in conferences. To the extent that was possible, and within the limits of my own competence and interest, I tried, in each case, to be responsive to the presumed preferences of those who solicited my contributions. Something of the geographic spread along with the international flavor of the presentations may be suggested by a listing of the sites: Bonn, West Germany (chap. 1); Pittsburgh, Pennsylvania (chap. 2); Kalamazoo, Michigan (chap. 3); Tallahassee, Florida (chap. 4); Niagara-on-the-Lake, Canada (chap. 5); Witten-Herdecke, West Germany (chap. 6); Chicago, Illinois (chap. 7); Lugano, Switzerland (chap. 8); Christchurch, New Zealand (chap. 9); Dallas, Texas (chap. 10); Bowling Green, Ohio (chaps. 11 and 15); Santa Cruz, California (chap. 18); Alpbach, Tirol, Austria (chap. 19) and Nagoya, Japan (chap. 20).

Fourteen of the essays have been published, some in varying departures from the versions included here, in separated and isolated journals or books. Only chapter 7 has been published in a widely circulated professional journal. Despite this availability, I include the essay here because it is the only place where I have attempted to apply my approach to issues of constitutional interpretation by the judiciary. I provide precise references to published versions of the separate essays in footnotes to the chapters. At this point, general acknowledgment of required permissions to reprint the materials should suffice.

Chapter 14, on the work ethic, has commanded as much of my interest and attention over the three years as have all of the other papers combined. Shortened versions of the argument have been presented, and published, but the extended paper included here contains elements of analysis that have not been previously developed. The analysis stands as a challenge to much of the orthodoxy in neoclassical economics, and, in thi˙ sense, it must be classified as both provisional and controversial. I consider this essay to be the most important one in the volume.

Three essays that were jointly authored with my colleague, Viktor Vanberg, are included. I appreciate his willingness to allow me to include chapters 5, 6, and 12.

Because they were written for presentation to general academic audiences, the technical content of most of the essays is minimal. A general understanding of the issues in political economy and social philosophy will, of course, facilitate appreciation of the arguments. But only with chapter 16, on the important book by David Gauthier, is nonfamiliarity with the literature likely to be damaging to comprehension.

Personally, I have found it both interesting and rewarding to discover that there remains more to be said on the age-old issues that are variously discussed in these essays. And I do not, by any means, consider that the arguments are yet near to exhaustion. If my energies do not flag, during the next three years I will surely write more essays on the same and closely related themes, and especially as I begin, along with others, to absorb into my psyche the impact of the momentous events of 1989.

Colleagues have been helpful as initial critics for many of the essays; I list these colleagues inclusively here: Peter Bernholz, Geoffrey Brennan, Roger Congleton, Hartmut Kliemt, David Levy, Jennifer Roback, Robert Tollison, Viktor Vanberg, Karen Vaughn, Richard Wagner, and Jack Wiseman. And, as usual for my books, my longtime assistant, Betty Tillman has kept me sufficiently organized to produce the papers here. I should also acknowledge the aid of Jo Ann Burgess, whose ability to rescue and revise drafts through the magic of electronics continues to amaze me.

Contents

Part 1
Political Economy and Constitutional Order

CHAPTER 1

The Domain of Constitutional
Political Economy

Richard B. McKenzie introduced the term, "constitutional economics,"[1] to define the central subject matter of a conference that he organized in Washington, D.C., in 1982. In his fortuitous addition of the adjective "constitutional" to the familiar disciplinary base, McKenzie provided precisely the combination of meaning that was needed to identify and to isolate a research program that had emerged as an integral, but distinguishable, part of the subdiscipline of public choice over the three decades of the latter's existence. "Constitutional politics" calls attention to the relevant subject phenomena but fails to convey the relevance and applicability of Economics, as a disciplinary base, in the examination and evaluation of the foundational rules of social order. By borrowing McKenzie's term, I was then able to suggest, and later to write, an extended entry on "Constitutional Economics" for *The New Palgrave*.[2] With these beginnings, the ongoing research program (which is readily translatable into the more inclusive "Constitutional Political Economy") attained full semantic legitimacy in the 1980s. The journal, *Constitutional Political Economy*, became the institutionalized complement.

This chapter describes the domain of the still emerging research program, the boundaries of which must be considered to be sufficiently provisional to allow for analytical developments along any of several now nonpredictable dimensions. My first task is to clarify the separate parts of the name itself, and to distinguish the usage of the partial terms from other applications. "Constitutional" economics must be shown to be different from "nonconstitutional," "orthodox," or "standard" economics. At the same time, constitutional "economics" must be shown to be different from constitutional "politics," as the latter may be commonly understood. Sections 1 and 2 are

---

A modified version of this chapter, entitled "The Domain of Constitutional Economics," was published in *Constitutional Political Economy* 1 (Winter 1990): 1–18.

1. Richard B. McKenzie, ed., *Constitutional Economics* (Lexington, Mass.: Lexington Books, 1984).

2. James M. Buchanan, "Constitutional Economics," in *The New Palgrave*, ed. John Eatwell, Murray Milgate, and Peter Newman (London: Macmillan, 1987).

designed to accomplish this task. My second task is to place or to locate constitutional political economy within a more inclusive intellectual tradition, and in particular in relation to classical political economy and contractarian political philosophy (sec. 3). My third self-assigned task, attempted in section 4, is to expose for criticism and to defend the central philosophical presuppositions upon which the whole constitutional economics enterprise rests. Section 5 introduces some of the more controversial issues concerning the role that perception, vision, and belief must play in constitutional economics, as in other areas of social inquiry. And I should note that some of the arguments advanced in this section may be viewed as personally idiosyncratic, even by some of my fellow constitutional political economists. It is also here that nonsympathetic critics may suggest, appropriately, that in some ultimate sense the whole enterprise is normative. This normative grounding must not, however, be used to deny the relevance of the wholly positive analyses that compare alternative structures from within the perspective defined by the hard core of the research program. The whole inquiry involves the study of rules, how rules work, and how rules might be chosen. But any such effort may be meaningless without some stipulation of the game that the rules are to describe.

1. Constitutional and Nonconstitutional Economics

There is a categorical distinction to be made between constitutional economics and nonconstitutional, or ordinary, economics, a distinction in the ultimate behavioral object of analytical attention. In one sense, all of economics is about choice, and about the varying and complex institutional arrangements within which individuals make choices among alternatives. In ordinary or orthodox economics, no matter how simple or how complex, analysis is concentrated on choices made within constraints that are, themselves, imposed exogenously to the person or persons charged with making the choice. The constraints that restrict the set of feasible choice options may be imposed by nature, by history, by a sequence of past choices, by other persons, by laws and institutional arrangements, or even by custom and convention. In the elementary textbook formulation of demand theory, for example, the individual consumer-purchaser confronts a range of goods available at a set of prices, but is restricted by the size of the budget. This budget is not within the choice set of the consumer-purchaser during the period of choice under scrutiny. Indeed it would seem unnatural or bizarre, within the mind-set fostered by ordinary economics, to consider the prospect that an individual might deliberately choose to constrain or limit the set of available choice options. Within this mind-set, the utility of the chooser is always maximized by allowing for choices over the whole range allowed by the exogenously determined constraints.

It is precisely at this critical point that constitutional economics, in its most inclusive definition, departs from the conventional framework of analysis. Constitutional economics directs analytical attention to the *choice among constraints*. Once stated in this fashion, economists will recognize that there is relatively little in their established canon that will assist in analyzing choices of this sort. To orthodox economists, only the elementary reality of scarcity makes choice necessary: Without scarcity there would be no need to choose. And it would appear to be both methodologically and descriptively absurd to introduce the artificial creation of scarcity as an object for behavioral analysis. Such bedrock conservatism presumably explains much of ordinary economists' inattention and disinterest in constitutional questions, at all levels.

If we move beyond the models of orthodox economics, however, even while remaining at the level of individual behavior, we observe that individuals do, in fact, choose their own constraints, at least to a degree and within some limits. Within recent decades, a few innovative thinkers from economics and other social sciences have begun studying the choice processes that are involved here (Elster, Schelling, Shefrin, Thaler).[3] The "economics of self-control" has reached the status of a respectable, if minor, research program, which may be destined to become more important in this era of emphasis on diet, exercise, health, and the environment. We must surely be sufficiently catholic to allow analysis in this "individual constitutional economics" to qualify for inclusion in the domain.

As they carry on within their own guaranteed private spaces, however, individuals would presumably subject themselves to a relatively small set of prior constraints. Individuals basically "trust themselves" to choose rationally when confronted with the externally imposed constraints that are dictated in their historically emergent conditions. If the choice among constraints, in all its complexity, is limited to the economics of self-control, or stated conversely, to the economics of temptation, there might be little to be gained in delineating a constitutional economics enterprise.

It is essential to acknowledge, near the outset of discussion, that individuals choose to impose constraints or limits on their own behavior, primarily, even if not exclusively, as part of an "exchange." The restrictions on their own

---

3. Jon Elster, *Ulysses and the Sirens* (Cambridge: Cambridge University Press, 1979); Thomas Schelling, "Egonomics, or the Art of Self-Management," *American Economic Review* 68 (May 1978): 290–94; Richard Thaler and H. M. Shefrin, "An Economic Theory of Self-Control," *Journal of Political Economy* 89 (April 1981): 392–406.

actions are accepted in return for the benefits that are anticipated from the reciprocally extended restrictions on the actions of others with whom they interact along the boundaries of private spaces and within the confines of acknowledged public spaces. That is to say, a domain of constitutional economics would exist even if individuals, in their private spaces, chose never to impose constraints on their own behavior. Note that by interpreting the individual's choice of a generalized constraint that restricts the actions both of others and himself or herself as a part of a reciprocal exchange, we have moved toward the familiar domain of orthodox economics. So interpreted, the individual who joins in a collective decision to impose a generally applied constitutional rule is not, at base, acting differently from observed behavior in a setting that involves giving up one desired good, apples, for another desired good, oranges. In the latter example, we can, without violating the meaning of words, say that the individual chooses to constrain, or to limit, the potential consumption of apples in exchange for the expanded opportunity to consume oranges. Expressed in this way, all that is required is that we classify the restrictions on others' actions as "goods" in the individual's preference function along with the more natural classification or restrictions on his or her own actions as "bads."

In this simplistic and individualistic perspective, the choice of a reciprocally binding constraint by individuals who are related one to another in an anticipated set of interactions becomes fully analogous to trade in ordinary goods and services, and, so treated, becomes quite different from the choice of a self-imposed constraint in the much more difficult economics of self-control, briefly discussed above.

Why have the practitioners of orthodox economics seemed so reluctant to extend analysis to include the reciprocal exchanges of liberties that are central to the domain of constitutional economics?

I can advance several related reasons. Economists, along with their peers in the other social sciences as well as other academic disciplines, have had no difficulty through the ages in implicitly classifying restrictions on some of the activities of some persons in the body politic to be "good." But the classification procedure has been quite different from the subjective evaluations presumed to be embodied in individuals' preference functions. The nonconstrained voluntary behavior is not classified to be "bad" because an individual simply disprefers such behavior in the ordinary way. Some such behavior is deemed to be "bad," and hence its rectification to be "good," on the basis of an externally derived criterion of "goodness" or "truth." The attributes or qualities of "goodness" and/or "badness" applied to actions of persons are treated as if they are intrinsically public, in the Samuelsonion taxonomic sense. An action cannot, properly, be adjudged to be "good" by one person without an implied generalization of such judgment to other persons. In this conceptualization, persons must, ideally, be brought into agreement on some ultimate classification of actions through a process that resembles scientific discourse. Agreement does not emerge from a trading process where differing interests are essentially compromised, with each party reckoning to enjoy some benefits while suffering some sacrifice of preferred position.

In some respects, it is surprising that economists have "jumped out" of their own analytical framework so readily when they consider the possible imposition of generalized constraints on behavior. They have expressed little curiosity in deriving justification for such constraints from a calculus of individual interests. Economists have, instead, been willing intellectual captives of idealistic political philosophers, and they have readily embraced variants of the Platonic and Hegelian mind-sets. Amartya Sen's use of the term "meddlesome preferences,"[4] by sharp contrast with such terms as "merit goods" and "merit wants," tends to focus analysis back toward a straightforward calculus of interests and away from nonindividualistic attributes of either goods or actions.

A second, and related, reason for economists' general failure to use the exchange setting when they consider the possible imposition of generalized constraints on individual behavior lies in the methodological dominance of the maximization paradigm. In the latter, "the economic problem" is defined as one of allocating scarce means (resources) among alternative ends. Choice is made necessary by the scarcity of means, and that which is desired (utility) is maximized when like units of resources yield equivalent returns in all uses to which they are put. In this elementary formulation, emphasis is almost exclusively placed on the choices that are made within the scarcity constraints that are, themselves, presumed to be beyond the scope for chooser selection. There is little or no attention paid to the identification of the choosing unit in this abstracted definition, and this feature allows for a relatively unnoticed transference of analysis from individual choice to "social" or "collective" choice on the basis of some implicit presumption that collectivities choose analogously to individuals.

This shift from individual to supraindividual choice was supported, and indirectly justified, by the emergence of macroaggregation and macroeconomic theory and policy during the early decades of the post-Robbins half-century. Target levels of macroaggregates (national product, rates of growth, levels of employment) were established to be objectively "good" and to serve as guideposts for choices to be made by collective entities (governments) subject only to the constraints imposed by natural scarcities and tech-

---

4. Amartya K. Sen, "The Impossibility of a Paretian Liberal," *Journal of Political Economy* 78 (January-February 1970): 152–57.

nological limits. By some implicit extension of the model for individual choice behavior, constrained only by external forces, governments came to be viewed romantically and were deemed capable of achieving "good," as defined for them by the economists and other social philosophers. Microeconomists had long been ready at hand to proffer policy advice to governments concerning ways and means to promote greater overall efficiency in the economy.

A third reason for economists' general failure to extend their analytical apparatus to the derivation of institutional-constitutional structure is to be found in their presumption that structural constraints are not, themselves, subject to deliberative choice, and, hence, to change. Economists have not neglected to recognize the relevance of institutional rules in affecting patterns of human behavior. Property-rights economics, in particular,[5] has opened up a research program that concentrates attention directly on the effects of alternative structures. For the most part, however, the emphasis here is on existing arrangements rather than on the comparative analysis involved in an extension to structures that might be designed and implemented.

Constitutional economics differs from nonconstitutional or orthodox economics along each of the dimensions that may be inferred from the reasons for neglect detailed above. Analysis is consistently individualistic, in the several senses that are relevant. The derivation of institutional constraints is based on a calculus of individual interests, which, in turn, requires the introduction and use of an exchange paradigm as opposed to the idealists' search for the unique "good." Furthermore, there is no extension of the choice calculus from the individual to collectivities, as such. Collective "choice" is factored down into the participatory behavior of individual members. Finally, emphasis is centered directly on the selection of rules, or institutions, that will, in turn, limit the behavior of the persons who operate within them. Institutions, defined broadly, are variables subject to deliberative evaluation and to explicit choice.[6]

As noted, at one extreme, constitutional analysis may be applied to the individual in total isolation, who may act solely in private space. At the other extreme, constitutional analysis is applied to the whole set of persons who make up the membership of the polity. This subcategory of research emphasis is the most familiar, since the very word *constitutional* tends to convey political connotations. The derivation of constraints on government does, indeed, occupy much of our attention. But the inclusive domain of constitutional economics also includes the derivation, analysis of, and justificatory argu-

---

5. Armen Alchian, *Economic Forces at Work* (Indianapolis: Indianapolis Liberty Press, 1977).

6. James M. Buchanan and Gordon Tullock, *The Calculus of Consent: Logical Foundations of Constitutional Democracy* (Ann Arbor: University of Michigan Press, 1962).

ment for rules that constrain both individual and collective behavior in a wide array of membership groupings, larger than the one-unit limit but smaller than the all inclusive limit of the whole polity. Clubs, trade unions, corporations, parties, universities, associations—these, and many more—exist and operate under constitutions that are amenable to scientific inquiry.

2. Constitutional "Economics" and Constitutional "Politics"

In section 1, I attempted to distinguish between constitutional and nonconstitutional economics. I propose, in section 2, to distinguish between constitutional "economics" and constitutional "politics," as the latter term may be generally and widely interpreted. As I have noted, most constitutional inquiry and analysis is concentrated at the level of the politically organized collectivity and is, in this sense, political. The distinction to be emphasized, however, is one of perspective rather than one that relates directly to either the form of organization or to the type of activity. If an exchange rather than a maximizing paradigm is taken to be descriptive of the inclusive research program for the discipline, then "economics" involves inquiry into *cooperative* arrangements for human interaction, extending from the simplest of two-person, two-good trading processes through the most complex, quasi-constitutional arrangements for multinational organizations. As noted in section 1, orthodox economics has rarely been extended to noncommercial or political activity, as such, but the exchange perspective readily allows this step to be taken.

The cooperative perspective, however, must be categorically distinguished from the contrasting *conflictual* perspective, which has been applied, almost automatically, to all political interactions, whether or not these are classified as constitutional. It will be useful here to examine the differences between the cooperative and the conflictual perspectives more carefully. The very term *politics* tends to conjure up a mental image of potential conflict among those persons who are members of the politically organized community. This conflict may be interpreted to be analogous to scientific disputes, in which separate participants or groups seek to convince one another of the "truth" of their advanced propositions. The age-old tradition of idealism in political philosophy conceives of all politics in this light, and, as noted earlier, the dominance of this model of politics has tended to discourage economists from political extensions of the exchange or cooperative paradigm. But, even if the teleological interpretation is rejected, politics may seem, by its very nature, to involve conflict between and among individuals and groups within a polity.

From the institutionally determined characteristics of collective decisions, the characteristics that dictate mutual exclusivity among the alternatives for selection (only one candidate can be electorally chosen) imply some ultimate division of the membership into two subsets, "winners" and "losers." This perspective almost directly suggests that politics is primarily, if not exclusively, a distributional game or enterprise, a process that involves transfers of value (utility) among and between separately identified coalitions of persons.

Note that the predominance of the distributional elements in the conflictual model of politics need not imply that the game be zero sum, although this limiting case may be useful for some analytical purposes. Conflictual politics may be positive, zero, or negative sum, as gains and losses are somehow aggregated over all participants (members). And this seems to be the natural model for analyzing politics so long as rules for reaching collective decisions require less than full agreement. If a majority, whether simple or qualified, is allowed to be decisive and impose its will on a minority, then the observed opposition of the minority to the alternative preferred by the majority can be taken to indicate that members of the minority expect to suffer utility losses, at least in a lost opportunity sense. In this model of conflictual politics, which appears to be descriptive of ordinary political activity, there seems to be no direct way of introducing a cooperative interpretation. A necessary condition for cooperation in social interaction is the prospect for positive expected gains by all parties, or, in the gainer-loser terminology, the prospect that there be no net losers. As a first descriptive cut, this condition seems to be foreign to the whole political enterprise.

It is precisely at this point, however, that constitutional politics, or politics at the constitutional level of choices among alternative sets of basic rules or constraints, rescues the cooperative model, at least in some potential explanatory and normative sense. As it operates and as we observe it to operate, ordinary politics may remain conflictual, in the manner noted above, while participation in the inclusive political game that defines the rules for ordinary politics may embody positively valued prospects for all members of the polity. In other words, constitutional politics does lend itself to examination in a cooperative analytical framework, while ordinary politics continues to lend itself to analysis that employs conflict models of interaction.

Generalized.agreement on constitutional rules that allow for the reaching of ordinary collective decisions by means that do not require general agreement is surely possible, as is empirically demonstrated in the context of almost all organizations. The analytical-scientific inquiry that involves comparisons of the working properties of alternative sets of rules along with the examination of processes through which agreement on rules may be attained defines the domain of primary concern. The use of the terminology "constitutional economics" or "constitutional political economy" rather than the somewhat more accurate "constitutional politics" is prompted by the linkage in scientific heritage between "economics" and "cooperation," by the inference of the appropriateness of the exchange, as opposed to the conflict, paradigm.

3. The Intellectual Traditions of Constitutional Political Economy

In sections 1 and 2, I attempted to set the research program in Constitutional Political Economy apart from ongoing programs within the interrelated and more inclusive disciplines of economics and political science. It would be totally misleading, however, to infer from my discussion that this research program has emerged full blown, as if divorced from any traditions of intellectual inquiry. As I have noted, constitutional economics, in its modern variant, did indeed blossom only in the second half of this century. But the program was not based either on a new scientific discovery, at least as usually defined, or on a new set of analytical tools. Constitutional Political Economy is best interpreted as a reemphasis, a revival, a rediscovery, of basic elements of earlier intellectual traditions that have been set aside, neglected, and sometimes forgotten in the social sciences and social philosophy.

These traditions are those of classical political economy and contractarian political philosophy. It will be useful to discuss each of these traditions briefly.

Classical political economy, represented especially in the works of Adam Smith,[7] was directed toward offering an explanation and understanding of how an economy (set of markets) would work without detailed political interventions and control. Smith's aim was to demonstrate that the *wealth* of the nation would be larger under a regime of minimal politicization than under the alternative closely controlled mercantilist regime. And the whole thrust of the argument was to the effect that all groups in the economy, especially the laboring classes, could be expected to share in the benefits promised upon the shift in regimes. The emphasis was on the generalization of expected gains over all persons and classes. The suggested change in the structure, or basic rules, that depoliticization involved was, therefore, within the feasible limits of potential agreement by all parties. The normative focus, again especially in Adam Smith, was not explicitly distributional. Only with the Marxist extensions of Ricardo's abstract analysis did interclass conflict enter into classical attention.

It is also important to recognize that the Smithean emphasis was not allocational in the modern economists' meaning of this term. The analysis was not designed to show that economic resources would be more effectively allocated to higher valued uses under a market than under a politicized re-

---

7. Adam Smith, *The Wealth of Nations* (New York: Random House, 1937).

gime, as measured by some external and objective standard of value. The aim was, instead, to show that the market order would allocate resources such that the evaluations (preferences) of individuals would be more fully satisfied, *regardless of what these evaluations might be.* In terms of his familiar example of the butcher, Smith's lesson was to show that self-interest in the marketplace works to supply meat for supper, provided that meat is what consumers want. There is no implication here that self-interest in the marketplace works to supply meat because meat is valuable in some nutritional sense as defined by experts.

So interpreted, therefore, Adam Smith's enterprise falls squarely within the domain of constitutional political economy. In a strictly positive sense, his analysis described both how the existing regime worked and how an alternative regime might work. And, since the alternative seemed to generate more wealth to all parties, as measured by their own standards, the normative extension of the positive analysis was quite straightforward. In this extension, the object upon which collective attention must be placed is the set of rules or constraints within which persons behave in their capacities as consumers-buyers and producers-sellers. The "laws and institutions" that define the economic-political order become the variables subject to possible adjustment and reform.

I have, in the immediately preceding paragraphs, selected elements from the tradition of classical political economy that seem to provide precursory foundations for the modern research program in Constitutional Political Economy. My treatment would surely be accused of bias, however, if I failed to indicate the presence of considerable ambiguity and confusion in the philosophical underpinnings of the classical economics enterprise. An interpretation of that enterprise in terms of classical utilitarianism would be quite different from my own; this alternative interpretation would stress quite separate elements of the tradition. The interpersonal comparability and aggregate measurability of utility were not explicitly rejected by the classical economists and, in a selected reading, these may be attributed, as presumptions, to their analyses. In this case, the whole enterprise becomes precursory to the maximizing rather than to the exchange paradigm in economics, with both allocational and distributional implications, and with a wholly different avenue for moving from the individual to the collective levels of choice. The categorical distinction between choices among rules and choices within rules all but disappears in the utilitarian configuration.

The elements of Adam Smith's intellectual enterprise become directly precursory to the research program in constitutional economics only when these elements are imbedded within the tradition of contractarian political philosophy, the tradition that was developed prior to, but became competitive with and quite different from, classical utilitarianism. From the seventeenth century, from the works of Althusius, Hobbes, Spinoza, and Locke[8] in particular, attempts were made to ground justificatory argument for state coercion on agreement by those individuals who are subject to coercion. This intellectual tradition invented the autonomous individual by shucking off the communitarian cocoon. The assignment to the individual of a capacity for rational independent choice, as such, allowed a "science" of economics and politics to emerge, a "science" that embodied a legitimatizing explanation for the emergence and existence of the state. In agreeing to be governed, explicitly or implicitly, the individual exchanges his or her own liberty with others who similarly give up liberties in exchange for the benefits offered by a regime characterized by behavioral limits.

The contractarian logic leaves open any specification of the range and scope for agreed upon coercive authority. The early contractarians and notably Hobbes, had no understanding of the efficacy of market order, as it might function under the umbrella of the protective or minimal state. This understanding was provided only in the eighteenth century and was fully articulated only in the great work of Adam Smith. Classical political economy, as appended to contractarian intellectual foundations, allowed the development of a scientifically based analysis aimed at comparing alternative structures of political-legal order, analysis that could introduce and use principles of rational choice behavior of individuals and without resort to supraindividualistic norms. Utilitarianism also rejected all supraindividual norms, as such, and grounded all norms in a calculus of pleasure and pain. Nonetheless, this Benthamite intrusion created ambiguity in the efforts to add up utilities over persons. In this way, the contractarian justification derived from conceptual agreement was obscured, and the way was opened for a nontranscendental utilitarian supersession of individualistic norms. The contractarian philosophical basis upon which classical political economy should have been exclusively developed was, at least partially, undermined and neglected for almost two centuries, only to be rediscovered in the research program of constitutional economics.

4. The Hard Core and Its Critics

Throughout this chapter I have referred to Constitutional Economics or Constitutional Political Economy as a *research program*, thereby deliberately using the Lakatosian classification. In this scheme, there exist elements in the hard core of the program that are rarely, if ever, challenged by those scholars

---

8. J. Althusius, *Politica methodice digesta* (1603), ed. C. J. Friedrich (Cambridge, Mass.: Harvard University Press, 1932); Thomas Hobbes, *Leviathan* (London: Everymans Library, 1943); John Locke, *Second Treatise of Civil Government* (Chicago: Gateway, 1955); B. Spinoza, *A Treatise in Politics*, trans. William McCall (London: Holyoake, 1854).

who work inside the intellectual tradition defined by the program. These central elements are taken as presuppositions, as relatively absolute absolutes, and, as such, they become, themselves, the constraints (the constitution) within which the scientific discourse is conducted. External intellectual challenges to the whole enterprise tend to be directed at these elements in the core of the program. The ongoing research within the constraints can, of course, proceed without concern for these external criticisms, but practitioners need to be aware of the core-imposed limits on the persuasive potential of the internalized analytical exercise.

For constitutional economics, the foundational position is summarized in *methodological individualism*. Unless those who would be participants in the scientific dialogue are willing to locate the exercise in the choice calculus of individuals, qua individuals, there can be no departure from the starting gate. The autonomous individual is a sine qua non for any initiation of serious inquiry in the research program. Individual autonomy, as a defining quality, does not, however, imply that the individual chooses and acts as if he or she exists in isolation from and apart from the community or communities of other persons with whom he or she may be variously associated. Any form of community or association of individuals may reflect some sharing of values, and, further, any individual's formation of values may be influenced by the values of those with whom he or she is variously associated in communities. The communitarian challenge to methodological individualism must go beyond the claim that individuals influence one another reciprocally through presence in communities. The challenge must make the stronger claim that individuation, the separation of the individual from community, is not conceptually possible, that it becomes meaningless to think of potential divergence between and among individual interests in a commınity. Stated in this way, it is evident that methodological individualism, as a presupposition of inquiry, characterizes almost all research programs in economics and political science; constitutional economics does not depart from its more inclusive disciplinary bases in this respect.

The communitarian critique does not often appear in such blatant guise. For constitutional economics, in particular, the critique apparently leaves the individualistic postulates unchallenged, while either implicitly or explicitly asserting the existence of some supraindividualistic source of evaluation. Individual evaluations are superceded by those emergent from God, natural law, right reason, or the State. This more subtle stance rejects methodological individualism, not on the claim that individuation is impossible or that individual evaluations may not differ within a community, but rather on the claim that it is normatively improper to derive collective action from individual evaluations. To the communitarian who posits the existence of some supraindividualistic scale of values, the whole analysis that builds on a base of an individualistic calculus can only be useful as an input in schemes of control and manipulation designed to align individualized preferences with those orderings dictated by the overarching norms for the community.

Concomitant with methodological individualism as a component of the hard core is the postulate of rational choice, a postulate that is shared over all research programs in economics. The autonomous individual is not only presumed to exist; this individual is also presumed to be capable of choosing among alternatives in a sufficiently orderly manner as to allow a quality of rationality to be attributed to observed behavior. For constitutional economics, the capacity for rational choice is extended to include a capacity to choose among constraints, both individually and collectively applied, within which subsequent choices may be made.

Rationality implies that choices may be analyzed as if an ordering of alternatives exists, arrayed in accordance with some scalar of "preferredness." We may, but need not, use the term "utility" to designate that which the individual calls upon to make up the ordinal ranking. At the analytical level, there is no need that the ranking correspond with any array of the choice alternatives that may be objectively measurable by some outside observer. The test for individual rationality in choice does require, however, the minimal step of classifying alternatives into "goods" and "bads." The central rationality precept states only that the individual choose more rather than less of "goods," and less rather than more of "bads." There is no requirement that rationality dictates choice in accordance with the individual's economic interest, as this might be measured by some outside observer of behavior.

The individualistic postulate allows the interests or preferences of individuals to differ, one from another. And the rationality postulate does not restrict these interests beyond the classificatory step noted. Homo economicus, the individual who populates the models of empirical economics may, but need not, describe the individual whose choice calculus is analyzed in constitutional political economy. When selecting among alternative constitutional constraints, however, the individual is required to make some predictions about the behavior of others than himself or herself. And, in such a setting, there is a powerful argument that suggests the appropriateness of something akin to the Homo economicus postulate for behavior.[9]

I have briefly discussed the individualistic and the rationality presuppositions of the research program. These elements are not controversial and they would be listed as components of the hard core both by practitioners and critics of constitutional economics. A less obvious element that is equally fundamental, however, involves the generalization of the individualistic and

---

9. Geoffrey Brennan and James M. Buchanan, *The Reason of Rules* (Cambridge: Cambridge University Press, 1985).

the rationality postulates to *all* persons in the political community. All individuals must be presumed capable of making rational choices among alternatives in accordance with individually autonomous value-scales. And this generalization does not allow derivation of collective action, whether or not directed toward choices among constraints, from individual evaluations on anything other than an *equal weighting*. To introduce a weighting scheme through which the evaluation of some persons in the community are deemed more important than other persons would require resort to some supraindividualistic source, which is, of course, ruled out by adherence to the individualistic postulate. In this sense, the whole of the constitutional economics research program rests squarely on a *democratic* foundation.

The identification of the elements in the hard core of the research program in constitutional economics allows for the simultaneous identification of its vulnerabilities. As noted, critics who call upon extraindividual sources of value cannot participate in the ongoing dialogue, nor can those skeptics who refuse to apply models of rational choice to the behavior of individuals as autonomous actors. To this point in its development, the program is vulnerable also in its failure to address the issue of defining membership in the community of persons over whom the postulates are to be applied. Who is to count as an autonomous individual? How are children to be treated, and at what age or stage of development does childhood cease with full membership in the community granted? How are the mentally and emotionally incompetent to be handled, and who is to decide who is incompetent? Is the community considered to be open to potential entrants?

These and related issues are relevant for inquiries in constitutional economics, but the program, by its nature, cannot address them readily. The starting point for analysis is a set of autonomous individuals, either already organized or potentially organizable in a political unit. Once the set is initially defined, the program can be extended to include examination and analysis of how the defined community itself addresses such issues. But the initial definition lies beyond the boundaries of any analytical construction within the program, as such.

5. Perception, Vision, and Faith

Nietzsche used the metaphor of viewing the world of reality through differing windows,[10] and Ortega y Gasset went so far as to define ultimate reality itself as a perspective.[11] In a sense, any research program involves a way of looking

---

10. W. Kaufman, *Nietzsche* (Princeton: Princeton University Press, 1950): 61.

11. José Ortega y Gasset, *Meditations on Quixote*, trans. Evelyn Rugg and Diego Marin (New York: Norton, 1961): 45.

at, and thereby imposing an order on, that which is perceived. This characterization applies particularly to any program in social science, where the ultimate object of inquiry is behavior in a social interaction process. I have on several occasions referred to the constitutional "perspective," which I have acknowledged to be different from other perspectives that might be used in examining and evaluating the interaction of individuals in social and/or political settings. This elementary fact, that perspectives differ or may differ, raises difficult issues in epistemology that cannot be ignored.

Consider, first, perception at its simplest level. Presumably, individuals are sufficiently alike, one to another, biologically that we see, hear, taste, smell, and feel physical phenomena similarly if not identically. We all see a wall as a barrier to movement, and no one of us makes an attempt to walk through walls. Someone who failed to perceive a wall as others do would be classified to be abnormal in at least one of the basic perceptual senses. As phenomena come to be increasingly complex, however, individuals may come to differ in their perceptions, despite the fact that, biologically, they continue to possess the same perceptual apparatus. Elementary sense perception must be accompanied by imaginative constructions that require some mental processing before a basis for evaluation, and ultimately for action, can be established.

As phenomena increase in complexity, the imaginative elements in perception increase relative to those that emerge directly from the senses. In this progression from the simple to the complex, the similarity in perceptions among persons must decrease. What may be called the "natural" way of observing phenomena fades away at some point along the spectrum. Individuals may then be brought into agreement on that which they observe only by entry into some sort of association of shared values or norms, which members, either explicitly or implicitly, choose. This statement may seem contradictory when first made; it may seem to state that persons choose how they see reality. But the statement becomes less challenging to ordinary notions when we replace "see" with "think about."

I have been accused of committing the naturalistic fallacy, in some of my own works, of failing to respect properly the fact-value, positive-normative distinction, and, hence, of deriving the "ought" from the "is," at least implicitly. I submit, however, that my critics mount such charges only because of their own confusion about the nature of perception of complex phenomena. If there exists no "natural" way of observing reality, some evaluation and choosing process is a necessary complement to the imaginative step that allows apparent chaos to be converted into order. We select the "is" that defines the hard core of our research program, and this holds true whether or not we are professional scientists. Within this "is," we can adhere strictly to the precepts laid down for positive analysis. But the normative implications that may be drawn are, indeed, derivative from the chosen perceptive framework, and could not, or would not, be otherwise available.

Constitutional economics is a domain of inquiry and discourse among scientists who choose to perceive social interaction as a set of complex relationships, both actual and potential, among autonomous persons, each of whom is capable of making rational choices. The domain, as such, cannot be extended to include inquiry by those who choose to perceive social interaction differently. There is simply no common basis for scientific argument, and ultimately agreement, with those who choose to perceive social interaction either in purely conflictual or purely idealistic visions. These visions are, indeed, alternative "windows" on the world. And the process through which individuals choose among such windows remains mysterious. How can empirical evidence be made convincing when such evidence must, itself, be perceived from only one vantage point at a time? The naïveté of modern empirical economists in this respect verges on absurdity.

When all is said and done, constitutional economics, for me, must be acknowledged to rest upon a precommitment to, or a faith in, if you will, man's cooperative potential. Persons are neither bees in hives, carnivorous beasts in a jungle, nor angels in God's heaven. They are independent units of consciousness, capable of assigning values to alternatives, and capable of choosing and acting in accordance with these values. It is both physically necessary and beneficial that they live together, in many and varying associations and communities. But to do so, they must live by rules that they can also choose.

CHAPTER 2

On the Structure of an Economy: A Reemphasis of Some Classical Foundations

The sovereign is completely discharged from a duty, in the attempting to perform which he must always be exposed to innumerable delusions, and for the proper performance of which no human wisdom or knowledge could ever be sufficient; the duty of superintending the industry of private people, and of directing it towards the employments most suitable to the interest of the society.

—Adam Smith, *The Wealth of Nations*

To those of us who share the view expressed so well by Adam Smith in my introductory citation, there is both "good news" and "bad news" in the global political economy of the early 1990s. The "good news" is reflected in the developing recognition that centrally planned economies everywhere remain glaringly inefficient, a recognition that has been accompanied by efforts to make major changes in internal incentive structures. More extensively, throughout the developed and the developing world of nations, the rhetoric of depoliticization and privatization has, occasionally, been translated into reality. The "bad" news emerges from the United States, where protectionist-mercantilist absurdities seem to be resurgent in the land.

These items prompt me to devote my attention exclusively to a restatement and reemphasis of what I think was Adam Smith's normative attitude on the structure of a national economy, and, by inference, on his attitude toward political-governmental directions for economic policy. Let me say at the outset, however, that I am not an exegetist, and that my concern is really not what Adam Smith may have said or failed to say. My concern is, instead, with articulating what I think would be a consistent position, for Adam Smith, in the context of the U.S. political economy in the 1990s. And you will not, of course, be surprised that I shall exploit yet another opportunity to present my own perspective on political economy generally.

I propose, therefore, to defend the categorical distinction to be made between the structure of an economy and the operation of that economy within

A shortened version of this chapter, entitled "On the Structure of an Economy: A Re-Emphasis of Some Classical Foundations," was published in *Business Economics* 24 (January 1989): 6–12.

such a structure. I shall argue that the appropriate domain for political economy, for politically directed reform as well as for discussion and analysis of that reform, is exclusively limited to structure. Efforts directed toward effectuating modifications of results that emerge only from complex interdependencies within structure are misguided, as are all canons of putative advice advanced by pundits who fail to understand the necessary distinction. My argument may be properly interpreted as a restatement of the positive case for laissez-faire that Adam Smith might have made had he used this term. Above all else, Adam Smith was a man of prudence, who would never have countenanced those fools of right or left whose caricatures through the decades have reduced a potentially meaningful slogan to polemical absurdity.

I shall proceed as follows. In section 1, I shall offer a precautionary tale about the dangers of terms that seem semantically and didactically useful but which may have the effect of making enlightened understanding more difficult to achieve. Functionalism, the familiar scourge of explanatory analysis in the other social sciences, also works its spell among economists. Section 2 is devoted to a necessarily foreshortened discussion of the order of an economy, as it operates within its own constraining structure. Section 3 examines elements of structure and analyzes relationships between structure and operations within structure. In section 4, I argue that elements of structure offer the only appropriate targets for reform. Finally, in section 5, I demonstrate how confusion in understanding the distinction between structure and operation-within-structure, between rules of the game and play within the rules, between process and end states, produces misdirected, and ultimately self-defeating, ventures in economic policy. The chapter falls clearly within "constitutional political economy," although, by comparison with some of my other papers, discussion here is concentrated on the structure of the economy rather than on the structure of the polity. In other words, the analysis examines the impact of politics on the economy, both in its positive and normative variants. The analysis does not, at least directly, introduce constitutional politics.

1. The "Functions" of an Economy

Any economist who was exposed directly to the teachings of Frank Knight at the University of Chicago or indirectly through access to one of the many elementary textbooks that incorporated elements of Knight's introductory monograph, "The Economic Organization,"[1] is familiar with the listing of the "functions" of an economic order. As initially presented by Knight, these are:

1. establishment of a scale of values,
2. organizing production,

---

1. Frank H. Knight, "The Economic Organization" (Chicago: University of Chicago, 1933), mimeograph.

3. distributing final product,
4. making provision for growth, and
5. adjusting demand to supply over periods of transition.

This listing is indeed useful, both semantically and didactically. It allows the student to focus on distinguishable categories of the economic interaction process, while continuing to recognize that the process, as it operates, carries out or performs the five functions simultaneously.

I want to suggest, however, that this Knightian introduction to our central subject matter may be misleading because it may be interpreted to imply that "the economy," "the economic organization," or "the economic order," accomplishes the listed functions, whether efficaciously or not, in some purposefully directed sense. If the economy, as such, has an acknowledged function or functions such as the establishment of a value scale, does it not seem to follow that the economy, modeled perhaps as a corporate actor or perhaps through its politically organized agents, acts in furtherance of the stipulated and functionally defined objective? Should we really be surprised when the state, in its perceived role as helmsman of the national economy, takes upon itself those tasks presumably assigned to it by the economists who purport to understand their own domain of scientific competence?

To interpret the listing in this way is, of course, a mark of misunderstanding and confusion, both of Knight's own purpose in setting it out, and of the whole interaction process that defines the central subject matter of our discipline. Indeed, we look to Adam Smith for one of the first explanations of how the economy does "perform" the listed functions without such functions, as such, being within the consciously pursued purposes of anyone, whether of the individual participant as buyer or seller in a market or the political agent for such a participant. It becomes functionalist fallacy to impute purpose to "the economy" from the observation that the listed functions are, somehow, carried out. The argument from result to conscious design has been, since the eighteenth century, the argument that the economist must counter. And it is but small exaggeration to say that the core of our discipline embodies the understanding that the observed results of economic process emerge without conscious design while at the same time they describe an order that is amenable to scientific analysis.

2. The Order of an Economy

I apologize for reemphasizing basic principles of economics that may seem both to insult your intelligence and to be remote from practical relevance. I submit, however, that these principles are ignored, forgotten, or deliberately violated in too much of what passes for learned wisdom in our profession. I submit that many modern economists do not know what they are talking about, or, more charitably, that they talk about a realm of discourse beyond that constrained by the origins and history of their scientific discipline.

Adam Smith laid out the boundaries. We take as our assigned task to understand and to explain how an economy generates patterns of order that incorporate achievement of our objectives without requiring either benevolence on the part of economic actors or explicit direction by political agents. The principle of spontaneous coordination of the market is *the* principle of our discipline. Perhaps the most widely cited statement in *The Wealth of Nations* is that which suggests that we get our supper's meat not from the benevolence of the butcher but from his regard to his own self-interest.

The butcher has a private pecuniary interest in having inventories of meat that will meet the demands of buyers. The qualities of desirability and availability take precedence over those qualities that may seem aesthetically superior by the butcher's own standards for the simple reason that the butcher seeks a larger relative share in the overall surplus generated by the nexus of trade and exchange among specialized participants. As we add the baker, the candlestick maker, and all of the other producing specializations in the modern complex economy, we explain the emergence of the set of goods and services that we observe, along with quality and locational characteristics. The butcher, in trying to meet the demands of buyers, who bring to the market their autonomous demands, along with all other potential and actual producers-suppliers and demanders, establishes the scale or standards of valuation, the first of the listed functions that we discussed earlier. This scale or standard emerges from the whole interaction process; it does not directly enter into the self-interest calculus of any participant. The butcher acts on the basis of strictly localized information concerning the demands of his or her clientele; the relative evaluation of beefsteak does not emerge as if from a poll of public opinion; it emerges from the set of interdependent choices made by sellers and buyers, each of whom responds directly to the incentives that he or she faces in a localized market setting.

The complex order of a market economy emerges from a large set of interlinked gamelike cooperative interactions between individual sellers and buyers, each of whom maximizes his or her utility in the localized setting of choice. No "player" in any of these gamelike interactions chooses on the basis of an ordinal ranking of "social states" that describe the possible economywide inclusive imputation of goods and services, postexchange. A "social choice" among "social states" (allocations, distributions, value scales) is, therefore, conceptually as well as practicably impossible, so long as any person is allowed to adjust behavior independently in the localized choice setting that is confronted.[2]

---

2. This point was central to my early criticism ("Social Choice, Democracy, and Free Markets," *Journal of Political Economy* 62 [April 1954]: 114–23) of Arrow's extension of his

3. Order within Structure

I have reemphasized the familiar proposition that, so long as individual buyers and sellers retain liberties to choose among the alternatives offered for sale and purchase in the separate markets, there can be no economywide "choice" of the particularized results of the economic interaction process, as these results might be described in terms of allocations, distributions, or evaluations. This conclusion holds independently of how any such attempted choice may be organized, whether under the auspices of an authoritarian regime or a democratically elected government. The results emerge from the whole set of interdependent choices made by individuals as these choices are constrained by the *structure* of the economy. In its inclusive definition, this structure must incorporate the resource and technology limits that describe the natural environment. These more or less immutable limits are not among my principal concerns here. My emphasis is placed instead on those elements of structure that are subject to purposeful modification and change.

The terminology of game theory is helpful. The structure of an economy describes what we may call the "rules" for the whole complex set of interdependent gamelike interactions between and among many players, each of whom acts in pursuit of a privately selected purpose. This interpretation of structure as a set of rules directly suggests that, as an individual chooses and acts within the structure, as he or she plays in the inclusively defined game, there is, and can be, no conscious or explicit consideration given to the possible choice among alternative sets of rules. For purposes of rational choice behavior in the economic process, the individual must accept the structure of the economy (the rules) as fixed, as a relatively absolute absolute that is not subject to his or her own privately orchestrated change. For example, the preexchange endowments that are within the recognized entitlements of any person are defined by and in the structure of the economy; such a person cannot, separately and independently, modify these endowments.

A distinction must be made between the individual's influence on the overall results of economywide interaction (on allocation, distribution, and evaluation) and the influence on the structure. As noted earlier, the results of economic interaction, within a structure, emerge from the localized private choices made by all participants. Each individual choice must, therefore, affect the aggregate result, even if no person, as chooser, has any conscious

---

impossibility theorem to apply to the results of market process (Kenneth Arrow, *Social Choice and Individual Values* [New York: Wiley, 1951]). Only in writing this chapter did I realize that, although stated quite differently and developed from a different perspective, Amartya Sen's demonstration of the paradox of the Paretian liberal comes ultimately to the same conclusion (Amartya K. Sen, "The Impossibility of a Paretian Liberal," *Journal of Political Economy* 78 [January–February 1970]: 152–57).

sense of his or her own influence on this result. Again a game analogy will be useful. A player chooses among strategies available under the rules that define the game; any player's choice will affect the solution that emerges from the choices of all the players, but no player "chooses" the solution, as such. By contrast, the rules or structure do not emerge from the within-rules choices made by participants; the structure remains necessarily independent of these direct in-structure or within-rules choices.[3]

The pattern of outcomes or results of the economic interaction process (allocations, distributions, evaluations) depend *both* on the individualized choices made in the whole set of interlinked exchanges and on the structure of the economy. I have argued that there can be no effective choice among alternative aggregate results, whether the attempt is made individually or collectively. Only the pattern of results is subject to deliberative change, and patterns can be changed only through effective changes in structure; that is, in the set of rules that constrain the exercise of individual choices to be made within the rules. I have noted also that the individual can exercise no influence on the structure of the economy as he or she chooses separately and independently among the options that he or she confronts. From this it becomes evident that any choice among alternative sets of rules must be, and can only be, collective. The structure of an economy, the set of constraints that limit the choice options of individuals, that define the feasibility spaces, is *public* in the classic sense. This structure is both nonpartitionable and nonexcludable. Any change in structure must, therefore, impact on all actors in the process, quite independently of how and by whom the collective action is motivated and carried out.

4. Constitutional Political Economy

The analysis of the working properties of alternative structures of an economy, alternative sets of rules and institutions that serve to constrain the choice behavior of participants within that economy, defines the domain for constitutional political economy in its positive aspects. Until recently, neoclassical economists tended to neglect the necessary interdependence between structure and potentially observable patterns of outcomes of the economic process. This neglect has been largely corrected by the emergence of the set of interrelated

---

3. The categorical distinction made here would be modified somewhat if we treat elements of structure as products of an evolutionary process. In this case, choice behavior within a structure might itself modify the development of structure over a sufficiently long period of adjustment. For my purposes, however, the categorical distinction made here serves a didactic function. By separating, both conceptually and analytically, the choices made within rules and the choices made among sets of rules, the appropriate domain of normative political economy may be much more clearly set forth.

research programs summarized under the rubric "the new political economy": law and economics, property rights economics, the new institutional economics, public choice. In each of these research programs, the focus of analysis is the impact of different structures of incentives on the choice behavior of economic actors and, through this impact, on the pattern of aggregative results in an economy.

The positive exercise must precede any normative judgment on structure, on any part thereof, whether directed at the status quo or at any proposed alternative. The only legitimate normative exercise involves institutional-structural comparison. Demonstration of "failure" against some idealized standard (efficiency, justice, liberty) that is not anchored in structural feasibility is irrelevant.

How are alternative structures to be arrayed in the normative exercise? What are the standards for ranking? Answers to these questions call for treatises, but I can be cryptic here, especially since I have written at near disquisition length elsewhere.[4]

There are two, quite separate responses to these questions that must be countered and shown to be untenable. The first is that which proceeds from the presumption that there is a unique, and agreed upon, objective, or objective function, for an economy that allows the working properties of alternative structures to be readily assessed. This direction of response, which continues to dominate the thinking of economists, reflects a carryover from idealism in political philosophy. Politics, inclusively defined, is conceived as the search for the "true," the "good," and the "beautiful," some ideal state of bliss waiting "out there" to be discovered or revealed.

As Adam Smith recognized so clearly, however, there is no agreed upon objective for the participants in an economic nexus, each one of whom seeks only to pursue his or her own privately defined aims (which may or may not reflect narrowly defined economic interest). Absent such agreement, there is simply no external standard by which alternative structures can be evaluated.

A second response commences from this very fact of individual differences. Each person, as a participant in the political-economic nexus can, presumably, array alternatives of structure as "better" or "worse" in terms of his or her own subjectively defined interest. From these observed differences among persons, the inference is then drawn that no normative judgment that transcends individual evaluation is possible. Hence, if we differ on the rank-

---

4. James M. Buchanan and Gordon Tullock, *The Calculus of Consent: Logical Foundations of Constitutional Democracy* (Ann Arbor: University of Michigan Press, 1962); James M. Buchanan, *The Limits of Liberty: Between Anarchy and Leviathan* (Chicago: University of Chicago Press, 1975); idem, *Freedom in Constitutional Contract: Perspective of a Political Economist* (College Station: Texas A & M University Press, 1978); idem, *Liberty, Market and State: Political Economy in the 1980s* (New York: New York University Press, 1985).

ing of structural alternatives, we fight; that is, the setting is one of pure conflict, out of which a single structure will emerge that satisfies the winners and coerces the losers.

I suggested previously that neither of these responses to the basic normative questions is acceptable. We must reject the presumed existence of an ideal standard, and we must also reject the nihilism implied by the absence of agreement. And at this point it is, I think, important to recognize, and to acknowledge quite explicitly, that in some fundamental sense many of us, as citizens, behave as if the structure of the economic-political order embodies legitimacy, which implies voluntary acquiescence in the coercion of the state without attribution of either omniscience or benevolence to political agents. That is to say, we live with each other neither as nihilists nor idealists. In an empirical, practical sense, we reconcile the absence of an ideal, agreed upon standard of evaluation and the implied conflict among individual objectives.

In a more formal exercise, we achieve this constitutionalist stance by the introduction of some means of dampening the potential for disagreement among individuals. Such means is provided in the use of something like a veil of ignorance and/or uncertainty, either conceptually or practicably, in the evaluation of alternative structures or constitutional rules. This device is, of course, familiar, from the works of John Rawls,[5] John Harsanyi,[6] Buchanan and Tullock,[7] and others.

The task of normative evaluation of alternative structures for an economy to be carried out after the positive exercise of comparison is assigned to individuals who are ignorant or highly uncertain about how the alternatives for structural choice will impact on their own identifiable interest. Such individuals will be led to agree, in their own interest, on structural features that exhibit many of the characteristics of the classical liberal social order.[8] And, the empirically observed acquiescence in the operation of many of the rules that define the existing structure suggests that, for many participants, there is implied agreement, even without the carrying through of the formal veil of ignorance evaluative exercise.

This contractarian-constitutionalist derivation of the elements of structure for an economy allows us to flesh out, in modern terms, much of Adam Smith's message that was left implicit in his own work. The construction here

---

5. John Rawls, *A Theory of Justice* (Cambridge, Mass.: Harvard University Press, 1971).

6. John Harsanyi, "Cardinal Welfare, Individualistic Ethics, and Interpersonal Comparisons of Utility," *Journal of Political Economy* 63 (August 1955): 309–21.

7. Buchanan and Tullock, *Calculus of Consent*.

8. For more extended discussion, see chap. 11, "The Contractarian Logic of Classical Liberalism," originally published in *Liberty, Property and the Future of Constitutional Development*, ed. Ellen Frankel Paul and Howard Dickman (New York: State University of New York Press, 1990), 9–22.

allows us to derive a regime of "laws and institutions" that offer protection to person and property on a nondiscriminatory basis, that enforce voluntary contracts among persons nondiscriminatorily, that protect the natural liberties of persons to enter into voluntary exchanges, that prohibit restriction on entry into trades, and that prohibit agreement on restrictive terms of trade. This listing, which could be extended and elaborated, contains elements of the structure that has come down to us in classical liberalism. Adam Smith was straightforward in suggesting that, within this broadly defined structure of an economy, there was no legitimate basis for directed interference by political agents.

The listing of constituent elements of structure that might be derived from the contractarian normative exercise can be extended to include, importantly, the political-legal guarantee of predictability in the value of the monetary standard or unit of account in the economy. Historically, observed political orders have rarely, if ever, provided this guarantee. The contractarian construction remains necessarily incomplete at critical elements of economic structure. While laws and institutions that protect the liberties of persons to enter and consummate voluntary exchanges command legitimacy directly, what are the limits suggested when voluntary exchanges affect other parties outside the exchange itself? The whole domain of externality, inclusively defined, does not find structural resolution directly in the initial normative exercise. As modern research has indicated, however, structural change that moves toward incentive-compatible imputation of rights may eliminate much of the contractarian ambiguity.

5. The Purposeless Economy

As my subtitle indicates, this chapter reemphasizes the classical foundations of political economy, and especially as these are reflected in the encompassing vision of Adam Smith. Even Smith, however, is subject to criticism in his selection of the title for his treatise. By calling attention to the *wealth* of nations, Smith may be interpreted as setting up a single valued criterion by which the functioning of an economy might be measured. As I have noted, a much preferred title would have been, "The Simple System of Natural Liberty," because what Smith demonstrated was that there is no need for us to conceptualize a single overriding or even an agreed upon purpose, aim, or objective for an economy, or for those political agents who may presume to take on the charge of furthering such purpose.

Properly understood, the economy has neither purpose, function, or intent. The economy is defined by a structure, a set of rules and institutions, that constrain the choices of many persons in an interlinked chain of gamelike interactions, one with another. For any individual, there are, of course, "better" and "worse" economies, but these evaluative terms translate directly into references to sets of rules or structures. Within any given structure, laissez-faire becomes the indicated policy stance, and this principle holds quite independently of the normative content of structure itself.

In one sense, there is absolutely nothing new or novel in what I have said in this chapter. But in yet another sense, the implications are revolutionary. The shift of emphasis to structure as the exclusive and only appropriate object for reform, along with the implied principle of laissez-faire applied to operation within structure, relegates to absurdity all proposals for reform supported on arguments from "national purpose," as well as all claims that the economy functions more satisfactorily if it is explicitly guided by presumably omniscient and benevolent political agents.

There are two separate, but related, aspects of the normative argument that I advance. The very definition of the economy as a structure, a set of constraining rules within which individuals seek to achieve their separately determined purposes, makes teleological direction of policy normatively self-contradictory. But alternative structures may be compared, and evaluated, in terms of their abilities to facilitate the accomplishment of the separately determined individual objectives. Since only individuals themselves can know what goals they seek, any direct delegation of authority to choose among structures reduces the information content of the constitutional choice process. The implied policy stance involves laissez-faire within constitutional structure and consensus in the ultimate choice of structure itself.

No claim is made here that adherence to the normative precepts outlined will resolve all issues. Even within the constitutionalist-contractarian paradigm, differences among individuals may arise both in scientific interpretation-explanation-prediction and in a choice of ultimate moral norms. As noted earlier, many features of the classical liberal position would be predicted to emerge from the contractarian procedural test. But the precise boundaries of the constitutionally chosen structural limits on individual voluntary association, as well as the constitutionally derived definitions of the protected spheres of individuals themselves, cannot be drawn from sources other than as revealed by those who count as members of the body politic.

Let us by all means continue to strive for, and to support, efforts to analyze the structure of the economy, and to seek consensus on means to make this structure more capable of allowing us, as individual participants, to further those separately defined objectives that we seek. Let us, however, guard against allowing intellectual confusion about what an economy is, to offer legitimatizing cover for the efforts of some persons and groups to impose their own purposes on others. Beware of those who pronounce on the economy's purpose.

CHAPTER 3

The Economy as a Constitutional Order

The occasion for this chapter was an assignment in which I was asked to assess the state of economic science, necessarily from my own personal perspective, which is, perhaps, less representative of median or mainstream evaluation than those perspectives offered by my other Nobel Memorial Prize peers in the same series. I shall make no attempt to be comprehensive here, although the implications of my whole argument for the economist's stance as both a positive and normative scientist involve major shifts in attitudes toward the disciplinary subject matter. I shall concentrate discussion on my understanding of what an economy is, from which inferential criticisms of research programs, didactic instruction, and policy implementation emerge, more or less as a matter of course.

I may succeed in attracting your attention by boldly stating two of these criticisms at the outset. First, there is no place for macroeconomics, either as a part of our positive science, or as a realm for policy action. Second, the appropriate mathematics is game theory rather than maximization of objective functions subject to constraints. These apparently unrelated criticisms emerge from understanding and interpreting the economy nonteleologically, as an *order*, rather than understanding and interpreting the economy teleologically, as an institutional arrangement that is to be evaluated in terms of relative success or failure to achieve assigned, system-defined objectives. In my title for the chapter, I have appended the word *constitutional* to the word *order* so as to indicate that my perspective differs both from those evolutionists who do emphasize the economy as an order but who, at the same time, deny that such an order can be "constituted," and from those who fail to make the distinction between constitutional and postconstitutional levels of choice.

In this introduction, let me also classify myself philosophically. I am a methodological and normative individualist, a radical subjectivist, a contractarian, and a constitutionalist. These descriptive attributes are familiar to those of you who may have been exposed to my published works over four decades. In a very real sense, these works are little more than my continuing

This chapter, untitled, was published in *The State of Economic Science: Views of Six Nobel Laureates*, ed. Werner Sichel, 79–96 (Kalamazoo: Upjohn Institute, 1989).

and considered assessment of the state of economics or political economy. I have always been, and remain, an outsider, whose efforts have been devoted to changing the direction of the disciplinary research program. There is perhaps less reason for me to take a reflective look at where we are scientifically than there is for those of my peers who have remained inside the dominant research program that describes what economists do. You would scarcely expect me to take on some new colors at this stage, and I assure you that there has been no recent conversion to a new paradigm. No one has had, or will have, occasion to label me as a holder of the conventional wisdom.

I shall proceed as follows. Section 1 examines the relationships between scarcity, choice, and value maximization within the domain of economics as scientific inquiry. My aim in this section is to demonstrate how these concepts, by having been placed in too central a role, have generated intellectual confusion. Section 2 extends the perspective to examine the appropriateness of macroeconomics in the subject matter domain of our discipline. Section 3 briefly treats the grand organizational alternatives and develops the notion that the conception of what the economy is, does have normative implications. Section 4 compares and contrasts the two approaches in terms of the shift from individual to social choice. Finally, in section 5, the argument is summarized.

1. Scarcity, Choice, and the Maximization of Value

I do not know what 1990s instructors in economics tell their students about the content of the discipline. Perhaps they simply ignore definitional starting points. But I do recall that, in the 1940s, economic theory (price theory) courses commenced with something like Milton Friedman's statement to the effect that economics is the study of how a particular society solves its economic problem.[1] And, at least in the 1940s, everyone knew that "the economic problem" was defined by Lionel Robbins as the allocation of scarce resources among alternative ends.[2] Scarcity, the inability to meet all demands, implies that choices must be made, from which it seems to follow directly that criteria for "better" and "worse" choices are required. These criteria emerge as some common denominator that allows the differing demands to be translated into a single dimension, which we then label as "utility" or "value." The "economic principle" offers the abstractly defined normative solution to the economic problem. Scarce resources are allocated among alternative uses to secure maximum value when a unit of each scarce resource yields equivalent value in each use to which it is put. Satisfying this norm maximizes value,

---

1. Milton Friedman, *Price Theory* (Chicago: Aldine, 1962).
2. Lionel Robbins, *The Nature and Significance of Economic Science* (London: Macmillan, 1932).

subject to the resource scarcity constraints. Economics, as a realm for scientific inquiry, does indeed seem to be reducible to applied maximization; the calculus seems surely to be its basic mathematics.

I want to suggest here that this economics, which is the economics that I learned both as a student and as a young professional, generates intellectual confusion and misunderstanding because it focuses attention inappropriately on scarcity, on choice, and on value maximization, while shifting attention away from the institutional structure of an economy, with the consequent failure to make elementary distinctions among alternative structures. Given the dominance of the Robbins formulation in the economic theory of the 1940s and 1950s, it is not surprising that market solutions were often modeled as analogous to planning solutions to the resource allocation problem. Economists proceeded as if "the market" embodies "social choices" among alternative allocations of resources, choices that may be compared with those that might emerge from the monolithic decisions of a single planner. Given the mind-set of mid-century, it is also not surprising that Arrow extended his impossibility theorem to market, as well as to political, choice.[3]

As early as 1962, in my presidential address to the Southern Economic Association,[4] I criticized the central role assigned to the maximizing paradigm in economics, and I called for a revival of "catallactics" (or "catallaxy") as the core of our discipline. My argument was that economics, as a social science, is or should be about trade, exchange, and the many and varied institutional forms that implement and facilitate trade, including all of the complexities of modern contracts as well as the whole realm of collective agreement on the constitutional rules of political society.

In a basic conceptual sense, the exchange process remains categorically different from the choosing process. In exchange, there is a necessary interaction between (among) separate actors (participants), no one of which can choose among "solutions." In exchange, each participant does, of course, make choices among alternative bids and offers (strategies). But these choices of any single participant are, at most, only a part of the interaction process. A solution to an exchange *emerges* only from the choices made, separately and independently, by all participants in the process. This solution, as such, is not explicitly chosen by any one of the participants, or by the set of participants organized as a collective entity. This solution is simply not within the choice-set of either individual actors or the collectivity.

This elementary sketch of exchange provides the basis for my early assertion that game theory offers the appropriate mathematical framework for

3. Kenneth Arrow, *Social Choice and Individual Values* (New York: Wiley, 1951).

4. James M. Buchanan, "What Should Economists Do?" *Southern Economic Journal* 30 (January 1964): 213–22. Reprinted in idem, *What Should Economists Do?* (Indianapolis: Liberty Press, 1979).

facilitating an abstract understanding of economics. In exchange, as in ordinary games, players or participants may be modeled as behaving to maximize their separately defined utilities, subject to the constraints separately faced, as defined by the rules, the endowments, and the predicted responses of other participants. The standard maximizing behavior embodied in rational choice models may, of course, be accepted for this analytical exercise. But, in exchange, again as in ordinary games, neither any single player-participant nor the set of players-participants, as a group, treats the outcome of the process as a maximand. The solution to the exchange process, simple or complex, is not the solution of a maximization problem, and to model it as such is the continuing source of major intellectual confusion in the whole discipline.

Equilibrium in any exchange interaction signals the exhaustion of the mutual gains, and this solution, as such, has behavioral properties that also describe positions of maxima for all choices. At equilibrium, no participant has an incentive to make further bids (offers) within the rules that define the structure of the interaction. In the equilibrium of the ideally competitive economy, there is no incentive, either for any single participant, or for any group of participants, including the all-inclusive group, to modify the results within the rules.[5] But what is maximized in this solution to the competitive "game"? That which is maximized, in any sense at all meaningful for behavior, is the value for *each* participant, as determined separately and subjectively, subject to the endowments initially possessed and to the expressed preferences of others in the nexus, as reflected in the bids (offers) made in markets. There is no "social" or "collective" value maximization, as such, in the exchange process, even in some idealized sense. Aggregative value, measured in some numéraire, is, of course, at a maximum in the solution, but this is a definitional consequence of the equilibrium. The relative prices of goods and services are themselves determined in the process of attaining the equilibrium, and it is only when these emergent prices are used that any maximum value, as an aggregate, can be defined.

Since an abstractly defined maximum for aggregative value cannot exist independently of the market process through which it is achieved, it is meaningless to refer to a shortfall in aggregative value, as such, except as some indirect identification of failure to exhaust gains from trade among participants somewhere in the nexus. Since participants are presumed able to make their own within-exchange choices, the political economist's hypothesis that value is not being maximized must be derived from observations that there exist impediments to the trading process, whether at the simple level of buyer-

---

5. In slightly more formal terms, the competitive equilibrium is in the core of the game. This conclusion holds only if the rules of the game are strictly defined and enforced, and especially in relation to the incentives offered to potential monopolizing coalitions.

seller exchange or at the level of all-inclusive complex "exchanges" in public goods.[6] The observing political economist is unable, even conceptually, to construct a "social welfare function" that will allow him or her to carry out a maximization exercise analogous to that which the planner for a centralized economy must undertake. For such a planner, his or her choices are analogous, even if at a different dimension of complexity, to those faced by any single participant in the exchange nexus.

2. Macroeconomics and Constitutional Political Economy

The basic and elementary distinction between the maximizing and the exchange paradigms supports the proposition that was advanced earlier concerning the suggested exclusion of macroeconomics from the domain of our disciplinary subject matter, at least macroeconomics as normally defined. That which is generated in the economic interaction process, whether or not represented as a formalized, abstractly defined equilibrium or solution, *emerges* from the separate and interdependent choices made by many participants, choices that are coordinated, whether efficaciously or not, through the institutional arrangements that define the economic structure. The economywide aggregated variables, such as national income or product, rates of employment, capacity utilization, or growth, are not variables subject to choice, either directly or indirectly, by individual participants in the economy or by political agents, who may presume to act on behalf of all participants as a collectivity, or any subset thereof.

It is intellectually confusing even to model "the economy" as if its normative purpose is one of maximizing income and/or employment, or, indeed, as if "the economy" has normative purpose at all. As noted earlier, any failure of the interaction process to generate maximum value must reflect failure to exploit gains from trade, whether simple or complex. This putative diagnosis calls attention to the structure itself, which may contain constraints that prevent the consummation of mutually advantageous trades.

Alternative structures are, of course, to be evaluated indirectly by observations of the patterns of results that are generated, and these results may be represented in terms of the familiar macroaggregated variables such as the level and growth of national product or employment. An economy that persistently generates wide swings in levels of income and employment would, appropriately, be deemed to be a *structural* failure, and such a pattern of results should offer incentives to investigate, locate, and identify the structural sources of the problem, leading ultimately to structural-institutional reform.

---

6. James M. Buchanan, "Positive Economics, Welfare Economics, and Political Economy," *Journal of Law and Economics* 2 (October 1959): 124–38.

The tragic flaw in Keynesian inspired macroeconomics lay in its acceptance, and, hence, neglect, of structure while concentrating almost exclusive attention on the prospects and potential for "guiding" the economy toward more satisfactory target levels of the aggregative variables. It is not at all surprising, when viewed in retrospect, that this monumental misdirection of scientific effort should have occurred, given the dominance of the maximizing paradigm during the critical years of mid-century. There was a general failure to recognize that the whole intellectual construction was inconsistent with a structure that allows for the independent choice behavior of many participants in the economic nexus. As Keynes himself recognized in his preface to the German translation of his book, the whole reinterpretation of the economic process in a normatively directed teleological model was more applicable to an authoritarian regime than to a democratic one.

I do not want to suggest, however, that the classical economists, at least those who were the targets of Keynes's direct criticism, were free of their own peculiar sort of blindness that led them, also, to neglect structural elements. In their implied presumption that results embodying satisfactory levels of the aggregative variables would emerge, independently of possible structural failures, these economists were ill-prepared to defend the discipline against the emotionally driven zealots for macroeconomic management.

The intellectual, scientific, and policy scenario should have been, and could have been, so different in those critical decades before mid-century. Little was really needed beyond an elementary recognition that the economic process functions well only within a legal-constitutional structure that embodies predictability in the value of the monetary unit, accompanied by a regime reform that would have been designed to guarantee such predictability. (In this respect alone, a unique window of opportunity was missed in the 1930s.) Macroeconomic theory, in both its lower and its higher reaches, need not have been born at all, along with the whole industry that designs, constructs, and operates the large macroeconomic models.[7]

3. Socialism, Laissez-Faire, Interventionism, and the Structure of an Economy

It is now widely acknowledged, both in theory and in practice, that socialism was (is) a failure. The socialist god is dead; the promise that was once associated with socialism, as an overarching principle for social organization,

---

7. Because of the near universal failure of economists to look at structure, then and now, we face, in the 1990s, even more potential unpredictability in the value of the monetary unit than we did in the 1920s. Given the inherent structural defect in our monetary regime, macroeconomic theorizing and the macromodels may be useful, if for no other reason than that our discretionary monopolists of fiat issue may use such models for their own purposes.

no longer exists. The romantic image of the state as an omniscient and benevolent entity, an image that had been around since Hegel, was shattered by the simple observation that those who act on behalf of the state are also ordinary humans, like the rest of us, who respond to standard incentives within the limited informational setting they confront. Centralized economic planning, with state ownership and control over means of production, has entered history as intellectual folly, despite the record of its having attracted the attention of so many brilliant minds in the first half of this century, and also despite the awful realization that efforts to implement this folly involved the needless sacrifice of millions of lives.

At the opposing end to socialism on the imagined ideological spectrum stands the equally romantic ideal of laissez-faire, the fictional image of the anarcho-capitalists, in which there is no role for the state at all. In this model, freely choosing individuals, who have somehow costlessly escaped from the Hobbesian jungle, will create and maintain markets in all goods and services, including the market for protection of person and possessions. It is as difficult to think systematically about this society as it is to think of that society peopled by the "new men" of idealized communism. Robert Nozick's derivation of the minimally coercive state was surely convincing even to those stubborn minds who held onto the laissez-faire dream.[8]

Any plausibly realistic analysis of social order, whether positive or normative, must be bounded by the limits set by these ideological extremes. The state is neither omniscient nor benevolent, but a political-legal framework is an essential element in any functioning order of human interaction. The analysis, discussion, and debate then centers on the degree or extent of political control over, and intervention into, the interaction process. The extended interventionist state remains a viable alternative in the ongoing political argument, and proponents for such a state are found among scientists and citizens alike, despite the general loss of faith in the socialist ideal. Opposed to the extended interventionist polity lies the minimal or protective state, tempered variously by acknowledgement of the appropriateness of both productive and transfer state elements.[9]

The question may be raised at this point concerning how these issues relate to my evaluation of the state of economic science, which was, after all, my assigned task for this chapter. I return to my central theme. My hypothesis is that the basic conceptualization of what "an economy" or "the economy" is,

---

8. Robert Nozick, *Anarchy, State, and Utopia* (New York: Basic Books, 1974).

9. A cynical observer might suggest that little, if any, scientific progress has been made since 1776, when Adam Smith first presented the antimercantilist argument from which modern economics emerged. Mercantilism (protectionism, interventionism) seems to have reemerged in the decades of the 1970s and 1980s in partial replacement for the acknowledged demise of socialism.

the paradigmatic vision of what it is that we are inquiring into and about, does, indeed, carry direct normative implications. In a real sense, my hypothesis suggests that divergent normative stances may reflect divergent *understandings* rather than different ultimate values. If this hypothesis is descriptively accurate, genuine scientific progress may be made at the level of fundamental understanding (methodology) as well as at the apparent cutting edges of some presumed invariant empirical reality.[10]

Applied somewhat more narrowly, my hypothesis is that the normatively preferred scope for state or collective intervention will depend directly upon the conceptualization of what the economy is, as the subject for scientific inquiry. That is to say, the normative debate on the turf bounded between the socialist and the laissez-faire extremes will reflect the divergent models of the observed reality. In a certain sense, *the ought is derived from the presumed is.*

Let me try to be more specific. I suggest that an accepted understanding of the economy as an order of interaction constrained within a set of rules or constraints leads more or less directly to a normatively preferred minimal intervention with the results of such interaction. By comparison and by contrast, an accepted understanding of the economy as an engine, mechanism, or means that is organized for the achievement of specifically defined purposes leads more or less directly to a normatively preferred stance of expediency in evaluating possible state or collective intervention with the interaction process.

Many textbooks commence with a discussion of the functions of an economy, as introduced by Frank H. Knight.[11] I have suggested (chap. 2) that even so much as a listing of "functions" for an economy may generate confusion and misunderstanding. If the economy, as such, is without purpose, how can we attribute functions to its operation? The economy-as-order conceptualization forces us to restrict evaluation to the relative success of the structure in facilitating the accomplishment of whatever it is that the separately interacting participants may seek. (Again the basic game analogy is useful. We evaluate the rules that describe a game by assessing how successful the rules are in allowing players to achieve those objectives that they seek in playing.)

The point here may be made emphatically in the simple example of a two-person, two-good exchange. Two traders are presumed to hold endowments in two goods, and these endowments are assumed to be mutually

---

10. As my great professor, Frank H. Knight, once remarked at the end of an impressively presented empirical survey, "proving that water runs downhill," which expresses my own verdict on much of what I see in the now-dominant empirical emphasis of modern economic research. I doubt if many economists are convinced by empirical evidence alone, although I acknowledge that the linkage between evidence and understanding remains mysterious.

11. Frank H. Knight, "The Economic Organization" (Chicago: University of Chicago, 1934), mimeograph.

acknowledged to be owned by the initial holders. The traders are observed to engage in exchange, and a posttrade distribution of endowments different from the pretrade distribution emerges. How do observing economists evaluate this simple exchange process? The two interpretations or understandings involve quite different exercises. The mechanistic, functionalist, teleological understanding introduces a presumed prior knowledge of individual utility or preference orderings, and the posttrade positions are compared with the pretrade positions, for each trader. If the comparisons indicate that each trader has moved to a higher level of utility, the exchange is judged to have been mutually utility enhancing.

The economy-as-order understanding proceeds quite differently. The economist does *not* call upon some presumed prior knowledge of the utility or preference functions of the two traders to be able to conclude that the exchange has been utility enhancing for each trader. He or she does not evaluate the results of exchange teleologically against some previously defined and known scalar. Instead, he or she adjudges the exchange to have been utility enhancing for each trader to the extent that the *process* itself has embodied attributes of fairness and propriety. If there has been neither force nor fraud, and if the exchange has been voluntary on the part of both traders, it is classified to have been mutually beneficial. When the economist analyzes the behavior of the traders in entering into and agreeing on terms of exchange, he or she may, if desired, use the language of utility maximization, provided that the exclusive emphasis is placed on individuals' behavior in maximizing their separately identified utilities, which are not observable independently.

Important implications for potential intervention in voluntary exchanges stem from the contrasting interpretations here. If the economist bases his or her evaluation on the relative success of the exchange in moving the traders higher on an independently existing utility scalar, he or she may be led to recommend intervention even in the absence of observation of force, fraud, or coercion in the exchange process itself. This approach provides the basis for paternalistic, merit goods arguments for collective interferences with voluntary market exchanges. The individual may not act to maximize his or her own utility. On the other hand, if the observing economist bases his evaluation exclusively on the process of the exchange itself, recommendations for collective intervention must be limited to proposals for removing barriers to trade, inclusively defined.

We can remain with the simple exchange example to discuss the role of agreement in the two interpretations-understandings of economic interaction, along with the place of the Pareto criterion in any evaluative exercise. Exchange involves agreement on the part of traders, both upon entry into trade and upon terms of trade. The emergence of a postexchange distribution of goods signals an equilibrium of sorts. The teleological interpretation of exchange does not call upon agreement for any critical purpose. The dual criteria are the separate utility scalars of our two traders, presumed known to the assessor prior to trade. If exchange moves each trader higher on the scalar assigned to him or her, the change is defined to have been Pareto superior. The welfare assessment can be positive without any necessary resort to interpersonal utility comparisons.

By contrast, the economy-as-order interpretation depends critically upon agreement as the criterion for assessment. Since there are no independently existent scalars, the only indication that traders have improved their position lies in their observed agreement. A positive welfare assessment becomes possible because the agreement has signaled mutually preferred change. Agreement is the means of defining Pareto (Wicksell) superiority, and it is the only means that exists.

4. From Individual to Social Choice:
Utilitarian versus Contractarian Foundations

The economist who conceptualizes the economy as a potential welfare generating mechanism or instrument may be unwilling to limit criteria of evaluation to separately imputed, individually identified scalars. Almost by necessity, and despite the acknowledged insupportability of a simplistic utilitarianism, some attempt will be made to derive meaningful measures for "social" or "collective" utility. This is the essential thrust behind the invention-elaboration-use of the social welfare function constructions in mid-century theoretical welfare economics, constructions that embodied both explicit introduction of ethical judgments and the relevance of the Pareto escape from direct interpersonal utility comparability. This whole exercise involved a search for a post-Robbins scalar against which the potential performance of the economy might be measured, a scalar that could be set up to exist independently of the performance itself. Success or failure of that which is evaluated, the economy or the market, is then determined from some comparison of observed results with those that might have been achieved. Modern economists who resorted to the social welfare function constructions, despite all their methodological and philosophical sophistication, have really not succeeded in escaping from the utilitarian foundations from which the whole maximizing allocationist paradigm emerged late in the nineteenth century.

If we shuck off the utilitarian trappings and simply abandon efforts to construct a scalar that will allow the evaluation of performance for the economy or the market, as such, we are then forced into an acceptance of the alternative conceptualization advanced here, that of the economy as an order, or structure, or set of rules, the performance of which is not to be evaluated in terms of results that are conceptually divorced from the behavior of acting individuals within the order itself. Within the order or structure, individuals engage in trade. If we then generalize the trading interaction and extend its application over large numbers of actors, we may begin to explain, derive, and analyze social or political interdependence as complex exchange, as a relationship that embodies political voluntary agreement as an appropriate criterion of legitimation.

The contractarian tradition in political philosophy offers the intellectual avenue that facilitates the shift of inquiry from simple market exchange engaged in by two traders to the intricacies of politics. Many critics balk at this extension. They may accept the centrality of voluntary exchange in economic process but remain unwilling to model politics in the exchange paradigm. By simple observation, so say such critics, politics is about conflict and coercion. How can we even begin to explain political reality by an exchange model?

The contractarian response requires a recognition of the distinction between the constitutional and the inconstitutional or postconstitutional levels of political interaction, a distinction without which any normative justification for political coercion could not exist, at least for the normative individualist. Conflict, coercion, zero-sum or negative-sum relationships among persons— these interactions do indeed characterize political institutions, as they may be observed to operate *within a set of constitutional rules*, that is, within a given constitutional order. The complex exchange model that embodies agreement among the many participants in the political "game" is clearly inapplicable here. But if analysis and attention are shifted to the level of rules, among which choices are possible, we can use potential and actual agreement among persons on these rules as the criterion for normative legitimacy. And such agreement may well produce rules, or sets of rules, that will operate so that, in particularized sequences of ordinary politics (single plays of the game) there may be negatively valued results for some of the participants.[12]

Note that there is a more or less natural extension from the simple model of market exchange to the complex model of constitutional politics. There is no categorical distinction between the economic and the political process; inquiry in each case centers on the choice behavior of individuals who act, one with another, to choose rules that will, in turn, constrain their within-rule choices that will, in their turn, generate patterns of results. Note also, however, that this politics-as-complex-exchange derivation is not readily available to the economist who remains trapped in the maximizing straightjacket.

5. The Political Economy as a Constitutional Order

I have fudged a bit in designating the title of this chapter as, "The Economy as a Constitutional Order." It should now be clear from my discussion that I

---

12. James M. Buchanan and Gordon Tullock, *The Calculus of Consent* (Ann Arbor: University of Michigan Press, 1962).

define the institutions of both the economy and the polity as belonging to an inclusive constitutional order that we may designate as "the political economy." The political economy is described by the whole set of constraints, or structure, within which individuals act in furtherance of their own objectives.

Defined exclusively, these constraints include physical and technological limits, including those embodied in human capacities, that can be taken as invariant. These "absolutes" are beyond my range of interest, except to note that much of the folly of the socialist idea stems from a failure to recognize the relative immalleability of human beings. My concern here, however, is with the set of constraints that are subject to deliberative change, and, hence, to choice.[13] Because these constraints are general and extend over all participants in the political economy, any choice must be, by definition, public, in the classic "public good" sense of this term. A shift in constraints for any one actor must apply for all actors.

Let me now return to the distinction made earlier between the constitutional and the inconstitutional levels of choice. Given any set of constraints, individuals will, separately and jointly, act in pursuit of their own interests and objectives. For some purposes, it is useful to take the existing constraints as a set of relatively absolute absolutes and to direct inquiry to predictions about the emergence of patterns of results. This domain of positive economics is productive, but it should not lead to the inference that these patterns of results can be modified to meet predetermined objectives, independently of any shift in the constraints themselves. Such effort must be paralleled by analyses aimed at predicting results that will emerge under alternative constraints, other rules of the game, other constitutional structures. As I noted earlier, the tragedy of the Keynesian enterprise lay in its failed effort to modify aggregative results directly, due to its oversight of any prospects for institutional-constitutional change.

If the political economy is conceived as being described, in part, by constraints that can be subject to explicit collective choice, attention is immediately drawn to prospects for constitutional-institutional change. Once again the game analogy is helpful; we change a game by changing the rules, which will, in turn, modify the predicted pattern of outcomes. If we diagnose the patterns of results observed to be less desired than alternative patterns deemed to be possible, it is incumbent on us, as political economists, to examine predicted results under alternative constraint structures. It is not legitimate to criticize, for example, an existing distribution of income or allocation of resources as being unjust, inequitable, or inefficient, without being able, at

---

13. I do not accept the implications of the analyses of some cultural evolutionists, who suggest that the basic institutions of social order evolve without conscious design and, by inference, suggest also that deliberate improvement in these institutions may be impossible, and, further, that attempts at improvement are harmful.

the same time, to demonstrate that some proposed alternative regime can be expected to generate distributions or allocations that will do better by the same standards.[14]

No one will, of course, be surprised that I have used the occasion of this chapter to present a varied reiteration of the case for constitutional political economy as the research program that should command the current attention of economists. As such, this research program involves both positive and normative elements. Some critics have often accused me of skirting dangerously close to, if not actually committing, the naturalistic fallacy, that of deriving the "ought" from the "is." I have never been concerned with such criticisms directly because, as noted earlier, in a certain sense we do derive "oughts" from our conceptions of what "is." The "is" that we take to be the economy does, indeed, have direct implications for how we ought to behave in our capacities as citizens who indirectly make collective choices among sets of rules. And let us be sure to understand that there is no "is" that is "out there" to the observing eye, ear, or skin. We create our understanding of the "is" by imposing an abstract structure on observed events. And it is this understanding that defines for us the effective limits of the feasible. It is dangerous nonsense to think that we do or can do otherwise.

---

14. Dan Usher, *The Economic Prerequisites to Democracy* (New York: Columbia University Press, 1981); Rutledge Vining, *On Appraising the Performance of an Economic System* (Cambridge: Cambridge University Press, 1984); Geoffrey Brennan and James M. Buchanan, *The Reason of Rules* (Cambridge: Cambridge University Press, 1985).

CHAPTER 4

The Justification of the Compound Republic:
A Retrospective Interpretation of
The Calculus of Consent

I have stated elsewhere[1] that the public choice perspective combines two distinct elements: the conceptualization of "politics as exchange" and the extension of the economists' model of utility maximizing behavior to political choice. *The Calculus of Consent* was the first book that integrated these two elements into a coherent logical structure.[2] It will be useful, in this short retrospective chapter, to compare and contrast the argument developed in *The Calculus of Consent* to those that were present in the nascent public choice analysis of the time, as well as in the then conventional wisdom in political science.

Kenneth Arrow published his seminal *Social Choice and Individual Values* in 1951;[3] Duncan Black's *Theory of Committees and Elections* appeared in 1958,[4] following earlier papers in the late 1940s and early 1950s. Anthony Downs published *An Economic Theory of Democracy* in 1957.[5] These three writers were all economists, as was Joseph Schumpeter whose book, *Capitalism, Socialism, and Democracy*, contained precursory, if widely neglected, parallels to the inquiries that followed.[6] In each case, analysis was grounded on the economists' model of utility maximization. Indeed, in the Arrow, Black, and later social choice constructions, the indi-

---

A modified version of this chapter, entitled "Justification of the Compound Republic," was published in *Public Choice and Constitutional Economics*, ed. James Gwartney and Richard Wagner, 131–38 (Greenwich, Conn.: JAI Press, 1988).

1. James M. Buchanan, "The Public Choice Perspective," *Economia delle scelte pubbliche* 1 (January 1983): 7–15.

2. James M. Buchanan and Gordon Tullock, *The Calculus of Consent: Logical Foundations of Constitutional Democracy* (Ann Arbor: University of Michigan Press, 1962).

3. Kenneth J. Arrow, *Social Choice and Individual Values* (New York: Wiley, 1951).

4. Duncan Black, *Theory of Committees and Elections* (Cambridge: Cambridge University Press, 1958).

5. Anthony Downs, *An Economic Theory of Democracy* (New York: Harper, 1957).

6. Joseph Schumpeter, *Capitalism, Socialism, and Democracy* (New York: Harper and Row, 1942).

vidual is defined as an ordinal preference ordering over alternative social states. Downs's work differs from the social choice strand of inquiry in that he modeled the behavior of political parties analogously to that of profit-seeking firms in a competitive market environment, but the construction, ultimately, is also based on the utility maximizing behavior of office-seeking politicians and interest-seeking voting constituents.

The missing element in all of these constructions is any justificatory argument for democratic process that embodies individualistic norms for evaluation. Arrow and Black seemed to place stability and consistency in "social choice" above any consideration of the desirability of any correspondence between individual values and collective outcomes. Downs seemed to be interested in the predictions of the results of majoritarian political process independently of any overriding of the desires of persons in minority preference positions. Arrow proved, dramatically, that consistent sets of individual orderings need not generate consistent social or collective results, under any rule. But he neglected any normative reference to the possible coercion of minority preferences or interests in any nonunanimous rule structure.[7]

These works left us with the dangling question: Why should an individual enter into a collective? These works presumed, without inquiry, that the individual was locked into membership in a political community and that the range and scope of the activities of the collectivity were themselves beyond the control of the individual and, by inference, beyond the boundaries of analysis amenable to any individualistic calculus. *The Calculus of Consent* differed from the precursory works in this fundamental respect. Our analysis embodied *justificatory* argument. We sought to outline, at least in very general terms, the conditions that must be present in order that the individual find it advantageous to enter into a political entity with constitutionally delineated ranges of activity or to acquiesce in membership in a historically existent polity.

The intellectual-analytical vacuum here was much more apparent in relation to the early extensions of economic methodology to political process than it seemed in then conventional political science inquiry. Precisely because the economists (Black, Arrow, and Downs) incorporated individual utility maximization explicitly in their analyses, possible differences among persons in preference orderings over political alternatives emerged as a central issue. In a model with identical preferences, problems addressed by Arrow, Black, or Downs do not directly arise. Once preferences over political choice options are presumed to differ, however, it is but a natural extension to consider the choice among political regimes.

---

7. Arrow's emphasis on stability and consistency in collective results to the neglect of individual interests was the primary target of my own criticism, "Social Choice, Democracy, and Free Markets," *Journal of Political Economy* 62 (April 1954): 114–23.

Normative political science at mid-century offered a dramatically different ideational environment. Influenced in part by Hegelian inspired idealism, the interest of the individual was treated as being embodied in the state and in politics as process. Even for many of those who could scarcely be classified as falling within this Hegelian tradition, politics was still conceived as a search for truth and goodness, a search from which a uniquely determinate "best" result (for *everyone*) emerges. One important strand of positive political analysis, based largely on the work of Arthur Bentley,[8] concentrated attention on conflicts among differing interests, but, in turn, tended to neglect the cooperative elements that are necessary to justify the game's being played at all.

If we remain within the presuppositions of methodological individualism, the state or the polity must ultimately be justified in terms of its potential for satisfying individuals' desires, whatever these might be. The state is necessarily an artifact, an instrument that has evolved, or is designed, for the purpose of meeting individual needs that cannot be readily satisfied under alternative arrangements. In this sense, the great game of politics must be positive-sum. If this fact is recognized, while at the same time the potential for conflict among differing individual interests is acknowledged, the basic exchange model of the economist is immediately suggested. In this elementary model, traders enter the interaction process with interests that conflict one with another distributionally but in a setting that offers mutuality of gain from cooperation.

This second element in the inclusive public choice perspective, that of "politics as exchange," is necessary for any justificatory argument. In adding this element to the utility maximizing models for individual choice behavior in politics, we were directly influenced by the great work of Knut Wicksell,[9] whom I have always considered to be the primary precursor of my own efforts in public choice, or, indeed, in political economy generally. Wicksell sought, along with a few of his European economist peers, to extend the range of economic analysis to the public or governmental sector of resource use. He sought a criterion for efficiency in the state or collective use of resources that was comparable to the criterion that had been formally specified for the use of resources in the market sector of the economy. What is the value of the collective use of a resource unit in the market? The only sources for valuation are the individuals who both enjoy the benefits of state financed services and pay the costs in sacrificed privately supplied goods. From this basic individualistic presupposition there emerged the Wicksellian unanimity criterion. If any proposed public or governmental outlay is valued more highly than the alternative market or private product of the resources, there must exist a

---

8. Arthur Bentley, *The Process of Government* (1908; reprint, Bloomington, Ind.: The Principia Press, 1935).

9. Knut Wicksell, *Finanztheoretische Untersuchungen* (Jena: Fischer, 1896).

scheme for tax-share allocation that will be agreed to by all citizens. If there is
no tax-sharing scheme that will secure unanimous approval, then the proposed
outlay fails the test. Note that this basic Wicksellian proposition incorporates
the epistemological humility of revealed preference as well as the Pareto
criterion for evaluation, both of which emerged as independently developed
ideas later.

In proposing departure from the established majority voting rule in legislative assemblies, Wicksell was suggesting a change in the effective political
constitution, the set of constraints within which political choices are made. He
shifted the ground for discourse. Rather than discuss the relative efficiency of
policy options under an unchanging rules structure, with little or no regard
either to what efficiency means or for any prospect for the desired option
being chosen, Wicksell sought to open up the structure of decision rules as a
variable that might be chosen instrumentally for the purpose of insuring that
collective action meet a meaningfully defined efficiency norm. Wicksell, of
course, recognized that the strict requirement for unanimity would offer incentives for strategic behavior to all participants, and that some relaxation of
this requirement might be necessary for practicable operation. By reducing
the requirement to, say, five-sixths of the voting members of the assembly, the
incentives for strategic behavior are dramatically reduced and, at the same
time, there is insurance against most, if not all, inefficient outlay.

Wicksell did not, however, move beyond the development of criteria for
evaluating policy alternatives one at a time and singly. He shifted attention to
a change in the rules for decision, from simple majority voting toward unanimity to insure against collective approval of projects that do not yield
benefits equal to or in excess of costs, *on any ordinary project*.[10] Wicksell did
not extend analysis to the operation of specific decision rules over a whole
sequence of time periods or separate categories of outlay, which might have
allowed for less restrictive criteria for single projects.

In *The Calculus of Consent*, Tullock and I made this extension beyond
Wicksell. We were directly influenced by discussions with our colleague at
the University of Virginia, Rutledge Vining, who hammered home the argument that political choices are among alternatives rules, institutions, and
arrangements which, as they operate, generate patterns of results that are, at
least in part, stochastic. We should then evaluate the working of a rule, any
rule, not in terms of its results in a particularized choice situation, but instead
in terms of its results over a whole sequence of separate "plays," separated
both intercategorically and intertemporally. Vining's insistence on the relevance of the analogy with the selection of the rules for ordinary games was

---

10. Wicksell exempted categories of outlay that were considered to be irrevocable commit-
ments, for example, debt interest.

part and parcel of the intellectual environment in Charlottesville, and the shift of the Wicksellian criterion from single projects to rules seemed a "natural" one for us to take.

In the confined Wicksellian choice setting, an individual, behaving non-strategically, will vote to approve a proposed collective outlay if he or she anticipates that the benefits he or she secures will exceed the tax costs. He or she will oppose all proposals that fail this test. If, however, the individual is placed in a genuine *constitutional* choice setting, where the alternatives are different decision rules under which a whole sequence of particular proposals will be considered, he or she will evaluate the predicted working properties of rules over the whole anticipated sequence. If, on balance, the operation of a defined rule is expected to yield net benefits over the sequence, the individual may vote to approve the rule, even if he or she predicts that he or she must, personally, be subjected to loss or damage in *some* particular "plays" of the political game.

By shifting the applicability of the unanimity or consensus criterion from the level of particular proposals to the level of rules, to constitutional rather than postconstitutional or in-period choices, we were able to allow for the possibility that preferred and agreed upon decision rules might embody size-able departures from the unanimity limit, including simple majority voting in some cases, and even less than majority voting in others. The constitutional calculus suggests that both the costs of reaching decisions under different rules and the importance of the decisions are relevant. And since both of these elements vary, the preferred rule will not be uniform over all ranges of potential political action.

The construction seemed to us to offer justificatory argument for something akin to the complex political structure that James Madison had in mind, much of which finds itself embedded in the constitutional framework approved by the American Founding Fathers. There is a justification for the compound republic, for constitutional democracy, that can be grounded in individual utility maximization, but the general argument does not allow the elevation of majority rule to dominating status. This rule, whether in the whole electorate or in the legislative assembly, takes its place alongside other rules, some of which may be more, others less, inclusive.

At the constitutional stage of choice among rules, our argument does, conceptually, require unanimous agreement among all parties. In this sense, we were simply advancing the Wicksell-Pareto criterion one stage upward in the choice-making hierarchy. As we suggested, however, agreement on rules is much more likely to emerge than agreement on policy alternatives within rules because of the difficulties in precisely identifying the individual's economic interests in the first setting. The rule to be chosen is expected to remain in being over a whole sequence of time periods and possibly over a wide set of separate in-period choices during each period. How can the individual, at the stage of trying to select among rules, identify his or her own narrowly defined self-interest? How can he or she predict which rule will maximize his or her own net wealth? He or she is necessarily forced to choose from behind a dark "veil of uncertainty." In such a situation, utility maximization dictates that generalized criteria, such as fairness, equity, or justice enter the calculus rather than more specific arguments like net income or wealth.

This construction enabled us analytically to bridge, at least in part, the gap between narrowly defined individual self-interest and an individually generated definition of what could be called the general interest. In this construction, our efforts were quite close to those of John Rawls, which culminated in his seminal book, *A Theory of Justice*.[11] Early papers published in the late 1950s had adumbrated the essential parts of the Rawlsian construction, and while our own construction was independently developed, we were familiar with the parallel efforts of Rawls.[12]

Our analysis differed from that of Rawls, however, in the important respect that we made no attempt to generate specific predictions about what might emerge from the prospective agreement among the contractors who choose rules from behind the veil of uncertainty. As noted above, our construction suggested that no single decision rule was likely to be chosen for general applicability over the whole range of political action. We used the construction to eliminate some sets of outcomes rather than to specify those sets that would be selected. By contrast, Rawls was led (we think, misled) to attempt to use the veil of ignorance construction to make specific predictions. He suggested that his two principles of justice would uniquely emerge from the preconstitutional stage of contractual agreement.

When constitutional stage politics is conceptualized as exchange among utility maximizing individuals, we are obliged to classify ourselves to be working within the social contract tradition in political philosophy. And precursors of *The Calculus of Consent* are found in the works of the classical social contract theorists rather than in the works of the idealists or the realists. What has been and remains surprising to me has been the reluctance and/or inability of social scientists and philosophers, and especially economists, to understand and to appreciate the relationships between the institutions of voluntary exchange, the choice among constitutional rules, and the operations of ordinary politics within such rules. James Madison clearly had such an understanding, which we tried to articulate in modern analytical language a

---

11. John Rawls, *A Theory of Justice* (Cambridge, Mass.: Harvard University Press, 1971).

12. We were not familiar at all with the construction of John Harsanyi ("Cardinal Welfare, Individualistic Ethics, and Interpersonal Comparisons of Utility," *Journal of Political Economy* 63 (August 1955): 309–21), which had appeared in the mid-1950s, but with quite a different normative purpose.

quarter-century ago. There has been some shift in both public and scholarly attitudes over twenty-five years, some shift toward recovery of the Madisonian wisdom. Perhaps *The Calculus of Consent* contributed marginally to this attitudinal change. But both "politics as pure conflict" and "politics as the quest for truth and light" continue as dominant models shaping both public and "scientific" views on collective action.

CHAPTER 5

Interests and Theories in Constitutional Choice

1. Agreement and Legitimacy in Constitutional Choice

The notion that agreement among all parties concerned is the fundamental principle by which the legitimacy of a community's basic constitutional order is assured seems to be widely shared across a broad range of otherwise quite different intellectual traditions. Upon closer examination it becomes apparent, however, that the notion of agreement takes on somewhat different meanings in different contexts, and that, accordingly, there exist systematically different interpretations as to what *kind of agreement* actually carries legitimizing force. In this regard various dimensions are potentially relevant along which "agreement" may be qualified, concerning, for instance, the conditions under which agreement is achieved, the process by which it is reached, or the way in which it is "revealed" (for example, verbal agreement vs. implicit agreement, original vs. ongoing agreement, etc.).

In this chapter we focus on the relation between the *social contract notion* and the *dialogue notion* of agreement, the former being represented by authors like John Rawls, David Gauthier, or James M. Buchanan, the latter by authors like Jürgen Habermas, Bruce A. Ackerman,[1] and James S. Fishkin. Our purpose is less in reconstructing the "genuine meaning" that the two notions carry in the specific contexts in which they have been put than in advancing a (re)interpretation that allows us to integrate social contract and dialogue into a more fruitful approach to the analysis of constitutional choice processes than either one of the two perspectives provides on its own. More specifically, we want to argue that the two notions—or, at least, certain of their crucial elements—can be viewed as naturally complementing each other if one explicitly separates the "interest-component" from the "theory-component" in human choice, two components that in rational choice theory are often inseparably blended in the concept of *preferences*. We suggest that

---

A modified version of this chapter entitled "Interests and Theories in Constitutional Choice" (with Viktor Vanberg), was published in *Journal of Theoretical Politics* 1, no. 1 (January 1989): 49–62.

1. Bruce A. Ackerman, *Social Justice in the Liberal State* (New Haven and London: Yale University Press, 1980).

the contractarian-agreement notion is primarily directed toward the interest-component while the dialogue notion can be most fruitfully seen as being concerned with the theory-component.

The chapter is organized as follows: section 2 is on the distinction between the two components of choice, the interest-component and the theory-component, a distinction that we argue to be of particular importance for the study of constitutional choice. Section 3 focuses on the interest-component and its relation to a contractarian-constitutional perspective, in particular to the "veil of uncertainty" and related theoretical concepts. Section 4 concentrates on the theory-component in constitutional choice. The Habermas notion of an "ideal speech situation" and related concepts are (re)interpreted as pertaining to the cognitive dimension. Some conclusions are drawn in section 5.

2. Interests and Theories in Constitutional Choice

The economist's standard interpretation of choice behavior is in terms of *preferences* and *constraints*. Preferences are considered to be reflected in a utility function over which a rational actor maximizes, subject to whatever constraints he or she faces. As commonly understood, the concept of preferences is purely about subjective values. It refers to an actor's evaluations of potential objects of choice. As it is commonly used, however, the concept typically has more than just an evaluative dimension. It is typically used in a way that blends *evaluative* and *cognitive* components, or, in other terms, that blends a person's *evaluations* of—or *interests* in—potential outcomes of choice and his or her *theories* about the world, in particular his or her theories about what these outcomes are likely to be.[2]

For many purposes it may be convenient to use the notion of preferences in a way that does not explicitly separate the genuinely evaluative components from the cognitive components. For some analytical purposes it may be useful, however, systematically to separate interests and theories as distinct elements in the choice process. How a person chooses among potential alternatives is not only a matter of "what he wants" but also of "what he believes," and for some kinds of choices an actor's beliefs or theories may play a most

---

2. For instance, a person's preference for, say, European-built over American-built cars does not simply reflect certain values or interests that he or she may harbor. It is heavily impregnated with factual predictions—or "theories"—about the consequences that are likely to result from buying a European rather than an American car, predictions that can turn out to be right or wrong, in contrast to the *genuinely evaluative components* of his or her "preference" that cannot be properly subjected to a true/false judgment. Talbot Page draws a distinction between "preference (utility)" and "belief (probability)" that in some respects parallels our distinction between interests and theories in "Pivot Mechanisms in Probability Revelation," (California Institute of Technology, 1987), mimeograph.

crucial role. We suggest that the second element is particularly important for constitutional choices, that is, for choices among rules.[3] It follows that constitutional analyses can profit from explicitly distinguishing between the evaluative and the cognitive dimension of constitutional choice.

The notion of consumer or household production, as advanced by Gary S. Becker,[4] provides a useful framework for stating somewhat more systematically the evaluative/cognitive distinction. In the context of the consumer production theory, the universe of potential objects of choice is divided into two subsets: On the one side, there are the "ultimate objects of desire" (food, shelter, sex, etc.) with regard to which all persons have the same invariant preferences, simply because of their common human nature. And, on the other side, there are those objects of choice that are potential inputs into the production of the ultimate objects of desire rather than being desired in and by themselves. The demand for these "instrumental" goods is a derived demand, derived from the demand for ultimate goods to the production of which they are expected to contribute. These "nonultimate" goods become the object of most choices that are empirically relevant for the purpose of social theory.

Independently of Becker's own specific interpretation, the usefulness of his conception for our purposes lies in the suggestion that people's preferences for "ordinary" objects of choice—like diet soft drinks, books, or karate cruises—are typically derived preferences, preferences that are an amalgam of preferences for more fundamental goods (like health, beauty, entertainment, social esteem, etc.) and theories about how these "ordinary" objects of choice contribute to the production of the more fundamental goods. To the extent that potential objects of choice are instrumental to the production of more fundamental goods, theories about their respective conduciveness in this regard obviously play a crucial part in a person's choice.

There is, one may say, an interest-component and a theory-component in almost any choice, from the choice among ice cream flavors to the choice of a mate, though, of course, the relative importance of the two components may dramatically vary over different categories. For many ordinary market choices, the theory-component will play a minimal role, while others may be heavily theory-laden. On the constitutional level, it should be obvious that people's theories about the working properties of alternative rules and rule-systems, and not just their interests in expected outcomes, are of crucial relevance to their choice behavior.

---

3. Although stated in different terms, the relatively greater importance of the theory component in constitutional, as opposed to ordinary, political choice was noted earlier in Buchanan's "Politics and Science," in *Freedom in Constitutional Contract: Perspective of a Political Economist* (College Station: Texas A & M University Press, 1977), 50–77, esp. 72ff.

4. Gary S. Becker, *The Economic Approach to Human Behavior* (Chicago and London: University of Chicago Press, 1976), esp. 131ff.

Constitutional choices are concerned with the choice of rules for a community or group of persons. By their very nature the rules that are to be chosen are *public* in the sense that they define the terms under which actions and transactions within the respective community may be carried out. That is, they affect everybody in the relevant community, though not necessarily everybody in the same way. In addition to their "publicness," constitutional choices are clearly of an instrumental nature. Rules are typically not objects valued in themselves. Rules are valued because of the pattern of outcomes that they are expected to produce.[5] We may use the term *constitutional preferences* to refer to a person's preferences over alternative rules or sets of rules, preferences that may be revealed in voting choices or in other ways. A person's constitutional preferences concern the ordering of rules that might be implemented in his or her community, or, stated differently, they describe the evaluation of the constitutional environment.

As noted earlier, constitutional preferences can be analytically decomposed into two components: *Constitutional theories* and *constitutional interests*. A person's constitutional theories are his or her predictions (embodying assumptions and beliefs) about what the prospective outcomes of alternative rules will be. These predictions may, of course, be arranged in a right or wrong scalar. His or her constitutional interests, on the other hand, are his or her own subjective evaluations of expected outcomes, evaluations to which the attribute "right/wrong" cannot be meaningfully applied. The cognitive and the evaluative components of a person's constitutional preferences are critically different in this regard, and because of this difference one should expect that the question of *constitutional agreement* raises different issues with regard to "constitutional interests" as opposed to "constitutional theories."

3. Constitutional Interests and Choice "Behind the Veil"

The contractarian agreement notion focuses central attention on the interest-component in constitutional choice. Social contract theories typically concern themselves with the issue of how agreement on rules can be achieved among persons with potentially conflicting constitutional interests.

One characteristic way of how a social contract theory may approach this issue is paradigmatically exemplified by John Rawls's *A Theory of Justice*.[6] In

---

5. As Friedrich A. Hayek states: "The rules of conduct . . . are multi-purpose instruments developed as adaptations to certain *kinds* of environment because they help to deal with certain *kinds* of situations," *Law, Legislation and Liberty*, vol. 2, *The Mirage of Social Justice* (London and Henley: Routledge & Kegan Paul, 1976), 2:4.

6. John Rawls, *A Theory of Justice* (Cambridge, Mass.: Harvard University Press, 1971).

Rawls's construction, the prospect of agreement is secured by defining certain "ideal" conditions under which constitutional choices are hypothetically made. The choosers are assumed to be placed behind a "veil of ignorance" that makes it impossible for them to know anything specific about how they will be personally affected by alternative rules. Ignorant about their prospective specific interests in particular outcomes, they are induced to judge rules "impartially." Potential conflict in constitutional interests is not eliminated, but the veil of ignorance transforms potential *inter*personal conflicts into *intra*personal ones. In the context of this chapter it is important to mention a second essential feature of the Rawlsian construction. While the persons behind the veil are assumed to be totally ignorant about their prospective *specific* interests in particular rules, they are, at the same time, assumed to be perfectly knowledgeable about the working properties of alternative rules. In our terminology, their constitutional theories are supposed to be perfect and noncontroversial. Informational problems with regard to the general workings of rules do not exist.

A standard objection against the Rawlsian type of contractarianism is that the conceptual reconstruction of some hypothetical agreement under ideal conditions carries little normative and explanatory significance with regard to actual constitutional choices that are made in a world where people are neither totally ignorant about their identifiable constitutional interests nor perfectly knowledgeable as far as their constitutional theories are concerned. Our discussion in the remainder of this chapter is, in part, about how the social contract notion may be employed in the analysis of constitutional choices that occur under such more realistic conditions.

In parts of what has become known as the "rent-seeking literature" in economics[7] there is a certain tendency to suggest that conflicts of interest are no less characteristic for choices among rules than for choices within rules and that, therefore, the idea of some genuine constitutional agreement is a mere illusion when placed in a real world context. People with identifiable specific constitutional interests will, it is argued, attempt to achieve implementation of rules that promise to be differentially advantageous to them, and their distributionally motivated struggle for "biased" rules will inhibit any mutually beneficial constitutional reform. Though rules may be conceivable that would allow for a "better" game, rules that would make everybody in the respective community better off, from this kind of rent-seeking perspective people's concern for their identifiable and conflicting constitutional interests will prevent them from actually realizing the potential gains from constitutional cooperation.

---

7. See, for example, James M. Buchanan, Robert D. Tollison, and Gordon Tullock, ed., *Toward a Theory of the Rent-Seeking Society* (College Station: Texas A & M University Press, 1980).

The rent-seeking skepticism is correct in its diagnosis that identifiability of particular constitutional interests in real-world settings makes agreement on rules more difficult to achieve. But it may be overly pessimistic to jump to the the conclusion that, under real-world conditions, genuine constitutional agreement is impossible. This diagnosis rules out the possibility that rational persons recognize the "rent-seeking trap" and engage in a concerted effort to escape. A more optimistic and, at the same time more realistic, approach should investigate the conditions under which, and the potential means by which, constitutional agreement may be facilitated in real, nonhypothetical choice situations.

It is, of course, true that in real-world settings people are typically not totally ignorant about their particular constitutional interests. But they are not perfectly certain about these interests either. In constitutional matters, people typically find themselves behind a *veil of uncertainty* that prevents them from accurately anticipating the particular ways in which they will be affected by the prospective workings of alternative rules. The veil of uncertainty can be more or less transparent, or, in other terms, its "thickness" may vary, dependent on certain characteristics of the actual choice situation. As the veil's "thickness" increases so will the prospect of achieving agreement.

The degree to which persons are uncertain about their particular, identifiable constitutional interests is not a determined and unalterable constraint. The variables that affect the veil's thickness can, to some extent, be manipulated, and rational actors may take deliberate measures designed to put themselves behind a thicker veil, thereby enhancing the prospects of realizing potential gains from constitutional agreement. Most important for these purposes is probably the fact that the degree of uncertainty is, in part, a function of the sort of rules that are under consideration. The essential dimensions here are the *generality* and the *durability* of rules.[8] The more general rules are and the longer the period over which they are expected to be in effect, the less certain people can be about the particular ways in which alternative rules will affect them.[9] They will therefore be induced to adopt a more impartial perspective, and, consequently, they will be more likely to reach agreement.[10]

---

8. On this issue, see Geoffrey Brennan and James M. Buchanan, *The Reason of Rules—Constitutional Political Economy* (Cambridge: Cambridge University Press, 1985), 28ff.

9. James M. Buchanan, "The Constitution of Economic Policy," *The American Economic Review* 77 (1987): 243–50, esp. 248.

10. The potential for rational actors deliberately to increase uncertainty in order to facilitate agreement is vividly described in the following quotation from F. A. Hayek:

That it is thus ignorance of the future outcome which makes possible agreement on rules . . . is recognized by the practice in many instances of deliberately making the outcome unpredictable in order to make agreement on the procedure possible: whenever we agree on drawing lots we deliberately substitute equal chances for the different parties for the certainty as to which of them will benefit from the outcome. Mothers who could never

It is not only through the veil of uncertainty that fairness may be induced and agreement facilitated in constitutional choice. An additional and independent factor, working in the same direction, is the *concern for stability*. The purpose of entering a constitutional agreement is the prospect of realizing gains that can be derived from operating under the respective constitutional constraints. The possibility of realizing such gains is not just a matter of securing some initial agreement; it is also a matter of continuing acquiescence in an ongoing cooperative arrangement. Stability refers to the viability of a constitutional arrangement over time. Rational actors can be expected to take considerations of stability into account when engaging in constitutional choice. And to the extent that fairness and stability of constitutional arrangements are interrelated, the concern for stability will induce a concern for fairness. It will do so, as mentioned before, in addition to, and independently of, the veil of uncertainty. The latter works by moderating the differences among identifiable constitutional interests. The concern for stability induces a preference for more impartial rules even in persons who may be perfectly aware of the particular effects that alternative rules will have on them. It is not the uncertainty about one's own particular position, but the anticipation that a constitutional arrangement is unlikely to be stable if it is only designed to serve one's own particular interests that will induce impartiality.

With regard to the potential relation between stability and fairness, it is important to distinguish between two aspects of the stability problem that are not always sufficiently separated in discussions on the issue, namely, the *compliance problem* and the *renegotiation problem*.[11] For a constitutional arrangement to be stable over time it has to command a sufficient level of compliance and a sufficient level of ongoing agreement. Both defection and pressure to renegotiate the terms of the arrangement will undermine the prospect of realizing the very benefits that motivate the constitutional agreement in the first place. Rational actors will, therefore, have a reason, at the constitutional stage, to be concerned about both problems and to incorporate appropriate precautions into their constitutional agreements. What is relevant for our purpose is that their constitutional concerns about compliance and renegotiation do not relate to the fairness issue in the same way.

---

agree whose desperately ill child the doctor should attend first, will readily agree before the event that it would be in the interest of all if he attend the children in some regular order which increased efficiency. (*Law, Legislation, and Liberty* 2:4)

11. An informative discussion on this issue is provided by Edward F. McClennen. On the distinction that is of relevance here, McClennen states: "[A] consensus on a principle of justice will be unstable not only if those who come to agree on it subsequently are prone to unilaterally defect from the agreement, but also if they are disposed to press for the rejection of that principle and the adoption of some other, that is, to press for a renegotiation of the social contract" (Edward F. McClennen, "Justice and the Problem of Stability," [National Humanities Center, 1987], mimeograph, 6ff).

Though there may be some indirect relation between fairness of rules and compliance with rules, the latter is certainly not a direct function of the former. That is, the fact that rules are perceived as fair by the relevant group of persons does not, per se, guarantee a willingness to comply with those rules. The compliance problem results from the fact that there are potential gains from defecting. Whether such gains exist or not is not per se dependent on the fairness properties. And to the extent that such gains exist, a compliance problem is present even with perfectly fair rules.[12]

There is a much more direct relation between the fairness issue and renegotiation. And it is with regard to renegotiation, rather than with regard to compliance, that the concern for stability can be expected to induce a concern for fairness. A constitutional agreement that favors particular interests may be achievable under "suitable" conditions, but such an agreement can be expected to be less robust with regard to potential changes in circumstances than fair arrangements.[13]

Finally, we should note that stability, in both the compliance and the renegotiation aspects, is necessarily a more important consideration in constitutional choice than in nonconstitutional or postconstitutional choice. By their very nature, rules imply quasi permanency; they are expected to remain in force over more than one period of time during which ordinary political choices are to be made within such rules as exist. This basic characteristic of rules insures that the present value (at the time of choice among rules) of predicted noncompliance or of agitation for renegotiation is substantially higher for long-term than for short-term rules. Hence, as increased durability may be deliberately invoked to thicken the veil, and to facilitate agreement, the concern for stability, in the process of reaching agreement, increases pari passu.

4. Dialogue and Reason in Constitutional Choice

The contractarian notion and the dialogue notion of agreement both imply a *procedural* criterion—as opposed to an outcome criterion—of legitimacy.

---

12. David Gauthier's theory in *Morals by Agreement* (Oxford: Oxford University Press, 1985) seems to be partly based on the assumption that there is some direct link between fairness and compliance. See, for example, Gauthier ("Morality, Rational Choice, and Semantic Representation—A Reply to My Critics," *Social Philosophy and Policy* 5[1988]: 173–221): "Stability plays a key role in linking rational choice to contractarian morality. Aware of the benefits to be gained from constraining principles, rational persons will seek principles that invite stable compliance. . . .An agreement affording equally favorable terms to all thus invites, as no other can, stable compliance" (189). On this issue, see also Viktor Vanberg and James M. Buchanan, "Rational Choice and Moral Order," *Analyse & Kritik* 10(December 1988): 138–60.

13. John Rawls discusses this issue in terms of the contrast between "acceptance as a mere *modus vivendi*" and *overlapping consensus*, the former being less robust since "its stability is

From both perspectives the legitimacy of basic constitutional principles is judged not against some predefined "ideal system" but in terms of the process from which these principles emerge. The normative focus is on the characteristics of the process of constitutional choice, not on characteristics of choice-outcomes as such. Furthermore, in both perspectives a "good" or "proper" process is defined as one that assures *fairness* or *impartiality* in the rules that emerge.[14]

The difference between the two constructions lies in their somewhat different understanding of the procedural characteristics that are to assure fairness. And it lies in their somewhat different interpretation of fairness itself. To the contractarian notion, the individuals' interests are the "basic inputs" into the constitutional process. The choice process is supposed properly to reflect these interests, whatever they may be. It is not considered a process in which these interests themselves are judged or rated in any way. Fairness is considered a matter of the constraints under which constitutional choices are made, not as a matter of the "quality" of interests that enter into such choices. In particular, it is the voluntariness of choice that, from a contractarian perspective, constitutes the essential prerequisite of fairness. Fairness and voluntariness of agreement are, in a sense, the same. Fairness is not defined independently of that upon which persons voluntarily agree.[15]

By contrast, within the dialogue or discourse theory framework the notions of agreement and fairness tend to carry a characteristically more "objectivist" or cognitive meaning in the sense of implying more than just the notion of intersecting or coinciding individual interests. Within this framework, constitutional agreement is not simply—as in the contractarian context—a matter of compromise among separate individual interests. Individuals' interests are not simply viewed as the basic inputs that the process of constitutional agreement is supposed properly to reflect. These interests are themselves to be evaluated and possibly transformed in the process of constitutional discourse. Whether this idea is (as, for example, by James S. Fishkin[16]) stated in terms of a distinction between "brute motivations" and "refined motivations" (where the former are to be transformed into the latter through "purging of bias and

---

contingent on circumstances remaining such as not to upset the fortunate convergence of interests" ("On Achieving Consensus Under Pluralism" [Harvard University, 1987], mimeograph, 7).

14. See, for example, James S. Fishkin, *Beyond Subjective Morality* (New Haven and London: Yale University Press, 1984), 24f and 95ff; Gauthier, *Social Philosophy and Policy*, 31f; Jürgen Habermas, *Moralbewusstsein und kommunikatives Handeln* (Frankfurt: Suhrkamp, 1983), 75ff.

15. It should be noted that our stylized characterization of the contractarian conception is supposed to focus on what we consider its essential difference from the dialogue construction. It is not necessarily intended to be descriptive of all variants of contractarianism.

16. James S. Fishkin, "Bargaining, Justice and Justification: Towards Reconstruction," (University of Texas, Austin, 1987), mimeograph, 16f.

indoctrination"); or whether it is (as, for example, by Jürgen Habermas[17]) invoked through the notion of an "impartial evaluation of the interests of all who are concerned" ("die unparteiliche Buerteilung der Interessen aller Betroffenen"): What is implied is a critical shift towards a "truth-judgment" interpretation of constitutional agreement.

Within the contractarian framework, agreement carries normative significance in and of itself. Agreed upon principles are considered legitimate simply because they are the ones that command agreement, not because agreement is indicative of some other "quality" that distinguishes these principles.[18] Observed agreement may be normatively qualified in terms of its *voluntariness*, that is, in terms of the constraints under which the parties involved express their agreement. But, in its contractarian sense, it cannot be meaningfully qualified in terms of a standard that goes beyond agreement itself. The claim to such qualification is, however, apparently inherent in the dialogue construction. According to Habermas,[19] valid or legitimate norms are not simply those on which persons under specified conditions happen to agree, they are those norms that deserve to be intersubjectively acknowledged because they embody some interest that is recognizably common to all persons concerned. And whether they deserve such recognition has to be examined in practical discourse. Constitutional agreement that emerges from ethical discourse has legitimizing force not simply because it is "agreement," but because it indicates that the agreed upon rules deserve to be classified as "equally good for everybody involved."[20]

To be sure, Habermas's style of reasoning typically leaves considerable room for interpretation, and one might argue that some of his statements can well be read in a way that is much less in contrast to a contractarian conception than our interpretation suggests. But Habermas himself explicitly notes the critical difference between his discourse notion and a compromise notion of agreement, emphasizing the cognitive claims of his own construction.[21] He

---

17. Habermas, *Moralbewusstsein und kommunikatives Handeln*, 78.

18. Jules L. Coleman's distinction between an "epistemic" and a "criterial, semantic" interpretation of agreement parallels the distinction that we want to stress here ("Market Contractarianism and the Unanimity Rule," *Social Philosophy and Policy* 2 [1985]: 69–114, esp. 106).

19. Habermas, *Moralbewusstsein und kommunikatives Handeln*, esp. 73–84.

20. Habermas, *Moralbewusstsein und kommunikatives Handeln*, 81:

In einem solchen Prozeß wird *einer dem anderen Gründe* dafür nennen, warum er wollen kann, dass eine Handlungsweise sozial verbindlich gemacht wird. . . .Und einen solchen Prozeß nennen wir eben den praktischen Diskurs. Eine Norm, die auf diesem Wege in Kraft gesetzt wird, kann "gerechtfertigt" heissen, weil durch den argumentativ erzielten Beschluß angezeigt wird, dass sie das Prädikat "gleichermassen gut für jeden der Betroffenen" verdient.

21. Habermas, *Moralbewusstsein und kommunikatives Handeln*, 81ff., in particular 82f.: "Im praktischen Diskurs versuchen sich die Beteiligten über ein gemeinsames Interesse klar zu

characterizes his construction as being critically dependent on the assumption that claims concerning the validity of norms carry a cognitive meaning and can be treated like truth-judgments.[22] And he strongly rejects the "skeptical premise that the validity of norms cannot be interpreted analogously to the validity of truth-judgments ("die skeptische Grundannahme, dass sich die Sollgeltung von Normen nicht in Analogie zur Wahrheitsgeltung von Propositionen verstehen lässt").[23]

As described, the contractarian and the dialogue interpretation of constitutional agreement appear to represent alternative and opposing views: *Agreement as compromise* versus *agreement as truth-judgment*. And, as intended by their authors, some of the conceptions advanced on the two sides may indeed be diametrically opposed. As mentioned earlier, however, our interest here is not in authenticity of interpretation. Instead, our interest is in exploring the potential for fruitful integration. And such potential clearly exists if the two constructions are interpreted in the context of the distinction between *constitutional interests* and *constitutional theories* as analytically separable components in constitutional preference and constitutional choice.

As stated in my earlier discussion on the relation between "Politics and Science,"[24] constitutional choice involves both individuals' genuine evaluations of alternative rules as well as their predictions about the working properties of such rules. Observed constitutional disagreement may reflect disagreement in either one or both of these components. And the process of reaching agreement can, conceptually, be discussed in different terms dependent on which one of the two components is concerned. To the extent that disagreement over rules reflects genuine differences in *interests*, reaching constitutional agreement is clearly a matter of compromise, of finding terms that are acceptable to everybody, and definitely not a matter of "discovering the truth." To the extent, however, that disagreement is a matter of differences in constitutional *theories*, the process of reaching agreement clearly is about "truth-judgments," and it can be properly compared to scientific discourse, to controversy over alternative theories in science.[25]

---

werden, beim Aushandeln eines Kompromisses versuchen sie, einen Ausgleich zwischen partikularen, einander widerstreitenden Interessen herbeizuführen."

22. Habermas, *Moralbewusstsein und kommunikatives Handeln*, 78: "Eine Diskursethik steht und fällt also mit den beiden Annahmen, dass *(a)* normative Geltungsansprüche einen kognitiven Sinn haben und *wie* Wahrheitsansprüche behandelt werden können, und dass *(b)* die Begründung von Normen und Geboten die Durchführung eines realen Diskurses verlangt. . . ." See also 131f.

23. Habermas, *Moralbewusstsein und kommunikatives* Handeln, 78.

24. Buchanan, *Freedom in Constitutional Contract*.

25. To quote from my earlier treatment:

The appropriate location for genuine constitutional choice seems to be somewhere between the limits imposed by the choice among scientific explanations on the one hand and the

Though interest components and theory components are conceptually separable inputs into constitutional preferences, there is, of course, no practical way of strictly separating them in actual constitutional choice. We cannot know with any degree of certainty whether, or to what extent, observed disagreement reflects "merely" differences in constitutional theories, or whether they are based on genuinely different evaluations. In this sense, acknowledgment of the legitimate role of potentially conflicting individual evaluations clearly excludes an interpretation that assigns, as Habermas does, a truth-judgment function to the constitutional process as such. Failure to reach agreement in actual constitutional discourse may, but need not necessarily, reflect disagreement in theories. Even with perfect agreement in the theoretical dimension, a potential for disagreement in evaluations may persist. And respect for such potential disagreement commands that the limits of "discourse" and the ultimate role and the need for *compromise* in constitutional matters be recognized.[26]

However, within the limits specified above, there is an obvious "role for reason," for science-like discourse in constitutional choice. Compared to ordinary market-choice, there seems to be a dramatic shift in relevance from the interest component to the theory component when choices among alternative rules are concerned.[27] Persons' preferences over alternative rules or sys-

---

choice among alternative publicly supplied goods on the other. There may be differences in individual evaluations of alternative rules—differences that may, in one sense, reflect basic value orderings. To this extent agreement will not be produced by open discussion. Something more than evaluation is involved in many cases, however. Individual differences may be based, to a large extent, on differing predictions about the working properties of the alternative rules under consideration. Within these limits meaningful discussion and analysis can take place, and the careful assessment of alternative models can closely resemble scientific process of the standard sort. (*Freedom in Constitutional Contract*, 72)

26. To quote again from my earlier discussion:

If politics at the constitutional level involves a process of discovery and exploration analogous to that of science, must we assume that there is a unique explanation, a unique set of rules which defines the elements of good society and which, once discovered, will come to be generally accepted by informed and intellectually honest men? . . . To some omniscient being . . . who can view man's interactions one with another solely in terms of his own evaluative criteria, the answer may be in the affirmative. But to man himself the existence of such singularity in solution seems highly dubious. Values would seem to differ, and perhaps even widely, even among enlightened men, and different men will tend to value different rules. My ideal "good society" need not be identical with yours in general or in its particulars even if we fully agree on the working properties of the alternative rules under discussion. (*Freedom in Constitutional Contract*, 75)

27. The difference between ordinary market choices and constitutional choices in terms of the dramatically greater role of theoretical components in the latter is discussed in Karen I. Vaughn, "Can There Be a Constitutional Political Economy?," (George Mason University, 1984), mimeograph, 10ff; see also Viktor Vanberg, "Individual Choice and Constitutional Constraints—The Normative Element in Classical and Contractarian Liberalism," *Analyse & Kritik* 8 (1986):

tems of rules do not simply reflect "basic values"; they are largely a product of their constitutional theories, and, therefore, may be changed through information that impacts on their theories. To the extent that persons' revealed constitutional preferences are informed by their predictions of the working properties of the rules that are under consideration, constitutional agreement can be facilitated by a process that systematically encourages critical examination and discussion of alternative theoretical constructions, separate from and independent of any procedural devices that aim at facilitating agreement in the interest dimension.

The dialogue or discourse notion can be fruitfully interpreted as drawing attention to the importance of the informational dimension in constitutional choice, even though its advocates might not agree to such a limited interpretation. The fact that the public discourse on rules—as political debates in general—is typically carried out by *reasoning arguments* but can be supposed to be motivated by *interests*, is sometimes taken as evidence that the political rhetoric is mere camouflage, concealing real interests. And there is a tendency—for example, in parts of the rent-seeking literature—to conclude from this that it is ultimately only interests and the power behind interests that count in the political process, while arguments and reason lack any power "of their own." Such an interpretation ignores the very fact that political discourse, carried out in terms of reasoning argument rather than simple declarations of interests, imposes effective constraints on how one may seek support for one's own proposals. And such interpretation distracts attention from the relevance of the genuinely *theoretical* components in all political and, a fortiori, in all constitutional preferences. Winning support for one's own visions and theories is an important part of the political process.[28]

5. Conclusion

In basically democratic societies, the rules that constrain the activities of members of the community, both in their private and political capacities, are "public goods" in the technical definition. These rules, whatever they may be and regardless of how they are selected, are equally constraining upon *all* members of the community. To the extent that persons share a *common* subset

---

113–49, esp. 141ff. It should be noted that our attention in the present context is exclusively on the relevance of the theory component. We deliberately ignore here the familiar problem of "rational ignorance" that is commonly stressed in comparisons between market choices and voting choices, that is, the problem that the incentives to be "well informed" are dramatically lower in the voting than in the market context, because of the systematically different expectations concerning the impact of one's own choice on oneself.

28. On this issue, see Thomas Sowell, *A Conflict of Visions* (New York: William Morrow, 1987).

of ultimate desires (for example, Hobbesian security), Beckerian Z-goods, that can only be met instrumentally through constitutional rules, the argument over alternative rules reduces to an argument over *theories*. If the desires that may be met through a constraining rule cannot be factored down into a commonly shared set, while, at the same time, the rules must be public in the sense noted, divergent *interests* must, somehow, be reconciled. At this level, discussion, dialogue, reason, and science lose the authority to generate potential agreement. Cooperation can replace conflict only if the different components of interests, held with varying intensities by persons, can be traded off or compromised with the results expressed, actually or symbolically, as a *social contract*.

Part 2
The Strategy of Constitutional Agreement

CHAPTER 6

The Politicization of Market Failure

Furthermore, there is no reason to suppose that the . . . regulations, made by a fallible administration subject to political pressures . . . , will necessarily always be those which increase the efficiency with which the economic system operates. . . .But equally there is no reason, why, on occasion, such governmental administrative regulation should not lead to an improvement in economic efficiency. This would seem particularly likely when, as is normally the case with the smoke nuisance, a large number of people are involved and in which therefore the costs of handling the problem through the market or the firm may be high.

—R. H. Coase, "The Problem of Social Cost"

Much of the externality literature has concentrated on the issue of whether or not what is diagnosed as "market failure" requires politically orchestrated correction and, if so, what the appropriate political measures should be. But what kind of "corrections" can the political process actually be expected to generate if a politicization of market failure occurs? Our purpose in this chapter is to address this question in a highly stylized and simplified model of both the externality-generating economic process and of the political decision-making process. We shall find it useful to differentiate between two cases that the standard interpretation of external effects tends to lump together. While the adjective "external" is normally understood as meaning *external* to the contracting parties, we shall make an explicit distinction between what we call "internal" and "external" externalities. As *internal externalities* we classify those effects that are *external* to a given contractual relation but *internal* to the group of contracting parties. As *external externalities* we classify those that are external to both the respective transaction and the group of contractors.

1. Private and Political Responses to Externalities

To "correct" for a negative externality is normally understood as making those parties who decide on the externality-causing activity account for the negative

---

This chapter was written jointly with Viktor J. Vanberg. A slightly modified version was published as "The Politicization of Market Failure," *Public Choice* 57 (May 1988): 101–13.

impact on third parties through an adjusted cost calculus. In Pigovian terms, correction means that the decision makers must take the full *social costs* of their actions into account. Such "correction" can, in principle, result from *private* as well as from *political* responses to externalities. The general principles of private correction have been lucidly analyzed in Coase's seminal, "The Problem of Social Cost."[1] As Coase pointed out, in the absence of transaction costs, the damage done to a third, nonconsenting party will, in any case, show up as an opportunity cost in an economic actor's calculation, whether he or she can be held liable in the existing legal system or not. The difference is only in the particular form these opportunity costs take. If the actor is liable it will be in the form of damages to be paid; if the actor is not liable it will be in the form of foregone payments that the third, harmed parties would be willing to make in order to induce the actor to restrict or altogether to abstain from the externality causing activity.[2] Whether the one or the other incidence of opportunity cost applies is obviously of distributional significance, but the Pigovian problem—the "divergence between private and social costs"—would not exist under Coasian bargaining, so long as transaction costs are negligible. Another type of private response to externalities, which may actually be considered a specific variant of the bargaining solution, would be a merger between an externality-creating and an externality-receiving unit (the farmer and the rancher in Coase's familiar and classic example). Such a merger will fully correct for any premerger allocative distortions. It internalizes the prior externality by insuring that the same decision maker secures the possible benefits of carrying out the damaging activity and the possible spillover costs that the activity involves.[3] Utility or profit-maximizing strategy dictates that the activity in question be adjusted to maximize net rent on the combined unit of operation.

Private responses to externalities, such as the bargaining or the merger solution, operate via some reassignment or rearrangement of rights within a given legal structure or, more generally, within a given framework of socially sanctioned rules and laws. In other words, private corrections are a matter of *in-period* adjustments among market participants—of trades made within a

---

1. In *The Economics of Legal Relationships*, ed. H. G. Manne, 127–67 (St. Paul: West Publishing, 1975). First published in *Journal of Law and Economics* 3 (1960): 1–44.

2. "(T)he Coase theorem . . . is based on the proposition that an implicit cost (the forgone payment from the farmer) is just as much a cost as is an explicit cost (the liability damage) . . ." (H. Demsetz, "When Does the Rule of Liability Matter," in *Economics of Legal Relationships*, 168–83, esp. 174.

3. It should be noted that "the same decision maker" may be a collective decision-making unit and that, in those cases, the structure of the decision-making process may have an impact on how the possible benefits and the possible spillover costs will be balanced against each other. We ignore this problem in the present, private-merger context. It will be of particular concern, however, in the later analysis of the political response to externalities.

defined institutional context. In contrast to such private responses, *political* corrections work via some change in the "rules of the game"; they imply some alteration in the rule structure itself.[4] Politicization, as such, amounts to an abrogation of existing prior legal "rights" concerning the activity in question. Political corrections are about *redefining* the rights that the market participants hold, not about *trading* defined rights. Where transaction costs render private bargaining or merger solutions nonviable,[5] political responses become particularly relevant, though it should be noticed that, independent of transaction costs barriers, negatively affected parties, for distributional reasons, may always have an incentive to take recourse to the political process.

Transaction costs typically increase significantly as we move beyond small-number to large-number interactions and, as a consequence, neither a merger nor a set of Coase-like bargained solutions may be predicted to occur.[6] This is often assumed to be relevant for many environmental issues such as air and water pollution, the classic example being the factory smoke that dirties the laundries of the many neighborhood housewives. If a viable private response to externalities in large-number interactions requires collective organization, the high organization costs may render politicization, that is, recourse to the existing organization called government, the cheaper alternative.

There are basically three forms that political responses to externalities can take: The legal structure can be redefined to make the externality-creating party fully liable for the damage it causes; the externality-causing activities can be made subject to some kind of direct regulation; or, finally, a tax can be imposed on the externality-creating activity.

The first alternative, though certainly a suitable instrument for distributional corrections, will not necessarily bring about a Pigovian allocational

---

4. On the distinction between private, in-period, and political constitutional responses to externalities, see Viktor J. Vanberg, "Individual Choice and Institutional Constraints—The Normative Element in Classical and Contractarian Liberalism," *Analyse & Kritik* 8 (1986): 113–49, esp. 123ff.

5. E. J. Mishan's comment is relevant here:

In the absence of government intervention, whatever the legal position, the unfavored party has a clear interest in trying to bribe the other party to modify the "uncorrected" output. Successful mutual agreement between the parties, however, presupposes that the maximum possible amount of the shared gains, G, in moving to an optimal position, exceeds their combined transaction costs T. . . . Failure to reach mutual agreement, on the other hand, can be regarded as prima facie evidence that $(G - T) < 0$. (E. J. Mishan, "The Postwar Literature on Externalities: An Interpretative Essay," *Journal of Economic Literature* 9 [1971]: 1–28, esp. 17).

6. For some necessary qualifications of the "large-number argument," see Buchanan, where the argument is made that not the large-number feature, as such, but "the presence of a 'publicness' interaction among 'consumers' or bearers of a potential external diseconomy is critical for the predicted failure of voluntary contractual arrangements" (James M. Buchanan, "The Institutional Structure of Externality," *Public Choice* 14 [1973]: 69–82).

improvement. Given the inherently reciprocal nature of the externality prob-lem,[7] a shift in the liability-rules may, if transaction costs matter, simply result in a shift from an excessive supply to an undersupply of the externality-creating activity.[8] An allocational net improvement could result, though, if the transaction costs barriers are "nonsymmetrical" in the sense that it is less costly to achieve a private bargaining solution under the new legal arrange-ment than under the old one.

Debates on political corrections of externalities concentrate on the *direct regulation* and *taxation* alternatives,[9] and it is those methods, particularly the latter, on which our analysis will concentrate. In contrast with the standard treatment in welfare economics, our interest is not in examining the "efficient regulations" or "efficient Pigovian taxes" that could be recommended for political implementation. Instead of assuming, as much of welfare economics implicitly seems to do, that there is some idealized efficiency-seeking despot to whom such policy recommendations can be suggested, our purpose in this chapter is to address the question that the welfare economists overlook, namely, can politicization of external diseconomies be expected to insure correction? Or, more specifically: Under what conditions could we predict that the political process would generate results that correspond, even if roughly, to those produced by genuine internalization of the external disecon-omy? Using a simple majority-voting model we shall analyze the outcomes of externality-correcting decisions that can be expected to result under different compositions of the voting population, compositions in terms of subgroups that are benefiting from and/or being harmed by an externality-creating ac-tivity, or neither or both.

---

7. "The question is commonly thought of as one in which *A* inflicts harm on *B* and what has to be decided is: How should we restrain *A*? But this is wrong. We are dealing with a problem of a reciprocal nature. To avoid the harm to *B* would inflict harm on *A*. The real question that has to be decided is: Should *A* be allowed to harm *B* or should *B* be allowed to harm *A*?" (R. H. Coase, "The Problem of Social Cost," 127f).

8. "(T)he assignment of rights to the . . . 'producer' of the external effect biases the outcomes in favor of an excessive supply of the diseconomy whereas the reversal of this assign-ment biases the results toward an undersupply of the diseconomy" (James M. Buchanan, "The Institutional Structure of Externality," p. 75f).

9. As Cornes and Sandler argue with regard to "policy intervention to deal with externalities":

The most celebrated form of intervention—suggested by Pigou and clarified, extended, and criticized by countless others—consists of a system of taxes and subsidies designed to distort individuals' choices toward an optimal outcome. An alternative to such manipula-tion of the price system involves the enforcement of quantitative constraints such as a set of environmental standards that must be maintained. (R. Cornes and T. Sandler, *The Theory of Externalities, Public Goods, and Club Goods* [Cambridge: Cambridge University Press, 1986], 48)

2. Majoritarian Voting and Direct Regulation

According to the standard interpretation of the notion of "external effects," the word *external* means: *External to the group* of those who take part in the decision to engage in the relevant activity. The implicit presumption is that the beneficiaries and the sufferers of the externality-creating activity are necessarily *different* sets of persons or firms. This presumption may be misleading in the case of externalities which are considered to occur in the context of transactions involving two or more parties, the case to which Pigou actually referred in his exposition of the issue.[10] In analyzing such cases, it seems to be more fruitful and appropriate to interpret the "external" as meaning external to the respective *transactions or contracts* rather than external to the transacting or contracting *parties*. Externalities in this sense may be *external* as well as *internal* to the parties to the transaction, two cases that, for reasons of terminological convenience, we propose to label *external externalities* and *internal externalities*.

Distinguishing between these two types of externalities by no means rules out that external effects may be both *internal* and *external*, in the sense defined. What is assumed is that these two types of effects can be usefully distinguished, not that all externalities can be exclusively classified into one or the other of the two categories. This distinction is particularly useful for our purpose of analyzing expected patterns of political responses to externalities. As an example for the following analysis, imagine a competitive industry that operates in a polity P and, in producing a good X, creates some environmental spillover damage. Members of the polity may or may not benefit from the externality-creating industry by consuming or not consuming good X. And they may or may not suffer from the spillover damage, dependent on where they reside within the community. All persons in the community are assumed to fall into one of the four categories that result from combining the two classifications, as indicated in the matrix below.[11]

---

10. In dealing with the divergences between social and private net products, Pigou referred to a situation where "one person A, in the course of rendering some service, for which payment is made, to a second person B, incidentally also renders services or disservices to other persons (not producers of like services) of such a sort that payment cannot be exacted from the benefited parties or compensation enforced on behalf of the injured parties" (A. C. Pigou, *The Economics of Welfare*, quoted here from R. H. Coase, "The Problems of Social Cost," esp. 149).

11. The distinction between categories $S(b,c)$ and $S(c)$ corresponds, of course, to the distinction between *internal* and *external* externalities. Incidentally, Mishan uses the notion of an "internal externality" in a sense similar to ours when he argues:

> [E]nvironmental spillovers . . . pose a problem not so much as between firms or industries, but as between, on the one hand, the producers and/or the users of spillover-creating goods and, on the other, the public at large. The implications are not diminished by the observation that, in important instances, the users of the spillover-creating goods and the affected public are all but indistinguishable—this being but a special case of external diseconomies

	Beneficiary-Consumer	Nonbeneficiary
Sufferer	$S(b,c)$	$S(c)$
Nonsufferer	$S(b)$	$S(i)$

If the beneficiaries and the sufferers of an externality-creating transaction are strictly different (nonintersecting) sets of persons—$S(b)$ and $S(c)$ in the matrix—any proposed politicization of the interaction places members of the two groups in directly opposing positions. Those who benefit from carrying out the activity will oppose any restriction or control, while those who suffer the spillover damages will support any restriction or control. If all persons in the relevant political community belong to one or the other of these two mutually exclusive sets, the simple majoritarian result will, of course, depend on the relative sizes of the two groups of constituents. Note that no member of either group prefers a solution that allows *some* restriction on the activity as opposed to no restriction or total prohibition. The person who is the beneficiary will clearly prefer that no restriction be placed on his or her freedom of action. The person who suffers spillover damage will equally prefer that the activity be altogether banned. In this two-group model of politics, a political solution that is analogous to that produced by merger or Coasian bargaining in the small-number setting seems beyond the range of the possible.

If, on the other hand, all members in the polity fall into category $S(b,c)$, that is, if they all consume good X and all suffer from the spillover damage, and if they all benefit and suffer to the same extent, then politicization would produce a solution analogous to a merger solution.[12] Each voter would balance the costs in terms of reduced consumption of good X against the benefits in terms of reduced spillover damages. And since, under our simplifying assumptions, all voters are affected in the same way, they will choose the efficient level of activity unanimously. Note that the same result cannot be achieved under private adjustment, since by individually and separately reducing his own consumption of good X a person in the polity cannot control the level of spillover damage.

---

internal to the activity in question. (E. J. Mishan, "The Postwar Literature on Externalities: An Interpretative Essay," 18; italics added)

12. In fact, as Coase has pointed out, politicization is in some sense analogous to a "supermerger": "The government is, in a sense, a super firm (but of a very special kind) since it is able to influence the use of factors of production by administrative decision" (R. H. Coase, "The Problem of Social Cost," 143).

If we modify the assumptions of our first scenario where all persons in the polity are classified into the two mutually exclusive sets of beneficiaries, $S(b)$, and sufferers, $S(c)$, and allow for some persons to be both beneficiaries and sufferers, $S(b,c)$, we may demonstrate that, at least under certain conditions, majoritarian solutions will produce results that are broadly analogous to those of mergerlike internalization. Consider an extremely abstract and unrealistic model. There are equal numbers of pure beneficiaries and pure sufferers of an external diseconomy. There is one person, however, who is both a beneficiary and a sufferer. Further, all beneficiaries are equal in the benefits secured from carrying out the activity, and all sufferers are similarly identical in the costs that they endure, both in total and over the range of action. The person who is both a beneficiary and a sufferer is equivalent, in benefits enjoyed and damages suffered, to persons in both of these separate sets.

In this highly simplified model, simple majority voting will guarantee that the efficient level of the activity will be selected from among the set of all possible alternatives that may be presented for a vote. This model is, by construction, equivalent to the merger in the two-person setting. The single person who is both beneficiary and sufferer effectively internalizes the externality, and since all preferences are single peaked, he becomes the median voter whose preferences determine the majoritarian outcome.

We may relax the extremely restrictive assumption to some degree without affecting this result. Suppose that, instead of postulating that there are precisely equal numbers of pure beneficiaries, $S(b)$, and pure sufferers of the diseconomy, $S(c)$, we allow the sizes of these groups to differ, while also allowing the size of the group that both enjoys benefits and suffers costs, $S(b,c)$, to be extended. Suppose that the polity is subdivided into the three subsets $S(b)$, $S(c)$, and $S(b,c)$, and assume, as before, that all members of $S(b)$ are identical, all members of $S(c)$ are identical, and all members of $S(b,c)$ are identical with members of the other groups on each side of the interaction. In this case, so long as

$$S(b,c) > [S(b) - S(c)] \tag{1}$$

the simple majoritarian result will be ideally efficient. Note that (1) may be satisfied even if $S(b,c)$ is quite small relative to the sizes of the two pure groups.

The efficient result emerges, of course, because of the single peakedness of preferences and because of the assumed equality among all beneficiaries and sufferers. The single peakedness feature of the model seems quite robust in ordinary diseconomy settings, but the assumption of equality among benefit and cost streams must, of course, be relaxed. We need not concern ourselves with the differences among the pure beneficiaries and the pure sufferers.

Presumably, each of the pure beneficiaries will prefer that the activity be unrestricted, regardless of the level of benefits secured; similarly, each of the sufferers will prefer that the activity be totally curtailed, regardless of the level of costs endured. Idealized efficiency need not emerge from simple majority process, however, once we allow for the prospect that the median-preference member of the $S(b,c)$-group may not enjoy benefits or suffer damages that are equivalent to the mean values for benefits and damages over the inclusive group. We need not carry out a detailed analysis of the many possible subcases here. So long as (1) is satisfied, the majoritarian result will always be located *between* the extreme solutions preferred by the pure beneficiaries on the one hand and the pure sufferers of the diseconomy on the other. That is to say, *some* restriction will be placed on the activity that embodies the diseconomy, but this politically determined restriction will fall short of total prohibition. So long as (1) is satisfied, members of $S(b,c)$ determine the majoritarian outcome, and these members, by virtue of their simultaneous enjoyment of benefits and sufferance of costs, are motivated to "merge" the two sides of the interaction in their decision calculus. Any failure to achieve idealized efficiency stems from a bias of the median voter's preference away from that preference that would incorporate mean values for benefits and costs.

To this point in the discussion, we have assumed that the alternatives presented for political (majoritarian) consideration are defined exclusively by levels of the externality-generating activity. That is to say, the alternatives are:

$R(0)$ = no restriction on the activity;
$R(1), \ldots, R(m - 1)$ = restrictions ranging from minimal, $R(1)$, to maximal, $R(m - 1)$;
$R(m)$ = total prohibition of the activity.

We may remain within this model and introduce the fourth category of members of the inclusive polity, $S(i)$, persons who are neither beneficiaries of the activity nor sufferers of the damage. So long as we retain the assumption that members of this set vote strictly in terms of their own interests, they will not directly participate in the electoral process, or, if they do participate, they will reflect no bias in the distribution of votes over the set of political alternatives. The addition of this fourth set of persons will not affect the results.[13]

3. Majoritarian Voting and Taxation

Pigovian welfare economists proposed that externality-creating activities be controlled indirectly by the imposition of corrective taxes (or subsidies for external economies) rather than directly by explicit political determination of

---

13. This conclusion depends critically, however, on the presumption that persons vote their interests. If expressive voting is introduced into the model, this result no longer holds. On the

activity levels.[14] They apparently failed to recognize that authorization of taxation for control opens an additional constitutional dimension for political action, with consequences that may be quite different from those predicted to emerge under conditions where politicization is limited to direct control.

As the simple analysis in section 2 showed, neither beneficiaries nor sufferers will prefer any nonextreme solutions. The levy of an ideally corrective tax will not, therefore, be preferred by either pure beneficiaries or pure sufferers *if the disposition of the tax revenues is disregarded.*[15] If, however, the return of tax proceeds is taken into account in voters' considerations of interest, this result need not hold. Beneficiaries of the activity, upon whom any tax is levied, will not, of course, prefer any attempted tax-induced restriction, even upon the guaranteed return of all tax revenues.[16] Sufferers of spillover damages may, however, prefer taxation to direct restriction, even if the latter may allow for total prohibition of the externality-generating activity, so long as they share in the tax revenues. That is to say, pure sufferers need not prefer the levy of prohibitive taxes on the activity. They may be able, through the utilization of taxation, to secure a rent over and beyond the benefits involved in a reduction in the extent of spillover damages suffered.

If *all* persons in the polity belong into category $S(b,c)$, if they all are equally damaged by and equally benefit (as consumer-buyers of good X) from the externality-generating activity, and if the revenues from the per unit tax are equally shared among all persons, then politicization will obviously insure full correction, whatever the particular political decision rule is. It will be in each and every person's interest to impose the idealized Pigovian tax.

---

issue of expressive voting, see Geoffrey Brennan and James M. Buchanan, "Voter Choice: Evaluating Political Alternatives," *American Behavioral Scientist* 29 (1984): 185–201.

14. A third alternative to direct regulation and to imposing a general tax is the auctioning of licenses to pollute. On the auctioning alternative, which we will not separately discuss in this chapter, see for example, J. E. Meade, *The Theory of Economic Externalities* (Leiden: A. W. Sijthoff, 1973), 65.

15. It should be noted that the issue that will concern us here, namely whether an "ideally corrective" tax will be chosen under political decision making is different from the issue of whether an ideally corrective tax is, in the absence of an appropriate transfer scheme, equivalent to a Coasian bargaining solution. On the latter issue see R. H. Coase, "The Problem of Social Cost," 161:

> Modern economists tend to think exclusively in terms of taxes and in a very precise way. The tax should be equal to the damage done and should therefore vary with the amount of the harmful effect. As it is not proposed that the proceeds of the tax should be paid to those suffering the damage, this solution is not the same as that which would force a business to pay compensation to those damaged by its actions, although economists generally do not seem to have noticed this and tend to treat the two solutions as being identical.

Also see James M. Buchanan and W. C. Stubblebine, "Externality," *Economica* 29 (1962): 371–84.

16. This aspect is more fully discussed in James M. Buchanan, "Market Failure and Political Failure," in *Individual Liberty and Democratic Decision-Making*, ed. P. Koslowski, 41–52 (Tübingen: J. C. B. Mohr [Paul Siebeck], 1987).

Compare this to a setting in which there are only two groups in the polity, $S(b)$ and $S(c)$, pure beneficiaries and pure sufferers. Assume that $S(c) > S(b)$ and that the tax proceeds are equally shared among all persons in the dominant majority coalition. The tax chosen by members of $S(c)$, here assumed equally affected, will be that rate which maximizes the difference between revenues from the tax and the costs incurred by spillover damages from the activity. This rate will (in all cases where the coalition cannot act as a discriminating monopolist) be such as to induce a level of activity *lower* than the efficient level, although at a level that is higher than the zero level that the same coalition would choose under the direct control instrument. Taxation allows members of this coalition to share in the rents that beneficiaries receive from the activity.

The rent-maximizing rate of tax, and associated level of activity, becomes analytically equivalent to the total prohibition of the activity in the direct control model. This solution emerges when members of the damaged group of voters hold an absolute majority. The solution that emerges when those who benefit from imposing the diseconomy are in the majority remains as before; there will be no tax levied and the activity will remain unrestricted.

We now introduce the third set of voters, $S(b,c)$, those persons who are both beneficiaries and sufferers of the externality. If these voters are in the determining position, that is, if condition 1 holds, the solution will be similar to that traced out in the direct control model. Because a person in the $S(b,c)$ group will be both a taxpayer (as a beneficiary-consumer) and a recipient of transfers (as a member of the dominant coalition), the distributional effects will be offsetting. The person in this group will, therefore, be motivated by the basic efficiency trade-off between benefits and costs that he or she faces. If the mean values of benefits and costs characterize the median voter, the majority-voting process will generate the ideally efficient outcome. If the median voter's position does not embody these mean values, there will, of course, be some departure from idealized efficiency. But the solution will be bounded, as before, by the two extreme limits.

In the direct control model of section 2, the introduction of a fourth constituency group, $S(i)$, persons who neither benefit from carrying out the externality-generating activity nor suffer damages from it, does not modify the majoritarian results so long as individuals strictly vote their own economic interests. This conclusion is dramatically changed as we allow the added taxing dimension. A person who is uninterested in the externality, per se, has a distributional interest in any tax revenues collected via the fisc.[17] A member of $S(i)$ will prefer a unit tax levied at the rate that will maximize total revenues so long as he or she anticipates being able to secure any positive share in the

17. For a similar argument, see Gordon Tullock, *Private Wants, Public Means* (New York and London: Basic Books, 1970), 77.

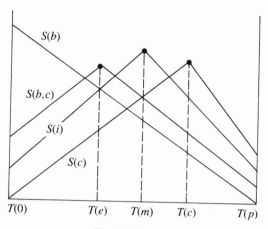

Fig. 6.1. $T(m)$, $T(e)$

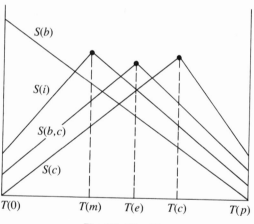

Fig. 6.2. $T(e)$, $T(m)$

return of revenues collected. The preferred tax rate for a member of $S(i)$ will be below that preferred by a member of $S(c)$, and the induced level of activity will be above that generated by the preferences of the latter. The relationship between the preferred tax rate of a member of $S(i)$ and a member of $S(b,c)$ is more complex, since the strict revenue-maximizing rate may lie above or below the rate dictated by personal efficiency considerations as optimal for a member of $S(b,c)$.

If we array rates of the unit tax along the abscissa, as in figures 6.1 and 6.2, we may depict the ordinal preferences of members of each of the four sets

($S[b]$, $S[c]$, $S[b,c]$, and $S[i]$). These rates of tax range from zero, shown by $T(0)$, to $T(p)$, that rate which insures total prohibition of the externality-generating activity. The preference ordering over the tax alternatives will exhibit single peakedness for each of the four representative persons. Hence, a stable majority voting solution is assured, regardless of the relative numbers of persons in each group.

Note that the possible outcomes are necessarily bounded by the tax rates $T(0)$ and $T(c)$, the latter being that rate of tax that will maximize the rent to those who are pure sufferers of the spillover damage. $T(c)$ is less than $T(p)$ because of the potential distributional gains secured from the return of tax revenues. If neither the pure beneficiaries, members of $S(b)$, nor the pure sufferers, members of $S(c)$, are in an absolute majority, the bound of possible majoritarian outcomes shrink to $T(e)$ and $T(m)$. The first, $T(e)$, is that unit tax preferred by the member of $S(b,c)$, the person who effectively "internalizes" the external effect within his or her own decision calculus. This preferred rate approximates, within the qualifications noted earlier, that rate which might be dictated by the orthodox efficiency criterion of the welfare economist. $T(m)$ is that rate of tax preferred by the member of $S(i)$, who is not directly affected by the externality, but who retains a potential interest in securing positive transfers from the distribution of the tax revenues. Note that the only difference between figures 6.1 and 6.2 is in the relationship between $T(e)$ and $T(m)$.

If $T(e)$ is less than $T(m)$, as in figure 6.1, and if beneficiaries and internalizers of the externality make up an absolute majority, the solution will settle at $T(e)$. If the sufferers and unaffected make up an absolute majority, the solution will settle at $T(m)$. If $T(m)$ is less than $T(e)$, as in figure 6.2, and if beneficiaries and unaffected make up the majority, the result will be at $T(m)$, the revenue maximizing tax rate. If sufferers and internalizers make up the majority in this case, the result will be $T(e)$.

4. Implications: Politicization and Efficiency

In our analysis, we have assumed that voters strictly vote their interests as defined by our classification into the four sets $S(b)$, $S(c)$, $S(b,c)$, and $S(i)$. As one recognizes that, in large number-settings, persons vote behind a "veil of insignificance,"[18] not considering their vote as being decisive for the overall outcome, it is easily conceivable that voting takes on a more expressive, rather than a strictly interest-oriented, character.[19] To the extent that such expressive voting actually occurs, the outcomes generated would, of course,

---

18. Hartmut Kliemt, "The Veil of Insignificance," *European Journal of Political Economy* 2, no. 3 (1987): 333–44.

19. See Geoffrey Brennan and James M. Buchanan, "Voter Choice."

depart from those which we predicted in the context of our simplified model of majoritarian voting. But there seems to be no reason to assume that expressive voting would systematically tend to generate outcomes that are closer to an efficient solution than the outcomes of directly interest-oriented voting. If expressive voting can be assumed to reflect political fashions, then, in the present climate, politicization would almost surely embody a bias toward excessive restriction.

The overall conclusion from our analysis is the negative one that politicization of market failure is unlikely to generate the ideally corrective measures that the welfare economist recommends. Only under very specific assumptions about the composition of the polity does the politically chosen solution approximate the efficient solution. Certainly, our model extremely simplifies the political decision-making process. But this does not imply that the problems diagnosed would necessarily be less severe under more realistic assumptions. Serious predictions about political corrections of market failure cannot be made without analysis of the actual working properties of the political process. The predicted results under politicization will depend on the political decision rule and on the relative sizes of the various sets of differentially interested persons in the polity.

CHAPTER 7

Contractarian Political Economy and Constitutional Interpretation

At the American Economic Association meetings in 1974, I presented a paper entitled, "A Contractarian Paradigm for Applying Economic Theory."[1] In that paper, along with others both earlier and later,[2] I argued that our subject matter is centrally a "science of exchange" or a "science of contract," and that the exchange paradigm takes precedence over the maximizing paradigm in our approach to analysis. This shift in the focus of positive inquiry carries normative implications. Conceptions such as aggregate efficiency in the allocation of resources become, at best, examples of functionalist error, along with the more explicitly normative variants of the social welfare function. The contractarian or catallactic approach to economic interaction suggests that systems or subsystems be evaluated in terms of the comparative ease or facility with which voluntary exchanges, contracts, or trades may be arranged between and among members of the community. Normative judgments take the form of statements that array "better" and "worse" *processes* (rules, laws, institutions) within which exchanges are allowed to take place. These judgments are categorically distinct from those that array and evaluate results or outcomes.

This shift in normative political economy has implications for the issues of constitutional interpretation debated by legal scholars and philosophers. These issues involve disputes along several related and intersecting dimensions: between judicial activism and nonactivism, between judicial deference to legislative authority and judicial independence; between strict constructivism and pragmatism; between original intent and legal environmentalism; between teleological and deontological conceptions of law. My purpose in this short chapter is to discuss some of these contractarian implications for con-

---

A modified version of this chapter, entitled "Contractarian Political Economy and Constitutional Interpretation," was published in *American Economic Review Papers and Proceedings 78*, no. 2 (May 1988): 135–39.

1. James M. Buchanan, "A Contractarian Perspective for Applying Economic Theory," *American Economic Review* 65 (May 1975): 225–30.

2. James M. Buchanan, *What Should Economists Do?* (Indianapolis: Liberty Press, 1979).

stitutional interpretation. This is a limited purpose, and I advance no direct and extended argument on either general philosophical issues or on points of debate in particular legal settings. Any identifiable contribution of the contractarian political economist must emerge from the differentially abstracted order that such a perspective imposes on social reality.

Section 1 covers the familiar distinction between an individualistic and a communitarian starting point. Because the argument here is indeed familiar, my discussion is restricted to statements without much supporting argument. The implication for legal interpretation of constitutional rules is almost self-evident. In section 2, I again go over analysis that I have developed at length in other writings, analysis that extends the catallactic paradigm from the economy to the political order, and, in particular, to the design, selection, and enforcement of constitutional rules. Section 3 examines the implications for judicial interpretation of the political constitution, and, in particular, the implications for the debate between strict constructivism and pragmatism and between original intent and legal environmentalism. In section 4 the argument is extended to the contractarian's stance in interpretative confrontation with rules that cannot find a logic in any contractarian ideal.

1. Normative Individualism

The primary question in any contractarian perspective on social order is the definition of the units that potentially engage in exchange. The economists' response here is straightforward; individuals enter into exchange, one with another, either to make direct trades of goods and services, or to create organizations (firms, clubs, states, associations) that, in turn, make such trades on their behalf. If the community exists as an organic entity in some sense prior to and independently of its individual members, and, further, if this community has its own supraindividualistic goals, the exchange perspective clearly breaks down. With whom could the inclusive community, as such, make exchanges?

If, however, the organic or communitarian paradigm is rejected in favor of an individualistic one, implications emerge that embody both methodological and normative content. If individuals, or organizations of individuals, are the units that enter into exchanges, the values or interests of individuals are the only values that matter for the quite simple reason that these are the only values that exist. Such terms as "national goals," "national interest," and "social objectives" are confusing at best. Individuals in a community may, of course, share values in common and they may agree widely on specific goals or objectives for policy directions to be taken by their political organization. But this very organization, like others, exists only for the purpose of furthering individual values and interests.

This summary of the normative individualist's position could be elaborated, but the summary is sufficient to suggest the direct implications for constitutional interpretation. The "good society" is that which best furthers the interests of its individual members, as expressed by these members, rather than that society that best furthers some independently defined criterion for the "good." The basic "rules of the game," the law, cannot be conceived as a means through which the community is shifted toward that which judges or intellectuals deem to be "good." Any teleological conception of the law, and of the constitution and of the role of the judiciary, is simply out of bounds under any contractarian or exchange conceptualization of social order.

2. Political Exchange

If we adhere strictly to the individualistic benchmark, there can be no fundamental distinction between economics and politics, or more generally, between the economy and the polity. The state, as any other collective organization, is created by individuals, and the state acts on behalf of individuals. Politics, in this individualistic framework, becomes a complex exchange process, in which individuals seek to accomplish purposes collectively that they cannot accomplish noncollectively or privately in any tolerably efficient manner. The catallactic perspective on simple exchange of economic goods merges into the contractarian perspective on politics and political order.

But how can ordinary politics as we observe it possibly be modeled as a complex exchange process in which individuals *voluntarily* participate, at least in any sense at all analogous to their participation in markets? Any attempt to extend the exchange perspective to politics seems absurd on its face, since we observe politics to be characterized by conflict rather than cooperation, best modeled as a game that is zero or negative sum. Coercion rather than voluntary participation seems to be the primary relationship embodied in politics. If, however, this coercion-conflict element is elevated to center stage, how can the state ever be legitimized or justified to the individual?

A way out of the apparent paradox is provided if we shift attention from ordinary politics, which is almost necessarily majoritarian, or, more generally, nonconsensual in its operation, to constitutional politics, which may at least approach consensual agreement, at least in its idealization. Individuals may generally agree upon the rules of the game within which ordinary politics takes place, and these agreed upon rules may allow for predicted net gainers and net losers in particularized political choices. The question of legitimacy or justification shifts directly to the rules, to the constitutional structure, which must remain categorically distinct from the operations of ordinary politics, which is constrained by the rules. As noted earlier, the argument that I have just sketched covers familiar territory, but its acceptance does have direct implications for judicial interpretation. The most critical of these implications stems from the categorical separation itself. There is a critically important functional role for judicial review. The "state-as-umpire" function is properly assigned to a branch of the political order that is separated from those branches that operate within the rules. Further, this function is conceptually, as well as operationally, different from ordinary politics. The judiciary, in its umpire role, must take a truth-judgment approach, an approach that is inappropriate in the workings of ordinary politics. The judiciary must determine whether or not the rules have been violated, whether or not a rule exists, or whether or not a rule applies to this or that case. These are truth judgments. It becomes absurd to introduce arguments based on such things as "compromises among interests" or "proper representation of interests" in the whole judicial exercise.

3. Changes in Rules

In an earlier paper, I classified the inclusive political order in terms of three separate functions.[3] The first involves the enforcement of the rules that exist. This embodies the role for judicial review that I have just discussed. The second involves the carrying out of ordinary politics within the rules that exist. This includes taxing, spending, and other activities within the broad rubric summarized as the financing and supply of public goods and services. The third function involves changes in the rules themselves, or constitutional reform. I have argued above that the judiciary, as an independent branch of the political order, properly operates within the first of these three functions. The legislative body, reflecting the interplay of group interests, properly operates within the second of these functions. The third function, that of changing the rules, is inappropriate both for the judiciary and for the legislative branch. The rules are changed only through the well-defined procedures for constitutional amendment, procedures that are explicitly more inclusive than ordinary legislation or judicial review. A straightforward implication of the contractarian complex exchange perspective on political order is that the judiciary oversteps its proper limits when it takes on the task of changing the basic rules within which the socio-economic-legal game is played.

If the judicial function is, and must be, restricted to interpretation of the rules that exist, specific guidelines for judges and courts charged with constitutional interpretation necessarily emerge. Parallel to this restriction on the scope of the judicial role is that placed on the legislative role. The legislature

3. James M. Buchanan, *Liberty, Market, and State* (New York: New York University Press, 1986).

also oversteps its proper limits when it moves beyond existing boundaries and itself makes changes in the constitutional order. From this it follows directly that the judiciary should not be deferential to legislative decisions when these have the effect of modifying the basic rules. In this respect, an activist, rather than a nonactivist and deferential court is required.

However, because the judicial role is itself limited to interpreting rules that exist, and cannot go beyond this, something akin to strict constructivism seems to be implied here. But the important point to be made is that the court should act as strict constructivist with respect to the constitutional rules that exist in the status quo when the case at issue is confronted. This status quo may, but need not, reflect generally accepted rules that are readily derivative from the original intent of those who designed and emplaced the written documents. The rules reflecting original intent may have been gradually modified by the historical case record to the point where there seems little connection with the rules that describe the status quo.

The indeterminacy in defining the status quo is unsatisfactory to many strict constructivists. How can a court define the rules that exist without direct resort to something like original intent? It is here that the court needs to rely on something akin to the modern economist's notion of rational expectations. Those rules in existence are those that best describe the set of individuals' expectations about the boundaries of political authority when the activities in question were carried out. An analogy from ordinary games may be helpful here. Suppose that the rule book describing the activities that may take place within a game, say, basketball, has remained unchanged for a number of years. But as the game has evolved, within the changing technology and changing skill levels of players, referees have gradually and incrementally modified the effective rules, for example, on walking with the ball. A new referee fulfills his or her role properly when he or she tries to enforce the rules that exist; he or she violates the assigned task when he or she tries to go back and enforce strictly the rules-as-written in the outdated rule book.

4. "Bad" Rules

The argument to this point is noncontroversial in the sense that the suggested implications for judicial interpretation of the constitution follow straightforwardly from the acceptance of the individualistic-contractarian perspective on political order. A more debatable set of issues arises as we focus attention on the stance of the judge, who fully shares the contractarian perspective, who is faced with the status quo existence of rules that reflect neither original intent nor plausibly justifiable extensions of such intent, and that, further, could never have passed any conceivable contractarian consensus test for legitimacy, even in some conceptual sense. That is to say, there may exist rules that are contained within the expectational set of both citizens and ordinary politicians, that have been imposed nonconsensually. Should the contractarian judge move beyond mere enforcement of the status quo in some attempt to dismantle "bad" law?

Much modern economic regulation (for example, minimum wage laws, rent control laws) presumably fits this category. Should the contractarian constitutionalist deem such laws to be nonconstitutional, despite the fact that prior courts have made judgments to the contrary? My argument suggests that if the prior judicial interpretations have been in place sufficiently long for these interpretations to have formed part of the rational expectations of both the citizenry and the acting political agents, it would not be appropriate for the contractarian judge to seek actively to change the rules. In this respect, my argument places me squarely on the Scalia side of the Scalia-Epstein debate.[4] Retrospectively, the court must defer to the status quo set of rules that exist, which may well embody prior judicial approval for legislation (including judicial legislation) that unconstitutionally shifted the boundaries of the consensual order. To move beyond such deference to the status quo and to assume an activist role in deconstruction, as guided by some ideal, even if this ideal be contractarian, opens up judicial review to precisely those dangers of abuse that Scalia warns against.

On the other hand, my argument suggests that the contractarian judge should be quite jealous in his or her protection of the existing rules from legislation and judicial intrusion that fails the consensual test. In a prospective or ex-ante sense, my argument places me on the Epstein side of the debate with Scalia. Deference to legislative authority, per se, cannot be justifiably derived from the three-stage contractarian model of political order outlined here.

Scalia argues that the courts should remain passive as legislatures act to constrain economic liberties. Epstein argues that courts should act to protect economic liberties, whether the legislation constraining such liberties has long existed and been upheld by prior court judgments or whether such legislation is recent or newly proposed. Neither Scalia nor Epstein makes the temporal cut that my argument implies. The contractarian position, as I interpret it, requires that the rules that exist, no matter how these might have come into being, be treated as relatively absolute absolutes and enforced by the courts until and unless these rules are changed by defined procedures for change.

My position does depend critically on some ability to define meaningfully just what the set of status quo rules is, an ability that is not centrally

---

4. Richard Epstein, "Judicial Power: Reckoning on Two Kinds of Error," in *Economic Liberties and the Judiciary*, ed. J. Dorn and H. Manne, 39–46 (Fairfax: George Mason University Press, 1987); and Antonin Scalia, "Economic Affairs as Human Affairs," in *Economic Liberties and the Judiciary*, 31–37.

important to either Scalia or Epstein. And in this respect I return to the importance of the expectational setting, to which courts should remain highly sensitive. Any legislatively orchestrated change that upsets the legitimately held expectations of citizens should be interpreted as a change in the constitutional structure, and, as such, should be prevented by the courts.

Consider the much discussed taking of property for public purpose. Modern courts have allowed legislatures authority to modify values of privately owned property within very broad public purpose limits. But there do remain limits, and wholly arbitrary intrusion would, presumably, be rejected even by modern courts. My position suggests that courts carefully draw such limits at the set of expectations held in the status quo, as properly measured.

In the three-stage functional classification imposed on political order by the contractarian perspective, the role for the judiciary is clear. The function of the judiciary is protection of that which is, which remains perhaps the most critical function for the maintenance of order and stability. The judicial branch serves a stabilizing, rather than a reformist or restorationist, role. The courts should protect what is, rather than try to promote what might be or try to restore what might have been.

CHAPTER 8

Prolegomena for a Strategy of Constitutional Revolution

This chapter amounts to an extended discussion stimulated directly by a paper presented by Professor Peter Bernholz at a Washington, D.C., conference in 1986, followed by comments of my own. Bernholz's paper was on prospects for reform in monetary constitutions, and my comments were entitled, "The Relevance of Constitutional Strategy."[1] In this further discussion, I shall examine prospects for genuine constitutional reform in the early 1990s. Is the time at hand when genuine constitutional revolution in Western countries may be possible? How could we recognize the elements of the socio-economic-political interaction process, including the attitudes of the participants, that might bring constitutional reform within the realm of the feasible? Can we identify steps that the political economist might take to direct or to channel discussion toward mutually beneficial changes in the rules of the political game?

In his paper, Bernholz limited his attention to prospects for change in monetary regimes, and he introduced a discussion of how separate interest groups might converge in support of regime change during specifically identifiable phases or stages of cycle described by differential rates of inflation. That is to say, the Bernholz argument suggested that the prospects for constitutional reform may vary with the situational setting and that an examination of the convergence and/or divergence among the separate interest groups may generate, for the observing political economist, a basis for a constitutional strategy. I propose here to go even further back in analysis, so to speak, and to examine the basic features of the "dilemma" that exists, prereform, in each of three "constitutions," the regulatory, the fiscal, and the monetary. Once these elemental features or characteristics have been identified, the problems faced in any reform strategy are more readily subject to analysis.

It will first be necessary to define, very briefly, what I mean by constitu-

---

1. Peter Bernholz, "The Implementation and Maintenance of a Monetary Constitution," *Cato Journal* 6 (Fall 1986): 477–512; James M. Buchanan, "The Relevance of Constitutional Strategy," *Cato Journal* 6 (Summer 1986): 513–18.

tional change, reform, or revolution. I shall, of course, be covering material here that I have discussed in many earlier books and articles. But a short summary, presented in section 1, seems essential in order to insure that my subsequent argument is understood.

After the summary statement of the constitutional perspective, I shall, in sections 2, 3, and 4, examine the distinct features in the separate diagnoses of the regulatory, the fiscal, and the monetary constitutions.

1. The Economy as a Constitutional Order

Those who conceptualize national economies as networks of macroaggregates that can be managed or manipulated for the purpose of promoting the achievement of macroeconomic objectives cannot understand what the terms "constitutional reform" or "constitutional revolution" mean. In this conceptualization, economic policy is straightforwardly teleological; there exist objectives worthy of achievement that are recognized by the authorities, and the economy must be guided toward such ends.

The constitutionalist perspective differs dramatically in its fundamental conceptualization of what the "economy" is. Here, the political economy is conceived as a *constitutional* order that, in itself, and, as such, embodies no independently defined objective or goal and has no function. The order is best described as a set of rules, or constraints, within which individuals, and organizations of individuals, interact, one with another, in promoting their own, individually initiated purposes. Patterns of outcomes or results (allocations, distributions, utilization, and growth rates) depend critically on the rules that constrain both private and public choices. And persons, generally, may judge some patterns of outcomes to be less desirable than others that might be generated under alternative rules. In such circumstances, there may be general agreement on a change in the rules, or constitutional reform.

It is essential to recognize that the choice of a rule (or a set of rules) within which a pattern of outcomes may emerge over a sequence of interactions is categorically distinct from the choice of an outcome or result that has well-defined characteristics. Policy is misdirected to the extent that it is motivated by the notion that specific outcome targets can be achieved. Even an ideally omniscient and benevolent authority could not choose an allocation of resources, a distribution of income, a rate of resource utilization, or a rate of economic growth. This proposition holds even if we totally ignore issues relating to the definition of what the ideals would look like in each case.

The social interaction process necessarily involves choices made by the many separate individuals and organizations in the economy-polity, each one of whom chooses subject to the constraints that are separately confronted. The many choices generate one outcome from among a whole set of outcomes that might emerge within the same set of constraining rules. To model policy as if the alternatives for "social choice" are outcomes amounts to a denial that participants retain independent powers of choice. Those who choose rules for games do not, in doing so, choose solutions; rather, solutions *emerge* from the choices of players made within the rules that constrain them.

Regardless of the ultimate location of political authority, whether this be concentrated in a single person, party, or class or dispersed among many persons who act through some collective decision-making institutions, any imposed, politically directed action or law must modify the constraints for all those who choose in any of the many capacities or roles. In this narrowly defined sense, any political action must be "constitutional." It seems preferable, however, to restrict the use of the term *constitutional* to those actions that have rules changes as their primary purpose.[2] The "economy as a constitutional order" is described by the set of rules within which individuals and organizations (including government) make choices and implement them in subsequent actions.

An existing constitution is evaluated through reference to the relative desirability of the pattern of outcomes that it allows the choices of participants to generate stochastically over a temporal sequence. The problems that arise in diagnosing "constitutional failure" are difficult and not well understood, even if we restrict attention to evaluation by a single person, whether this person be an active participant or an outside observer. My concern here is not, however, with such problems, as difficult as these may be.[3] My concern is with the comparative evaluation of an existing set of rules made by the many separate persons in a constitutional democracy, where basic changes in structure are made, ideally, only upon consensual agreement.

It is, first of all, self-evident that any agreement on the diagnosis of a constitutional order is enormously more difficult to achieve than the making of a diagnosis itself by a single person, or even by a group of persons who share evaluative norms. In particular, if the status quo set of rules, or some part thereof, is consensually diagnosed as needing reform or change, players must not only agree that the "game" played out within the existing rules is negative sum, in some appropriately defined opportunity cost sense, but, also, there

---

2. Taxation offers an example. Any tax will modify the constraints faced by individuals in the polity, even the lump-sum tax that is often used for benchmark comparisons by public finance theorists. But a tax levied for the purpose of financing public outlay, which will change constraints for individual choice, is not exclusively aimed at accomplishing the behavioral change induced by the modification of constraints. In the terminology suggested here, only the latter tax is to be considered "constitutional."

3. See Rutledge Vining, *On Appraising the Performance of an Economic System* (Cambridge: Cambridge University Press, 1984), for a concentrated treatment of some of the issues in constitutional diagnoses at the level of the individual evaluator.

must be agreement upon the alternative set of rules that is predicted to yield higher utility levels. The monetary regime offers a good example. There may be general agreement that an existing regime "fails" in comparison with some alternative regime, but agreement may break down on the identification of the alternative with which the existing regime is compared. The discretionary authority of national central banks may be judged to be nonpreferred by all parties, but the preferred alternative may be a gold standard by some and a rule-directed fiat system by others.

Is it not absurd to think that the required consensus could ever be attained? Will not there be at least some major groups in a polity that will consider any existing rules preferred over any alternative? I do not underestimate the magnitude of the challenge here. But, by way of precaution, we must keep in mind that, if there is no agreement possible on any change, then the existing set of rules is, in this sense, to be considered optimal. The simple logic of Pareto criteria tell us that if an existing state of affairs is to be evaluated as Pareto-inferior, there must exist at least one alternative that is Pareto-superior. The challenge to the political economist is to locate the set of changes that will command general agreement.[4]

2. Features of the Regulatory Dilemma

I propose to examine, in turn, three areas where constitutional failure seems to be present in Western democratic nations, three "constitutions." I shall try to outline, in each case, elementary features of the prereform setting. This step is required *before* any discussion-analysis of possible change in rules.

In this section, I consider the general area of "regulation," by which I refer to the direct intrusion of politicized controls over market interaction. The familiar examples are political controls over (or interferences with) terms of potential voluntary exchanges of goods and services: controls over wages, prices, interest rates, rents, entry into and exit from occupations, industries, and locations. In each case, the political controls are motivated by producer group interests, which seek to secure benefits (monopoly rents) at the expense of the citizenry generally. Any change in rules that prohibits such political control is clearly not to the particularized interest of any such potentially favored group if the policy issues affecting that group are taken one at a time and in isolation. The potential or actual beneficiary group or class will never

4. For a statement of this general methodological position, see James M. Buchanan, "Positive Economics, Welfare Economics and Political Economy," *Fiscal Theory and Political Economy* (Chapel Hill: University of North Carolina Press, 1960), 105–24. Also see W. H. Hutt, *A Plan for Reconstruction* (London: Kegan Paul, Trench, Trubner, 1943).

freely assent to piecemeal constitutional change. The particular interest of the group will be damaged in the process.

By contrast, each group that finds itself the beneficiary of the regulation that protects its own particular interests is itself damaged by regulations that serve to generate particularized benefits to other groups and interests. Each group would, in its *constitutional* interest, prefer that all of the other regulations be removed and that exchanges be allowed unrestricted domain over these sectors of economic life. If this generalized conflict between the individual's particular interest and his or her constitutional interest is acknowledged, then the way seems open for a general agreement that will prohibit, constitutionally, any political interference with the freedom of voluntary exchange. If the number of producer groups that secures political protection becomes sufficiently large, the losses suffered, even by a protected producer group, may outweigh any gains from the protection. In this setting, the members of all protected producing groups, along with nonproducers in the economy, will agree on a change in rules that eliminates protection over *all* groups.

The essential feature of this prereform regulatory setting is described in the classical Prisoner's Dilemma. Given the constitutional rules of the game, as they exist, producer groups maximize utility by seeking protection under the state's regulatory umbrella. As more and more groups succeed in this effort, a point is reached where members, even of those groups that are protected by regulation, are worse off than they would have been or would be in the absence of political regulation generally. But the generalization feature is worthy of emphasis here; it would not be in the utility-maximizing interest of any protected group to seek removal from the protective umbrella of regulation in isolation from the other protected groups. Constitutional reform can only be successful if it is sufficiently *general* to bring in large numbers of separate producer interests and remove all of these, simultaneously, from the regulatory umbrella.

3. The Potential for Reform in the Fiscal Constitution

The central flaw in existing fiscal constitutions lies in the absence of any constraint on the debt financing of current public consumption. The impact of the Keynesian revolution in economic policy was to repeal effectively the balanced budget norm for fiscal prudence. Post-Keynes, political decision makers have felt free to exercise their natural proclivities to spend without taxing currently, proclivities that are based on the desire to meet demands of constituents. As I have argued on numerous occasions and in many forums for three decades, the suggested constitutional reform is simple and straightforward and represents the implementation of a central principle of classical public debt theory. The constitution should be changed to include a prohibition of debt financing of outlay on currently consumed publicly provided goods, services, and transfers.

Note, however, that the basic features of the prereform status quo here, with the observed regime of continuous deficit financing, are quite different from those that are present under the protectionist regulatory regime discussed in section 2. The fiscal status quo cannot be modeled in terms of the classical Prisoner's Dilemma, where individuals' particular or operational interests may conflict with their more generalized constitutional interests. Any argument for constitutional reform must incorporate recognition of the distinct structural features. In the ongoing deficit regime, persons living now, in their capacities as current recipients of publicly financed benefits or in their capacities as current taxpayers, secure net utility gains at the direct expense of persons who will occupy beneficiary-taxpayer roles in future periods. (There will, of course, be some overlap between these groups.) Deficit financing of current consumption is a pure intertemporal transfer. And, like all transfers, no efficiency gains are available that, even conceptually, would allow the potential gainers from a change in the rules (future-period taxpayer-beneficiaries) to compensate the potential losers (current-period taxpayer-beneficiaries). The argument for constitutional change must, therefore, be grounded differently from the interest-based logic of regulatory reform.

There are two separable features of the argument here, each of which is derived from a feature that is familiar in nonfiscal applications. In the first, we ignore the collective decision aspects of fiscal choice and concentrate exclusively on the individual. Here any change in the rules that will restrict debt financing of current consumption must call upon some argument from the "economics of temptation." The individual who recognizes his or her own possible "weakness of will" in future periods may choose to impose upon himself or herself binding constraints that will effectively prevent his or her situational responses, as those responses might be dictated by in-period utility maximization. This precommitment logic has been discussed by Elster, Schelling, Thaler, and others in such examples as forbearance from tobacco, alcohol, food, and sex. Somewhat more generally, the argument may be extended to personally derived norms against pure consumption borrowing.

A second part of an argument for change in fiscal rules requires the introduction of the collective aspects of choice. Even in settings where an individual might not, upon reflection, choose to bind himself against consumption borrowing, he or she may well agree to bond or precommit the collective of which he or she is a member. Individuals may do so because they do not "trust" fellow members to refrain from "temptation," and because they recognize that, in majoritarian settings, they cannot effectively forestall *un-*

desired political choices.[5] One or both of these elements may generate a consensus that a balanced budget rule should be adopted, despite the recognized current-period loss.

There is, however, an implication of the constitutional reform logic here that is not present in the regulatory example. Because rule changes here do, indeed, impose acknowledged current-period utility losses, relative to utility levels enjoyed in the absence of the change, consensus building may require that implementation be lagged over several periods. This time lag requirement is not central to reform in the regulatory constitution, as previously discussed.

Also, as the discussion suggests, the moral or ethical dimensions of the comparative evaluation of the status quo and the alternative regime becomes important in the fiscal constitution, whereas such dimensions may remain relatively insignificant in the thrust for regulatory depoliticization. Deficit financing of current public consumption involves a more blatantly unjust transfer from future-period to current-period taxpayer-beneficiaries than the more diffuse transfer from consumers to producers in the regulatory setting. Quite apart from this difference in generality, there are also "excess burdens" produced by politicized interference with voluntary exchanges, the elimination of which offers a "cushion" for working out agreed upon compromises on rules changes. No such "excess burden" exists in the pure intertemporal transfers reflected in deficit financing. Only some introduction of a moral argument can oppose the play of self-interest here.

4. Potential Change in Monetary Rules

In the paper referred to earlier, Bernholz suggested that the dynamics of the inflationary process offer opportunities for implementing change in the monetary structure. In his analysis, nonconstrained discretionary authorities exhibit consistent inflationary bias due to pervasive political pressures. As the authority responds by reducing the value of the monetary unit, the interests of government and of debtors, both existing and potential, are promoted at the expense of creditors. As potential creditors (lenders) recognize the inflationary patterns and make predictions concerning its continuance, they will demand and be able to secure protection of value through modified terms of intertemporal exchange. As this adjustment takes place, the earlier gains from inflation, to the government on the one hand and to debtors on the other, may be squeezed out, and, in some cases, converted into net losses. At some

---

5. For elaboration of the argument here, see chap. 21 in James M. Buchanan, *Liberty, Market and State: Political Economy in the 1980s* (New York: New York University Press, 1986), 229–39.

appropriate point in the dynamic sequence, there can be a genuine convergence of debtor and creditor interests on a shift in structure toward a regime that embodies predictability in the value of the monetary unit.

Predictability, in and of itself, implies pure efficiency gains to all potential transactors who use money as a medium of exchange or store of value. There is an "excess burden" in nonpredictability that is analogous to that involved in politicized interferences with market exchanges, and this "excess burden" can provide a cushion for securing agreement among different interests. Note here that the efficiency-based argument for predictability is not the same as the argument for *stability* in the value of the standard, at least in any direct sense. On the other hand, if a change in regime insures predictability in the value of the monetary unit, there should arise no conflict among interests (for example, debtors and creditors) as to the direction or rate of change in this value through time. If all transactors make the same prediction as to the temporal path of change in the standard's value, and if the regime insures that these expectations are fulfilled, there is no difference in first-level efficiency between inflationary, stable, and deflationary patterns. Efficiency differences here, which may be minimal, arise only from differences in the resource costs of using money relative to other standards for storing value.

5. The Welfare Politics of Constitutional Change

I have entitled this chapter "prolegomena" for a strategy of constitutional revolution. My central point has been that we must understand the characteristic features in the diagnosis of regime failure in each of the three cases examined before proceeding to suggest specific reforms. This approach suggests, in turn, that the prospects for securing constitutional change need not be so dismal as pessimistic political economists sometimes seem to accept. With reference to both the regulatory and the monetary constitutions, there can arise some convergence of special interests in support of change; the thrust need not come from some effective representation of the generalized and diffuse interests of nonorganized and nonorganizable consumers. In regulatory reform, the very multiplicity of special interests who seek, and get, regulatory protection from the state may, at some point, insure that these interests, in their roles as consumers, will recognize the negative-sum aspects of the rent-seeking game in which they are all involved. In monetary reform, the dynamics of the inflationary sequence will possibly generate a convergence of interests on basic structural change at the appropriate point in the sequence.

In the fiscal constitution, the reform in the rules that will replace the regime of permanent deficit financing with one of balanced budgets is not as amenable to any convergence of interests as the other constitutional sectors examined here. The overt conflict of interests here is not between groups within the existing population (between producers and consumers in the regulatory case, between debtors and creditors in the monetary case), but between "generations," or between temporally defined sets of taxpayers-beneficiaries. Some motivation other than the current interests of persons, whether organized in special interests or diffused and generalized, must describe any thrust toward the introduction of constitutional checks.

It may seem, in some respects, surprising that the agitation for constitutional change seems to be greatest precisely in this area where the interest-based thrust for change would seem weakest. On the other hand, the observed agitation seems to have produced relatively little effective change. Perhaps we can explain the differences in the three regimes, along with the prospects for dramatic constitutional change, by the characteristic features of the diagnosis after all. Because both the regulatory and the monetary rules are ultimately vulnerable to pressures from interest-driven coalitions in support of change, the excesses of departures from the dictates of efficiency-defined ideals may have been more limited. The protectionist intrusion of the modern state may be limited by the recognition that, if it extends beyond certain limits, it becomes self-destructive in the interest-driven polity. The monetary authorities, seeking always to protect their own bureaucratic interest, may reckon on the interest group feedback from too extensive an exercise of the inflationary engine. There is no such limitation internal to the fiscal profligacy that describes the financing of modern states; the relatively greater agitation for change in fiscal rules arises precisely because there are fewer constraining internal checks.

CHAPTER 9

Achieving Economic Reform

Economists, along with others, agree that economies "work better" when governments keep out of the way and allow voluntary market exchanges to operate within a legal framework that protects property rights and enforces contracts. And to "work better" means to produce a higher valued bundle of goods and services. But governments do not restrict their activities to protective functions; governments, everywhere, in greater or lesser degree, interfere with the workings of markets. Economic reform, then, becomes the inclusive term that refers to institutional changes in the direction of liberating free exchange from politicized intervention.

What is the starting point? Why is economic reform needed at all? Why is it so difficult to achieve? What are the prospects for economic reform in the 1990s? These questions dictate the organization of my efforts in this chapter.

1. Here and Now

As many of you know, I have always insisted that would-be reformers of economic and political institutions acknowledge the simple existential fact that reform, improvement, or change is tethered to the "here and now" as a starting point. I continue to be surprised by those romanticists among us who advance policy nostrums in blissful ignorance of this fact. But "here and now" embodies a multiplicity of dimensions and this cautionary warning gets us nowhere in itself. We need to go further and to specify what we are talking about. That which exists in the "here and now" which is relevant for my discussion is described in a set of individuals who are organized variously in an interlinked set of institutional arrangements, including a polity, normally a nation-state. These individuals have, in turn, a set of rights, claims, duties, and obligations to or against the other participants-members through the institutions in which they cooperate, and these rights, claims, duties, and obligations are themselves defined in the same set of rules or procedures that specify both constraints on individual and institutional behavior and procedures for changing the rules. In summary, we can say that a "constitution" offers a comprehensive description of the rules within which the socio-economic-political game is played. The constitution that exists defines the "here and now" that becomes relevant for my purpose, and effective improvement or reform must involve changes in this defined structure of rules.

2. But How Do We Know That Improvement Is Possible?

Let it be acknowledged that change commences with the status quo. But how do we answer Dr. Pangloss? Why does not the very existence of the rules for social order imply their functional rationality? Absent some rational role, why would the rules that we observe have ever evolved into everyday usage or have been explicitly chosen and maintained through time? And, indeed, is not the primary task for social scientists, and especially political economists, one of locating explanations for observed institutions of order? And does not any diagnosis of structural defects reflect the presumptive arrogance of "rationalist constructivism," against which Hayek has warned us?[1]

I place myself on record here in opposition to this element in Hayek's thought, and, more specifically, in opposition to other modern political economists (many of whom have Chicago moorings), who invoke "transactions costs" barriers to explain the absence of the complex trades or agreements on rules changes that might seem to be mutually beneficial by the criteria of theoretical welfare economics. But I also, and at the same time, place myself on record alongside William H. Hutt, who never ceased from diagnosing putative structural failures when he observed the existence of politicized barriers to voluntary exchanges.

In a 1959 paper,[2] I suggested that the analysis derived from theoretical welfare economics did offer the political economist the bases for advancing hypotheses for changes in rules, hypotheses that could find confirmation only in the attainment of consensus, hypotheses that would be effectively falsified in the absence of such attainment. This stance allows the political economist to infer, by hypothesis, a shortfall in potential well-being when he or she observes politicized barriers to voluntary exchanges among persons, but it does not allow the derivative normative inference that such barriers should necessarily be removed by a presumed benevolent government. The stance here forces upon the economist the secondary chore of working out schemes of compensations between potential net gainers and potential net losers that any changes in rules must involve. The distributional elements of any proposal for reform are necessarily combined with allocational elements in any search for prospective consensus.

---

1. F. A. Hayek, *Law, Legislation, and Liberty*, 3 vols. (Chicago: University of Chicago Press, 1973, 1976, 1979).

2. James M. Buchanan, "Positive Economics, Welfare Economics, and Political Economy," *Journal of Law and Economics* 2 (October 1959): 124–38.

3. The Simple Logic of Agreement
on Pareto-Relevant Reform

In this section, I shall first present the basic logical principles of the Pareto optimality construction in abstract terms, but applied to the stance of the political economist outlined above. I shall then proceed to illustrate these principles through a simple and familiar example, that of politicized control over the price of rental housing.

The political economist observes some politicized interference with the freedom of persons to engage in voluntary exchange transactions. The existing situation is adjudged to be nonoptimal or inefficient in the Pareto sense. There must then exist some alternative situation in which all persons could be made better off, by their own evaluation, or some persons made better off and no others worse off than in the existing setting. From this definitional or classificatory starting point, there follows the conclusion that there must also exist some means of moving from the initial, nonoptimal position to an alternative, optimal position in a way that will damage no one in the economic nexus. This allows the further inference that there must then exist some means of securing agreement on the part of all parties to make the shift in question.

Let us now apply this analysis to rent control. The economist diagnoses rent control to be inefficient. The rental price on old housing is below equilibrium levels, there is a shortage of such housing, and waiting lists and various "key price" arrangements have become substitute rationing devices. The price of new housing, which is exempt from control, is above the price of old housing by more than any meaningful equilibrium price differential.

If presented as a simple proposal to abolish rent control, there would be immediate opposition by those persons who claim rights to existing old housing units. This opposition would prevent the emergence of consensus on the proposal for change. The task for the political economist is to work out the minimal set of compensations that would be required to "buy out" the claims held by those who live in the old housing subject to control and, at the same time, work out some scheme whereby these compensations may be voluntarily financed by others in the community. Owners of old housing could be a major source for such "taxes," and prospective tenants who have previously been denied easy access to such housing would also be willing to meet some share of these financing requirements.

The logic is straightforward. If the rent control rule is Pareto inefficient or nonoptimal, there must exist some scheme of potential compensations and payments that will prove possible and upon which consensus may be attained. If there is no such scheme possible, the observing political economist must acknowledge that his initial classification of the rule as inefficient is in error.

4. Why and How, Then, Can Inefficient Arrangements Continue to Exist?

The reasoning is impeccable, and there is little or no disagreement among economists in the classification of politicized interferences into value-reducing and value-enhancing sets. Why, then, do we observe pervasive and continuing politicized restrictions on voluntary exchanges among persons, restrictions that almost all economists would label value reducing, like rent controls? And why do such restrictions persist once they are in place? And, further, why do new intrusions into the liberty of persons to make voluntary exchanges continue to emerge from political process. If such intrusions are genuinely value reducing, as economists agree, what prevents the working out of agreed upon schemes that will both eliminate existing interferences and prevent new ones from arising?

I shall discuss these two questions separately. First, I shall address the issues that arise in attempts to secure economic reform by removing existing interferences with voluntary exchanges. Second, I shall extend the analysis to efforts to forestall or prevent the politicization of markets that are operating without specific controls. I shall, in both cases, use the rent control example where applicable.

Suppose that an observing political economist adjudges an existing regime (for example, rent control) to be value reducing. Accepting the stance outlined above, this economist advances a reform package that includes removal of the controls along with compensation payments to those who claim rights or entitlements in the status quo, and, also, tax payments or contributions from those members of the community who could expect to secure net gains from the removal of the restrictions. (With rent control, the package would involve removal of controls over rental housing prices, along with compensations to those who claim "tenant rights," financed by tax payments from those who are expected gainers, owners of controlled units and others who are denied access to the stock.) The elementary logic suggests that there should exist many such schemes that could command generalized assent.

The economist, whom we presume has done his or her work well, is likely to be shocked by the negative reactions to this proposal, when it is advanced as a hypothesis for general approval. And this economist is likely to face continuing frustration when, as, and if differing schemes for effecting the reform are put forward. Persons and groups whose well-being would be predicted to increase, and perhaps substantially, may nonetheless reject, out of hand, any and all schemes that involve their payment of compensation to other persons who would be predicted to lose, and perhaps substantially, from the proposed change in market restrictions.

To understand the central problem in achieving economic reform it is necessary to examine the bases for the apparent refusal of potential gainers to participate in the "complex exchange" that promises to yield net benefits to all members of the community. Why do such persons, (such as the owners of controlled housing units), act in ways that seem contrary to their own economic interests?

Two separate but somewhat related explanations may be suggested. The potential gainers from suggested reform may refuse to acknowledge the *entitlements* or *rights* of those who would be damaged by removal of the restrictions on market exchanges. To offer compensations to those who seem to be unfairly advantaged by existing arrangements, even if it is recognized that such compensations would be required to secure the agreement needed to make the reforms, would violate canons of rough justice. And these canons or principles may dominate the straightforward calculus of economic self-interest.

A separate, but somewhat related, reason why potential gainers from proposed economic reform may refuse to participate in any overall scheme that requires any contribution toward the financing of compensations to potential losers emerges when we examine the political calculus of the former. Full treatment here would require an intellectual excursion through much of elementary public choice theory; a summary description must suffice. Most politicized restrictions or controls over the liberties of persons to enter into voluntary exchanges emerge from the workings of ordinary democratic politics, within which decisions are reached by *majority* coalitions in legislative assemblies or parliaments, decisions which are then imposed on the full membership of the polity. Those who are losers, in some opportunity cost sense, from prior enactments of market restrictions, may consider themselves to have been coerced by the will of an opposing majority coalition. And these losers, who would be the potential gainers from the removal of the restrictions, may hold out positive prospects for the organization of a different and politically successful majority coalition that will, in its turn, impose its own will on members of the majority that enacted the restrictive legislation in the first place. In this imagined scenario, those who stand to gain by economic reform may anticipate securing the desired reform without compensation paid to those who stand to lose. And a rational calculus may dictate that investment in efforts to build new majority coalitions may be more productive than investment in the direct payment of compensation designed to secure the agreement or acquiescence of the potential losers from the proposed change.

The effects of this political choice calculus in preventing agreement on economic reform measures that promise to yield benefits to all parties, given appropriate compensations, are related to differentials in expectations among the separate groups of participants. If prospective gainers from removal of market restrictions anticipate the effective formation of a new majority coalition which will act to repeal the restrictions, why should they pay compensations to the losers? But if these expectations are in error, and those who are in place and protected by existing controls (for example, tenants in old housing) anticipate continuing political dominance, the status quo can surely be predicted to prevail. In contrast, to the extent that prospective gainers become less hopeful of being able to form successful new majority coalitions they become more willing to finance compensations. And, conversely, to the extent that prospective losers become less secure in their maintenance of majority support, they become more willing to accept compensations that are within the relevant choice-set of those who must finance them.

We now shift attention to the different, but related, set of questions involving possible ways and means of preventing the interferences that seem to be characteristic of the working of democratic politics. If, in some way, political behavior could be constrained to insure that value-reducing restrictions on exchanges would never be imposed, there would never arise the need for economic "reform" of the sort under discussion here.

Again, we can locate a source of difficulty in a failure of majoritarian politics to allow a separation to be made between allocational and distributional objectives. A majority coalition may impose economic control measures that clearly reduce value in order to attain desired distributional results. (For example, if tenants in old housing units form a majority coalition, they may impose rent controls simply to keep their own housing costs down, with no regard to the overall waste in economic resources that the control generates.) If, before any such measure could be enacted, prospective beneficiaries should be required to get the agreement of prospective losers, no value-reducing restrictions could be put in place. But, or so the argument might go, why should members of an effective majority coalition, or their legislative representatives, feel obliged to attain the consent, through appropriate compensations or otherwise, of those who are members of the opposing minority? Does not "democracy" mean "rule by majority"?

So long as such an attitude describes both public and intellectual-academic understanding of what "democracy" is all about, we can only predict continued, politically motivated interferences with the liberties of persons to enter freely into exchanges one with another. Until and unless *constitutional* constraints are placed upon the authority of legislative majorities to intervene in the workings of the economy, there will be no means of forestalling the continuing need for economic "reform," defined as the dismantling of prior interventions.

To suggest that political actions aimed at intervening in economic exchanges must pass a constitutional test need not rule out, in any way, all such interventions. Constitutions contain within their rules further rules that define how changes in rules are to be made. But constitutional politics is necessarily more inclusive than within- or postconstitutional politics. A simple majority is not (or should not be) sufficient to implement genuine constitutional change. Hence, proponents and advocates of economic intervention would be required to secure the assent of something more than a bare majority. And in an idealized, and admittedly limiting, case, constitutionally authorized political interventions into markets could take place *only* if such interventions are value enhancing rather than value reducing.

Merely to suggest that intervention into the economic process should be placed out of bounds for majoritarian legislative politics may be labeled subversive, especially in view of a century of socialist inspired and romanticized misunderstandings about the relative efficacies of markets and politicized alternatives. But this century of confusion has surely come close to running its course. It is time to restore an understanding of the relationship between effective democracy and constitutional order.

5. Economic Reform and Distributional Conflict

The discussion to this point suggests that the central problem of achieving economic reform, or of preventing institutional changes that would make future reform desirable, is not, in itself, *economic*. The problem is, instead, that *the economy* (by which term I refer to the interaction of persons and groups in an interlinked nexus of market transactions), becomes the institutional setting within which *distributional* conflicts are resolved through *political* means. The logic of the Paretian welfare economics sketched out in section 3 is based on the implicit presumption that such conflicts have been resolved or, alternatively, have been relegated for resolution to some arena that is independent of economic process. This logical exercise is helpful in suggesting that a separation between the basic conflicts over claims to value among persons and groups and the voluntary contractual exchanges of values among persons and groups is conceptually, and also institutionally, within the possible.

The political economist, as such, can contribute nothing directly to the dialogue concerning conflicting claims and rights to shares in value. The political economist can, however, provide a measure of the social waste of value that is involved when conflicts over claims are settled through politicized intervention into markets. (Return to the rent control example. The political economist cannot offer a scientific judgment concerning whether or not the tenants of old housing units should be subsidized at the expense of other groups in the community. The political economist can, however, demonstrate that the subsidization in the form of rent ceilings destroys potential value.)

The possible achievement of economic reform through some institutional conversion of indirect subsidization of particular groups through market intervention into direct subsidization through fiscal transfers faces much the same difficulty discussed earlier with reference to the payment of compensations. Groups that benefit through indirect subsidization or protection by market distortions recognize that direct fiscal subsidization intended to generate equivalent distributional patterns will secure relatively less political support. Arbitrary and discriminatory programs of direct fiscal transfers designed to match the distributional effects of piecemeal interferences with market exchanges would not stand scrutiny when evaluated against generalized criteria of fairness or justice, no matter what ultimate form these criteria may take. And the political economist can, indeed, offer some assistance here in pointing out the discrepancy between the attainment of idealized distributive norms and the arbitrary patterns that emerge from politicized markets, quite apart from the demonstrable resource waste. Through such an exercise, the advocates of continued market distortion can be forced into blatant expressions of particularized distributional objectives and away from arguments cloaked in terms of advancing generalized norms.

6. Economics, Politics, and Prospects

The logic of Paretian welfare economics tells us that the removal of politicized intervention in voluntary market exchange can be orchestrated in such a way that everyone in an economy can be made better off, and by his or her own reckoning. This theorem provides the economist with both a scientific raison d'être and a basis for hope. The economist need not take sides among gainers and losers since, by the Paretian logic, all persons can become gainers from economic reform. And because persons can be presumed to pursue their own interests, there must always remain the hope that, ultimately, rationality will prevail in the choice among institutions.

At the same time, however, the logic of democratic politics, and especially majoritarian politics, tells us that the separation between the operation of the market economy and persisting distributional conflict is unlikely to be secured, thereby insuring that the economist's hopes will remain unfulfilled. It does remain possible however, to say something further about the prospects for reform, at least in terms of an attempted identification of those situations and settings in which economic reform seems most likely to occur.

First, consider a setting where major shocks have essentially destroyed and disrupted the legal-economic-political order; specifically, consider the upheavals generated in the aftermath of major war or revolution. In this setting, there exist no effective rights and claims to values in a status quo; hence, there can be little overt opposition to the emergence of relatively nonpoliticized exchange arrangements that may not have been present prior to the disruption.

And, if there are economists in the wings who have prepared a reform agenda, we might predict that a market order substantially free of political encumbrances might emerge, with the predictable consequences of economic prosperity and growth. Mancur Olson has used this argument persuasively to explain the economic rise of Germany and Japan in the years following World War II, a war that destroyed the institutional base in both countries.[3] William H. Hutt also relied on the disruptions of the institutional arrangements in Great Britain during World War II to make possible his proposed plan for reconstruction which did involve compensatory adjustments for groups that might make claims against some return to the prewar status quo ante.[4] As we know, Hutt's proposal did not succeed.

It is important to emphasize that, even when possibly favorable conditions for economic reform exist, there must be an available agenda for action ready for implementation, an agenda that has been prepared by political economists. The Freiberg or Ordnungspolitik school served this function admirably in postwar Germany, as did the so-called Chicago boys in post-Allende Chile.

Prospects would remain bleak indeed if economic reform could only take place in the upheavals of major wars or revolutions. We can identify a different, and nonwar, setting that offers the opportunity for effective removal of politicized controls over the workings of markets. If a national economy undergoes a historical experience during which, due both to falsified theoretical principles and to the workings of interest-group majoritarian politics, many separate markets have come to be politicized, either by direct interferences with freely established prices or, alternatively, by direct governmental enterprise operation, a "constitutionlike" shift toward the opening of markets may come to be feasible. The economy that has come to be overburdened with a whole set of restrictions will be inefficient in a readily demonstrable sense, and especially so in comparison with other national economies. Participants even in politically protected markets will be able to reckon the general costs of continued widespread politicization. Resistance to depoliticization (privatization) will be less acute on the part of members even of protected industry and consumer groups if the proposed reform is presented as a "package" that embodies similar treatment over a whole set of industries. That is to say, generalized economic reform that incorporates changes in the organiza-

---

3. Mancur Olson, *The Rise and Decline of Nations* (New Haven: Yale University Press, 1982).

4. William H. Hutt, *Plan for Reconstruction* (London: Kegan Paul, Trench, Trubner & Co., 1943).

tion, operation, and control over many sectors may offer more prospects for political success than piecemeal reforms that pick off one or a few industries at a time. If stated as a hypothesis, we could say that the more socialized is the economy, the higher the prospects for economic reform.

I noted only in passing the relevance of the openness of an economy to international comparisons. Almost regardless of internal distributional pressures, a nation cannot long retain inefficient politicized controls over those sectors of its economy that produce for foreign markets. And, further, to the extent that inefficiencies in nonexport sectors exert spillover effects on economies generally, we should predict that small national economies with important export sectors should experience fewer difficulties with securing effective depoliticization than large national economies. This sketch of an analysis yields a hypothesis. If, as, and when the small national economies of Eastern Europe (Hungary, Poland) come to be increasingly opened, we can expect more by way of growth-producing economic reform than elsewhere over the ensuing decades. By comparison, in large internal economies where conflicts among domestic distributional interests dominate international considerations, and where socialization-politicization has not been extended to absurd limits (for example, United States), we must, I think, remain relatively pessimistic about the implementation of economic reform.

To this point, I have not mentioned ideology or conversion to organizational principles as a source or motivation for economic reform. But the influence of ideology should not be totally left out of the account. The depoliticization of the British economy that occurred during the late eighteenth and early nineteenth centuries was surely due, in part, to the conversion of political leaders to the normative principles advanced by the classical political economists. Sober assessment of the modern mind-set in the academies of the 1990s suggests that there is scant prospect for any intellectually led rediscovery of laissez-faire as an explicit normative ideal for social organization. This negative assessment must, however, be accompanied by an acknowledgement of near total uncertainty about the direction to be taken by the intellectuals of the world in the post-Marxist, postsocialist epoch that has so suddenly emerged upon us. Confronted with the discredited socialist alternatives, where are the intellectual critics of free markets to turn?

It seems at least to be within the possible that the leading centers of effective economic reform will be the postsocialist economies, which may well outdistance those mixed economies where extensive politicization did not describe the middle century but where, at the same time, the politicization that did occur is held in place by the exigencies of domestic distributional conflict.

CHAPTER 10

Economists and the Gains from Trade

> The consumer is sovereign when, in his role of citizen, he has not delegated
> to political institutions for authoritarian use the power which he can ex-
> ercise socially through his power to demand (or to refrain from demanding).
> —William H. Hutt, *Economists and the Public*

In earlier writings,[1] I contrasted two starting points for the inquiry of economists: (1) the two-person, two-good exchange model which immediately calls
attention to the mutuality of gains-from-trade, and (2) the one-person, or
Crusoe model, which immediately draws attention to the allocation of scarce
resources among alternatives aimed at maximizing utility. These two initiating
methodological thrusts can, of course, be integrated, and the work of almost
any economist incorporates elements of both. It is nonetheless helpful to
classify economists in terms of these two starting points. Such a classification
can offer a basis for evaluation that enables us to identify and appreciate the
internal consistency of apparently disparate contributions.

For somewhat different, although related, reasons, I should place Knut
Wicksell,[2] Ronald H. Coase,[3] and William H. Hutt[4] squarely in the first, or
gains-from-trade, category, the category that I apply self-consciously to my
own efforts. As I have argued at some length elsewhere,[5] I should locate my
own professor, Frank H. Knight, in both categories simultaneously, a characterization that explains a source of ambiguity in his work. The overwhelming

---

A modified version of this chapter, entitled "Economists and the Gains from Trade," was
published in *Managerial and Decision Economics* (Special Issue 1988): 5–12.

1. James M. Buchanan, "Better Than Plowing," *Banco Nazionale di Lavoro Quarterly
Review* 159 (December 1986): 359–76.

2. Knut Wicksell, *Finanztheoretische Untersuchungen* (Jena: Fischer, 1896).

3. Ronald H. Coase, "The Problem of Social Cost," *Journal of Law and Economics* 3
(October 1960): 1–44.

4. William H. Hutt, *A Plan for Reconstruction* (London: Kegan Paul, 1943).

5. James M. Buchanan, "The Economizing Element in Knight's Ethical Critique of
Capitalist Order," *Ethics* 98 (October 1987): 61–75.

majority of modern economists fall clearly into the second category; identification by name is unnecessary.

The focus of my discussion in this chapter is on two early books by
William H. Hutt, *Economists and the Public* and *A Plan for Reconstruction*.
These books can be best appreciated if the gains-from-trade emphasis is
stressed as the characteristic feature. In these books, as in all of his works,
Hutt was an articulate reductionist. He demonstrated early in his career an
ability to cut through mazes of analytical complexity and to isolate and to
identify the elementary principles relevant to the issues discussed.

In section 1, I shall show how the reductionist use of the gains-from-
trade model allowed Hutt to mount effective criticism of observed economic
policy and to suggest directions for institutional reform. In section 2, I relate
Hutt's proposals to those advanced by Knut Wicksell four decades previously.
In particular, I identify what seem to me to be differences in epistemological
presuppositions for normative analysis. In section 3, I compare Hutt's analysis with that associated with Ronald H. Coase. In section 4, I describe Hutt as
an authentic classical liberal, distinguish this position from those who do not
quite qualify, and, finally, point out some of the problems that the classical
liberal faces in public persuasion. Section 5 offers summary conclusions.

1. Gains from Trade

Let me first follow up the distinction between a gains-from-trade or exchange
perspective and an allocational or maximizing perspective by comparing and
contrasting both the diagnostic and the reformist proclivities that emerge more
or less naturally from each. The economist whose foundational base is
catallaxy tends to locate breakdown or failure of an observed or imagined
economic process in restrictions on, or prohibitions of, the freedom of individuals to enter into mutually beneficial exchanges. Market failure, by definition, means that there exist unexploited gains-from-trade, and the economist
diagnoses such failure by identifying the barriers that prevent the potential
gains from being exploited by the persons whose interests would be served by
their removal. By comparison, the economist whose foundational logic lies in
a maximizing calculus tends to define breakdown or failure as a shortfall in
aggregate value below that which might maximally be achievable. More
familiarly, his or her emphasis is put on the inefficiency reflected in the
misallocation of resources that he or she observes. Market failure, as defined,
implies inefficiency in resource use, and the economist performs his or her
diagnostic task when he or she identifies departures from those conditions that
must be satisfied to insure optimality. The observed relationships between and
among prices and costs, as these seem to be faced by market participants,
offer the basis for evaluation.

The two approaches to diagnoses of market failure yield differing norma-tive implications concerning potential correction. The gains-from-trade econ-omist, having diagnosed failure through identification of a restriction on the liberty of participants, calls, quite simply, for a removal of the barrier, inde-pendently of explicit reference to the subsequent predicted shift in allocational results. By contrast, the allocational economist, having identified failure by specific distortions in resource use, calls explicitly for a shift in allocation, independently of direct reference to the institutional setting.

The seemingly straightforward comparison of the two positions taken by economists, as sketched out above, masks a difference in the definition of the individual economic actor implicit in each position. The gains-from-trade economist defines an individual, as potential trader, by both preferences *and* endowments. Further, the distribution of resource endowments among indi-viduals is presumed settled and legally protected. The allocational economist defines an individual strictly in terms of a preference or utility function with-out necessary reference to resource endowments. In this analytical construc-tion, efficiency or optimality in resource use is defined in terms of individual values, but these values are "disembodied" in the sense that they are not directly tied to endowments. For this reason, the allocationist, as such, may even have difficulty in identifying restrictions on economic liberties to ex-change and especially in distinguishing such restrictions from those involved in establishing the pretrade distribution among individuals.

Nowhere is the gains-from-trade source of Hutt's inquiry more clearly evident than in the early chapters of *A Plan for Reconstruction*. Here the institutional setting under examination was the economy-polity of Great Brit-ain upon entry into World War II. This political economy was characterized by many and varying restrictions on the economic liberties of individuals, restric-tions that were defended in each and every case by the arguments of presum-ably sophisticated economists as well as by those persons and groups who held putative claims to the capital values embodied in the existence and continuation of the restrictions. The potential gains in capital values that would have been produced by a removal of the restrictions existed only as an imagined opportunity foregone, and this was sensed only by the economist who thoroughly understood the principles upon which the market order func-tions. In Hutt's earlier book, *Economists and the Public*, he had laid out these principles, and he had also traced the subversion of these principles in the work of economists, commencing with the ambiguities that emerged in the influential work of John Stuart Mill, and carried forward in the work of W. S. Jevons and many others.

I suggested earlier that Hutt was a reductionist in his application and use of the gains-from-trade criterion to condemn restrictions on economic liberties whenever and wherever these were observed to be present. Hutt made no attempt to classify restrictive practices, whether publicly or privately organized, into two sets, those that were to be condemned and those that were, somehow, to be condoned. Hutt was among a very small band of social scientists who exhibited elementary consistency in the normative stance accorded to economic value. If persons are restricted in their liberties to engage in voluntary exchange, value is, by definition, less than it could be in the absence of such restrictions. What criterion may be introduced to distinguish those exchanges that exclusively or primarily increase value to the exchanging parties from those in which the values to these parties are achieved at the expense of parties external to agreement?

In *Economists and the Public*, Hutt introduced the now familiar notion of "consumers' sovereignty," which provided the criterion he needed. (Hutt's introduction of consumers' sovereignty, in and of itself, should warrant him a significant place in the history of economic terms in this century.) Value to consumers of final products and services—this becomes the test that may be used to make the distinction between voluntary agreements that pass the ultimate value test and those that do not. Any restriction or barrier to freely negotiated economic exchanges of the ordinary sort must harm consumers. Similarly, and conversely, any implementation of an agreement through which agreeing parties gain at the expense of third parties may also generate net harms. John Stuart Mill, along with many others, did not understand this critically important difference. Their whole normative edifice crumbled because of the failure to condemn voluntary contracts (or public surrogates) that reduced value to ultimate consumers.

From the mid-nineteenth century, normative discourse, with accompanying developments in economic policy, was drained of the clarity that had been present in the works of the earlier classical writers, notably Adam Smith. Further, the increasing politicization of the economy weakened the carryover force of the common law, which had embodied, in rough terms, the appropriate distinction between value-enhancing trades and restrictive agreements. The gains that parties sought to secure, either through public or private agency, from agreements on sharing or dividing markets, on fixing prices or wages, on joint negotiations—these are not properly enforceable as gains-from-trade. These are, instead, gains from restrictions on trade, and as such, they are subject to normative condemnation on the principle of consumers' sovereignty. The state's enforcement and protection of individuals' liberties of contract cannot be extended to contracts made in restraint of trade.

As noted, there was no distinction made, in Hutt's analysis, between privately organized and publicly organized restrictions on trade. There was no argument for direct government restrictions on exchanges based on some putative "general interest" until and unless such restrictions could be demonstrated to be beneficial to consumers. State intervention in markets to protect or to enhance value positions attained or potentially attainable for or by producer interests, including particularly the interests of the owners of factor inputs, stands condemned on the principle of consumers' sovereignty.

2. Restrictions and Reform

The normative implications that follow from an identification of restrictions on value-enhancing exchanges seem straightforward. If the objective for policy reform is the maximization of utility for individuals, as consumers, subject to the preferences of others, along with a distribution of endowments, then such reform consists in the elimination of the identified restrictions. And, indeed, such has been the convention of reformist advice proffered to governments and to political leaders by economists generally, who have normally assumed, even if implicitly, that governments would act benevolently upon, and therefore follow, the advice so offered.

As early as 1896, Knut Wicksell warned against such a presumption by economists, and he called for a totally different approach to normative political economy. He was directly concerned with the structure of taxing-spending decisions, and his criticism was specifically aimed at the rather empty pronouncements of the public finance economists on principles of taxation, which they advanced independently of any consideration of the spending side of the fiscal account and also independently of any consideration of the institutional structure within which fiscal choices are made. Wicksell suggested that, if improvements in fiscal outcomes are desired, the advising economist should concentrate attention on the structure of the political decision process, on the incentives that were faced by legislators who were ultimately responsible, electorally, to their constituencies. The interests of constituents, in turn, must reflect both tax costs and spending benefits.

As I have argued at length, and variously, Knut Wicksell deserves recognition as the most important precursor of the whole research program in public choice, or at least those aspects of the program with which I have been personally identified.[6] Wicksell's objective was to construct a criterion for efficiency in fiscal decisions, by which he meant the satisfaction of the demands of individuals as consumers of collectively financed goods and services, analogously to the satisfaction of consumer demands in the competitive market for private goods and services. In Hutt's later terminology, Wicksell was seeking to establish institutional requirements that would insure that the principle of consumers' sovereignty is met through governmental provision of goods and services, alongside the operation of the market or private sector. By

---

6. My Nobel Prize Lecture in 1986 was devoted to a detailed elaboration of the Wicksellian foundations for normative economic policy. See James M. Buchanan, "The Constitution of Economic Policy," *American Economic Review* 77 (June 1987): 243–50.

the very nature of the problem that he confronted, Wicksell was forced to adopt what I have called a gains-from-trade perspective. He could not call on the formal properties of decentralized competitive equilibrium to assist in any diagnosis of failure or success or to provide criteria for satisfaction of the welfare norm. By necessity, Wicksell was compelled to adopt the criterion of *agreement*, interpreted as that which emerges as the end state of any voluntary exchange process. As this criterion was extended to the fiscal choice process, the "voluntary exchange theory" of normative public finance was born.

I had discovered Wicksell's major contribution in 1948 (by accident), and my translation of the central part of this contribution was published in 1958. Somewhat later, in 1959, I used the basic Wicksellian construction to lay out what I considered to be an internally consistent methodological position.[7] Sometime after publication of my methodological paper, probably in 1961, Professor F. A. Hayek called my attention to William H. Hutt's book, *A Plan for Reconstruction*, a book that was unknown to me. Hayek recognized the parallel between the Wicksell-Buchanan analytical structure for normative economics and that which he recalled in Hutt's book. Hayek's suggestion made me search out and read Hutt's 1943 book (I was already familiar with *Economists and the Public*).

There were parallels in the two analyses, but I discovered that there were also major differences between the Wicksellian and the Huttian normative perspectives. These differences seem reinforced by my recent review of these two contributions. The epistemological presuppositions of the two constructions are quite different, along with several points of relevant emphasis. We can perhaps better understand Hutt's book by juxtaposing his whole enterprise against that of Wicksell.

As I have noted above, Wicksell was required by the nature of the problem he faced, and as he conceived it, to utilize *agreement* as the ultimate test for the mutuality of gains from the complex exchange that any taxing-spending choice represents. He was led, therefore, to introduce the rule of unanimity as the benchmark institution for fiscal decisions. Only if some tax-sharing scheme should at the same time be agreed to unanimously and provide sufficient revenues to cover outlays could a spending project be guaranteed to be value enhancing or efficient. Although he presented the whole construction under the rubric of "justice," Wicksell's emphasis, as I interpret it, was on the epistemological properties of agreement. That is to say, it is only upon the observed agreement of all parties that the observing economist could adjudge

---

7. The translated part of Wicksell's book, *Finanztheoretische Untersuchungen*, appeared as "A New Principle of Just Taxation," in *Classics in the Theory of Public Finance*, ed. R. A. Musgrave and A. T. Peacock, 72–118 (London: Macmillan, 1958). The methodological essay was James M. Buchanan, "Positive Economics, Welfare Economics, and Political Economy," *Journal of Law and Economics* 2 (October 1959): 124–38.

a project to be value enhancing in net. Absent such agreement, as revealed, there was no means through which the values placed on the project by benefiting parties might be ascertained. The rule of unanimity was required, ideally, in order to establish the existence of consensus, without which a project proposal could not be evaluated.[8]

A second feature of the Wicksellian construction deserves notice as we compare it with Hutt's reconstruction exercise. Wicksell was aiming to establish rules for making fiscal choices in a legislative assembly that would remain in being for a sequence of budgetary periods, during which many ordinary taxing and spending projects would be presented for acceptance or rejection. None of the projects described institutions that were already in existence and which carried with them valued claims held under putative ownership of separately identified persons and groups.

With this summary statement of Wicksell's construction, we may proceed to examine Hutt's plan for postwar reconstruction. The first difference refers to the institutional setting, tied to the Wicksell objective discussed immediately above. By contrast with Wicksell, Hutt's target was the whole structure of restrictions that was embodied in the more or less permanent institutions of the British economy, as it had existed prewar. These restrictive institutions had established for identified persons and groups specific claims that were highly valued and which rational persons would seek to protect. Hutt considered the wartime emergency disruption as a once-and-for-all opportunity to put matters right, to eliminate long-established practices, through one fell swoop of reform and reconstruction. Hutt's enterprise was genuinely "constitutional," in the sense of structural change, rather than a Wicksell-like change in political rules for making decisions. Once the restrictions were swept away, the only requirement was that heed be paid to the normative advice of classical liberal political economists. Hutt did not sense the possible policy consequences of majoritarian rules in legislative bodies. In this respect, his enterprise was less sophisticated than that of Wicksell.

The central parallel between Wicksell and Hutt lies in their common recognition that effective normative economics required something more than railing against either arbitrary tax schemes or observed restrictive practices on some absurd presumption that a benevolent government would, willy-nilly, act directly on the advice so offered. But there were subtle differences in the epistemological grounds for such commonly shared departures from the orthodox stance of political economists. As noted earlier, Wicksell recognized that governments are driven by the interests of constituents and that *consensus*

---

8. The Wicksellian construction was shifted to the constitutional level of choices among rules in James M. Buchanan and Gordon Tullock, *The Calculus of Consent: Logical Foundations of Constitutional Democracy* (Ann Arbor: University of Michigan Press, 1962).

is required in order to get political change. Hence, reform proposals must embody a set of changes that will secure consensus which will, in its turn, serve to ratify, on normative grounds, the changes themselves.

Hutt was substantially more self-confident, and confident in the ability of the observing economist, to locate market failures through the identification of restrictions on economic liberties, a confidence that stemmed, perhaps justifiably, from the type of exercise involved. Hutt did not seek *consensus* for its own sake, either as the unique means of determining whether or not an observed practice was value reducing or value enhancing. Nor did he refer explicitly to consensus or consensus building in terms of the politics of reconstruction, although this may well have been an underlying element in the discussion that seemed too obvious to examine. Explicitly, Hutt seemed to ground his plan, which did embody buy-out and compensation schemes on a large scale, on the injustices and inequities that might accompany any major institutional change. The following statement indicates the thrust of Hutt's argument.

> . . . the vested interests may be, and on grounds of social justice, indeed, *must* be "bought out," "compensated." And we shall suggest . . . firstly, that this be done in such a way that the distributive injustices of restrictive privileges will dissolve in posterity, and, secondly, that the burden on the productive system may be immediately dissolved and so incidentally furnish the funds requisite for compensation.[9]

Note that this statement appears in Hutt's 1936 book, which suggests that *A Plan for Reconstruction* can be interpreted as little other than a detailed working out of the general position outlined seven years before. The argument seems to be that individuals and groups, perhaps through no fault of their own, found themselves locked into positions of being beneficiaries of various restrictive practices. They held claims under the existing scheme with some legitimacy, and the wholesale confiscation entailed in any noncompensated reconstruction would violate all precepts for justice.

Examined from our vantage point in the 1990s, *A Plan for Reconstruction* seems naïve and unsophisticated in its implicit presumptions about the political efficacy of bureaucratic administration. In keeping with the intellectual fashion of the 1930s and 1940s, Hutt's overall plan involved the operation of a complex set of commissions and boards, peopled by lawyers, civil servants, and economists who would genuinely serve the "public interest." Hutt acknowledged that, in proposing the plan, he was engaged in an act of

---

9. William H. Hutt, *Economists and the Public* (London: Jonathan Cape, 1936), 65; italics in the original.

social engineering, put forward in the institutional chaos and disruption of war as a means of "seizing the day" before the structure should be allowed to rigidify into its established prewar patterns of restrictiveness. In this particular respect, Hutt's vision matched that of Mancur Olson, some forty years in advance.[10] Hutt clearly saw that a relapse into restrictionism would insure unnecessary harm and suffering.

We should not be too critical of Hutt for his failure to anticipate contributions made by public choice economists decades after these books were written. Almost necessarily, Hutt wrote these books burdened with a part of the economists' mind-set of the times. What is important is that *A Plan for Reconstruction* is driven throughout by Hutt's reductionist emphasis on the simple equation between the existence of restrictive practices on the one hand and unexploited gains-from-trade on the other. The set of direct and indirect compensations, the income guarantees, the devices for bureaucratic administration and adjudication—these aspects of the book tend to be rejected out of hand by modern classical liberals. But the Hutt of the 1940s considered these to be small costs to pay for the improvement promised, and costs that could readily be paid from the value surplus that full exploitation of the potential gains would make possible.

(As a digression, we may ask a question about the general intellectual mind-sets of the decades of the 1890s and the 1940s. Did Wicksell's much more skeptical attitude toward political decision makers reflect a characteristic of his times, a characteristic that changed markedly over the forty years that separate these two economists?)

3. "Reform" without Restriction

William H. Hutt and Ronald H. Coase are a half-generation apart in age, Hutt being the senior of the two. Both economists were educated at the London School of Economics, and both have explicitly acknowledged the direct and indirect influence of the same two scholars, Edwin Cannan and Arnold Plant. We should, therefore, expect to find parallel strands in their analyses and attitudes, despite the genuine originality that makes each of these economists a man unto himself.

And parallels there are, parallels that we may readily identify if we return to my initial classification of both as gains-from-trade economists. I have suggested that the main theme of Hutt's efforts may be described as: "If

---

10. In his book, Olson argues that the relatively rapid growth rates of Japan and Germany during the early postwar years, as compared with the growth rate for Great Britain, were due, at least in part, to the destruction of institutional rigidities consequent on military defeat, a destruction not matched in the economic structure of the victors. See Mancur Olson, *Rise and Decline of Nations* (New Haven: Yale University Press, 1982).

restrictions on economic liberties exist, there exist unexploited, and hence potentially exploitable, gains from trade." This theme leads Hutt to look persistently for restrictions, whether privately or publicly organized, and to advance normative schemes for removal of such practices whenever and wherever they occur.

This theme has its obverse: "If there are no restrictions on economic liberties to exchange, there exist no nonexploited gains from trade." This obverse rendering of the theme can be readily associated with the contribution of Ronald H. Coase, in a sense more specifically than any association of the first version with Hutt. If ownership rights are well defined and legally protected, and if no restrictions exist, individuals will act to exploit all of the opportunities from exchanges among rights independently of the pattern of ownership. This now famous Coase theorem has been central to the development of the whole "law and economics" research program since the early 1960s. We can predict, retrospectively, that Hutt, who was always engaged in the development and applications of the positive variant of the theme here, would have found the Coase theorem to be an almost self-evident proposition.[11] The shock waves that the theorem sent through the ranks of professional economists, even among those who were normatively sympathetic to the positions taken by Coase (or by Hutt) provides clear, if indirect, proof that the allocationist mentality dominated the discipline in 1960, as indeed it does in the 1990s. Only by some institutionally blind and epistemologically arrogant concentration on the conditions required for optimal or efficient resource allocation (the equalities between marginal private and marginal social costs, à la Pigou) could the self-evident character of the Coasian proposition be called into question.

The normative implication of the Coase theme is, expectedly, also the obverse of that associated with Hutt's. For the latter, if restrictions exist, remove them in order that gains-from-trade may be exploited. For the former, for the Coasian theme, if no restrictions are observed present, laissez-faire. The appearances of inefficiency, based on observations of apparent market failures, are just that, mere appearances, and presumably reflect some failure of observers to reckon on the accompanying existence of transaction costs that must be present in any exchange, which can only occur with an institutional setting. There is no inconsistency between the sometimes zealous reformist thrust that identifies restrictive practices in order to seek to eliminate them,

11. I can justify my classification of Wicksell, Hutt, and Coase in the same gains-from-trade category by recalling, autobiographically, my own initial reactions to the Coasian proposition when first presented among faculty colleagues at the University of Virginia in the late 1950s. Coming at the Coase theorem from a Wicksellian perspective, I found the theorem almost self-evident, and I specifically recall the surprise felt when Coase reported back to us about the controversial reaction to his presentation of the theorem at the University of Chicago.

and the apparent quiescence in the face of apparent allocational failures in the absence of observed restrictions. Both attitudes are cut from the same cloth; both are characteristic of the gains-from-trade economist.

4. The Limits of Classical Liberalism

William H. Hutt was an authentic classical liberal, and this characterization was nowhere better exhibited than in the book, *Economists and the Public*, which remains, in several respects, his best work. As I have noted, Hutt does not commit the libertarian blunder of extending his defense of the liberties of individuals to enter into ordinary voluntary exchanges to a defense of the liberties of individuals to enter into voluntary agreements in restraint of trade. His measuring rod is always ultimate value to consumers, the role that is universally shared among all individuals in the economy-polity. The norm of consumers' sovereignty carries through in all of Hutt's discourse.

There are very few authentic classical liberals, especially if we require internal consistency between their positive analysis and its normative implications. For the economist whose methodological starting point is allocational, such consistency is likely to be difficult if not impossible to maintain since there is no central emphasis on process as opposed to results. The dominance of the allocational thrust in modern normative economics, along with the inconsistencies that this fosters, has been partially responsible for the failure of classical liberalism to be more effective as a coherent social philosophy. I suggest, however, that there are also more fundamental limits to the persuasiveness of classical liberalism, limits that may be identified even in the works of authentic representatives, such as William H. Hutt.

I should commence, however, with a more targeted criticism leveled against those economists who share a broadly classical liberal persuasion but who, nonetheless, fall strictly within the allocational camp. Their normative emphasis is, as suggested, on efficiency in resource use. And, as has often been noted, arguments promoting abstract efficiency as a social objective gain few adherents. Hence, these arguments carry relatively little by way of potential for garnering votes in any electoral process. Efficiency, as a norm for policy, carries little or no emotive thrust, and economists should never have been surprised that their unqualified advocacy of efficiency-enhancing changes in structure falls on deaf ears.

The authentic, classical liberal who adheres to the basic gains-from-trade perspective on the discipline of economics represents an advance on his or her counterpart who comes from the allocational camp. The gains-from-trade economist, if he or she remains consistent, does not place arguments from efficiency, as such, in the front rank of his or her rhetorical presentation. His or her reform emphasis is directed toward the removal of restrictions, with the enhanced value in exchange relegated to a position of necessary consequence. This, roughly stated, is the stance that describes Hutt's economics.

A further step could readily be taken by the gains-from-trade economist that is more difficult for the allocationalist. But it is a step that Hutt does not himself explicitly take. All emphasis on gains in exchange value could be dropped, and an argument against restrictions on liberties to exchange could be mounted on grounds of simple justice. Adam Smith's "justice of natural liberty" could be moved to center stage. It has always seemed to me that this offers a more persuasive base for generating public and political support for the freedom of exchange than any argument from utility, value, or efficiency. On the other hand, the argument from justice may lapse more readily into a generalized defense of the liberty of voluntary contract with no readily available means of making the distinction between contracts, exchanges, or agreements that concentrate benefits on the trading parties and those in which the benefits are secured from the imposition of spillover harms on others. Some criterion analogous to Hutt's consumers' sovereignty must enter the evaluative exercise at some point.

The modern public choice economist, who may also seek to further the normative principles of classical liberalism, may succeed where his or her colleagues fail, at least with some of the unpersuaded. Rather than stressing either the superior allocative efficiency of the market process or the potential for exploiting unenjoyed gains from trade through the removal of restrictions on economic liberties, the public choice economist calls direct attention to the predicted and the observed failures or breakdowns in the institutional alternatives to market interactions. Markets fail, especially when evaluated against idealized efficiency norms. And institutional correctives to market failures also fail, even if these are cleverly designed by authentic classical liberals like Hutt. A *Plan for Reconstruction*, in particular, conveys the notion that if only the institutional structure could be redesigned by economists who are guided by the precepts of classical liberalism, all just might be well. In that small book, Hutt, along with his economist peers of all ideological persuasions, remained an institutional-political idealist of sorts, while he, again with his peers, looked quite critically at the economic process.

There remains, however, a more fundamental weakness in the position of the classical liberal, again as exemplified in the early works of W. H. Hutt, a weakness or deficiency that very substantially reduces the normative impact of the total argument. I refer to the absence of an ultimate ethical criterion against which reform measures are to be tested. Hutt himself recognizes the problem here, in his defense of his norm of consumers' sovereignty. Consider the following statement.

> It will now be suggested that values under natural scarcity in response to consumers' sovereignty are the only ones that can be taken as providing

the ideal control of society's activities. The basis of our contention is as follows: Rejecting all systems of absolute ethics and aesthetics, judgment as to the goodness or badness of the result of any valuation process can only be personal; so that we have no more satisfactory criteria of the goodness of society's preferences in the objective expression than we have of the goodness of individual taste. But under our assumption of the absence of absolute standards, it seems that there is only one *conceivable* criterion of the desirability of values for which we can expect general acceptance, namely, that the forces determining them have been social, not private. It is for this simple reason that *liberty* (which we regard as practically synonymous with *tolerance*) must be regarded as a higher over-ruling principle.[12]

The appeal here to consumers' sovereignty (carefully qualified and interpreted) is perhaps persuasive to economists, but there is no easy response to someone who asks: Why consumers? A response that calls upon a value maximization criterion is likely to be misunderstood, and vague references to utility maximization will quickly run afoul of distributional objections. The alternative that appeals directly to the rights of persons freely to engage in exchange, which is the base of any argument from justice, may seem to rest on arbitrary assertion.

What is the most satisfactory underlying political philosophy for classical liberalism? If we reject both the utilitarian and the natural rights positions, what are we left with? To me, the answer here has always seemed obvious. *Contractarianism* is the one generalized philosophical position consistent with the classical liberal defense of freedom of exchange. Indeed, contractarianism can be interpreted as little more than an extension of the paradigm of free exchange to the broader setting. And, importantly, the extension adds ethical content that seems absent in the truncated stance that describes Hutt's efforts.

Is a specific collective action justified, or can a justificatory argument in its support be made? Is a specific rule or institution justified, or can a justificatory argument be mounted in its defense? Hutt would apply his consumers' sovereignty test. Does the action or the rule operate to benefit individuals acting independently as ultimate consumers? But why single out this role of individuals to the exclusion of all others?

The contractarian can offer a way out of the dilemma that may seem to be left dangling in the Hutt enterprise. The contractarian shifts the question: Could the proposed action or the observed rule possibly secure unanimous consent (in the limit) of all participants affected if the direct effects, positive and/or negative, cannot be imputed to identified parties? Or, in terms that

---

12. William H. Hutt, *Economists and the Public*, 282; italics in the original.

have been made familiar since the seminal work of John Rawls,[13] could the proposal or the rule have been agreed upon by all persons behind a sufficiently thick veil of ignorance and/or uncertainty such that no identification of prospective gainers and losers is possible? This elementary contractarian test does, I think, lend operational support, at least conceptually, to Hutt's norm of consumers' sovereignty, properly interpreted, but it also possesses a more appealing ethical base because it applies to individuals in *all* roles. Further, the contractarian test becomes conceptually more precise in its ability to make the required distinction between acceptable and unacceptable voluntary agreements. By shifting "voluntary exchange" upward to the constitutional level of choices among rules, the consensual or general agreement test may be applied.

I do not suggest here that contractarian logic can be used to generate ethical support for the whole comprehensive program of classical liberalism, as this program is normally understood and presented. The contractarian test cannot rule out the possible influence of what A. K. Sen has called "meddlesome preferences,"[14] even if identification of the holders of such preferences is removed from the exercise. There are "gray" areas of potential institutional change and policy action over which the contractarian test remains silent, whereas the consumers' sovereignty test may seem definitive.[15] I should argue, nonetheless, that the contractarian foundations do lend support to the classical liberal principles for social order over most of the domain that interest such authentic representatives of the tradition as W. H. Hutt, and that this ethical support may more than offset the apparent losses in definitiveness on the in-between or "gray" areas of normative political economy.

5. Conclusion

In this chapter, I have used the arguments in two samples of Hutt's work as bases for developing and elaborating my characterization of gains-from-trade economists, in their positive and normative roles. *Economists and the Public* stands as one of Hutt's best contributions, and it deserves much more attention than it received when it appeared (and subsequently). It warrants reading by modern social scientists. (I have long urged that this book be reprinted.)

A Plan for Reconstruction is a dated effort that reflects, in part, the engineering urges of the economists of its time. Further, it includes rather tedious discussions of institutional proposals that retain little modern rele-

---

13. John Rawls, *A Theory of Justice* (Cambridge, Mass.: Harvard University Press, 1971).

14. Amartya K. Sen, "The Impossibility of a Paretian Liberal," *Journal of Political Economy* 78 (January-February 1970): 152–57.

15. See John Gray, "Contractarian Method, Private Property, and the Market Economy," (Oxford: Jesus College, 1986), mimeograph.

vance. This book does not warrant careful reading in 1990. On the other hand, credit must be given to Hutt for his recognition that fundamental institutional reform requires that attention be paid to the interests of those persons and groups that have legitimately valued expectations embodied in any status quo. Such recognition alone places William H. Hutt among the select few political economists and classical liberals who are, at base, realistic rather than romantic reformers.

CHAPTER 11

The Contractarian Logic of Classical Liberalism

I propose to examine the possible derivation of constitutional protection of voluntary exchanges between persons, and organizations of persons, from contractarian criteria for evaluation. Membership in the polity is assumed to be well defined, and each individual is to count equally in the ultimate determination of rules. Hence, legitimacy emerges only upon unanimous consent.

If agreement is to be brought within the range of the possible here, some means of bridging the gap between well-identified individual interests, which will conflict, and the common or general interest, defined by the emergence of agreement, is necessary. The veil of ignorance and/or uncertainty, accompanied by some sense of the quasi permanency of rules and institutions, offers the only means that seems fully consistent with the contractarian perspective. The question then becomes: Behind a sufficiently thick veil of ignorance and/or uncertainty, will the individual in some hypothesized constitutional stage choose to insure protection for voluntary contractual exchanges? Or, if he or she chooses to protect some exchanges and not others, where and how will a distinction be made?

Initially, the question seems straightforward, but closer examination suggests that the basic meaning of "voluntary exchange" must be clarified. What, precisely, is involved in an exchange between two persons?

1. A Simple Example

Consider the simplest possible example in which Persons A and B hold initial and fully partitioned stocks of two potentially exchangeable goods, Apples

---

The title of this chapter is a deliberately borrowed emendation on that used in Russell Hardin's provocative paper, "The Utilitarian Logic of Liberalism," *Ethics* 97 (October 1986): 47–74. There are parallels as well as major differences between Hardin's analysis and my own.

The substantive results of my analysis are closer to those reached by John Gray in his more inclusive, and differently directed, paper, "Contractarian Method, Private Property, and the Market Economy," (Oxford: Jesus College, 1986), mimeograph.

A modified version of this chapter, entitled "The Contractarian Logic of Classical Liberalism," was published in *Liberty, Property and the Future of Constitutional Development*, ed. Ellen Frankel Paul and Howard Dickman (New York: State University of New York Press, 1990), 9–22.

and Bananas. Prior to entry into a trading relation, A holds a stock of Apples; B holds a stock of Bananas.

It is semantically appropriate, as well as logically useful, to say that A has rights in Apples, and B has rights in Bananas prior to entry into exchange. Indeed, without some such legal or mutually respected set of rights, trade, as an institution, would not be possible.[1] But precisely what does having rights in the initial stock of Apples allow A to do? Presumably, these rights allow A to prevent others from consuming, from eating up or otherwise using, the Apples in A's initial endowment without A's consent. Person A is protected in these respects by his or her rights to the Apples; Person B is similarly protected in his or her rights to Bananas.

As Armen Alchian emphasized in his early and seminal work on the economics of property,[2] exchange involves a transfer of rights. After a trade, there has been a shift in ownership of at least some of the Apples and some of the Bananas. Note, however, that the initial definition of rights, as such, does not include entry into potential exchange. As an institution, exchange requires that there be some initial assignment of rights to goods, as indicated, but it also requires some assignment of liberties to enter into a market and to make bids and offers. Person A, in our example, holds initial rights to his or her Apple endowment; he or she does not hold any initial liberty to offer these in exchange for B's Bananas.

In the strict two-person setting, such a liberty for A will be within the sphere of authority of Person B, which he or she may or may not grant to Person A. Person B may, simply, refuse to deal with Person A; B may withhold any liberty of A to enter into a bargaining process, or market. Note that such action on the part of B would not, in any way, transgress on A's rights to the Apples in his or her initial stock. Person B may, on the other hand, allow A the liberty of entering into the exchange process while, at the same time, Person A may allow B a similar liberty. If this reciprocal granting of liberties to enter exchange takes place, Person A will make offers of Apples for Bananas, and Person B will make offers of Bananas for Apples. Exchange will take place with a resultant transfer of rights to the units of goods that change hands.

This highly stylized example may seem analytically otiose, since neither person would seem to have any possible interest in withholding the liberty of entering the exchange process from the other, at least so long as we stay within the dimensions of the two-person, two-good model and do not allow noneconomic considerations to enter motivations. I shall demonstrate, however, that the distinction between rights and liberties does become relevant in

---

1. It is possible to derive the initial imputation of such rights from a contractarian logic. On this, see James M. Buchanan, *The Limits of Liberty: Between Anarchy and Leviathan* (Chicago: University of Chicago Press, 1975).

2. Armen Alchian, *Economic Forces at Work* (Indianapolis: Liberty Press, 1977).

more complex models and that the use of these terms can be helpful in reaching a provisional answer to the basic question posed earlier. I hope to show that agreement may be reached on constitutional protection for the reciprocal exchange of liberties to contract that facilitates the voluntary transfer of rights, but that constitutional protection cannot be similarly justified for the exchange of liberties that do not facilitate any transfer of rights, even if this exchange of liberties is itself wholly voluntary on the part of the parties involved.

An alternative formulation would include, with the set of rights to initial endowments, the ability to enter into the contracting process with parties on the other sides of potential exchanges. This formulation would have the semantic advantage of not requiring reference to liberties to enter exchanges, but it has the disadvantage of requiring that some of the rights involved in the exchange process could possibly be made inalienable. That which is defined to be a liberty to enter exchange or contract in my preferred terminology becomes that dimension of rights that are made alienable by agreement in the constitutional decision process under the alternative terminology.

2. Enlarging the Example

Consider now an enlarged, if still highly stylized, example of potential exchange in Apples and Bananas. There are now two persons, A_1 and A_2, both of whom initially have rights to stocks of Apples. There are also, say, ten persons, $B_1, B_2, \ldots, B_{10}$, each one of whom has initial rights to a stock of Bananas. In this trading community of twelve persons, we assume that, initially, each person has allowed every other person the liberty of entering a market or exchange relationship. Under these conditions, trade will take place as in the two-person model.

In this setting, however, we should note that persons A_1 and A_2 may well find it mutually advantageous to agree, voluntarily, on a reciprocal alienation of some of the liberties to exchange that have been granted to them by the B's. Person A_1 might, for example, agree to give up any liberty of entering into an exchange process with persons B_6 through B_{10} in exchange for A_2's agreement to give up any liberty of entering into a trading relationship with B_1 through B_5. This sort of contract may be mutually advantageous to the A's because, in this way, each can achieve a monopoly position with respect to a subset of the buyers for Apples. Each of the A's can thereby expect to secure a somewhat larger share of the producers-consumer's rents in the community than that share anticipated under the competitive adjustment in the absence of the market-sharing contract. The agreement will tend to make the A's better off at the expense of the B's who, because of their larger numbers, are assumed unable to organize a fully effective offsetting market-sharing arrangement.

If we now introduce the contractarian-constitutionalist perspective, and place any person behind an appropriately defined veil of ignorance and/or uncertainty, it seems clear that voluntary exchanges like that between the two *A*'s just discussed would *not* be provided constitutional protection. That is to say, the legal rules chosen behind the veil would not allow market-sharing agreements to be enforced. Behind the veil, no person could predict his or her status as an *A* or *B*. Even in this pure exchange setting, any agreement between persons on the same side of any market will insure that value will be destroyed. On the other hand, and by contrast, all agreements that result in an exchange of rights to goods and services across both sides of markets will be predicted to be value enhancing. These latter agreements or contracts will be provided legal enforceability under the agreed upon constitutional structure.

The results here are, of course, familiar. Contracts made in restraint of trade were traditionally unenforceable under the common law. These contracts may involve market shares, as in our simple example, but they may also extend to the setting of prices, along with other characteristics of the terms on which goods and services may be offered on markets. Any such contractual agreement may be interpreted as a mutual exchange of liberties to contract with persons on the other side of markets. In the simple setting here, where we limit analysis to fully partitionable goods and services that involve no spillover or external effects, any voluntary agreement by same-side traders to give up any of the liberties of dealing with other-side traders insures that value will be destroyed. Goods and services will be prevented from moving to their most highly valued uses, as determined by the evaluations placed on them by the participants in the potential exchange nexus.

3. Politicizing the Example

Let us now assume that voluntary *private* contracts in restraint of exchange are legally nonenforceable within the setting of the same example, that which includes two *A*'s as sellers of Apples, and ten *B*'s as sellers of Bananas, with trades restricted to those that directly involve transfers of Apples and Bananas. The legal rules are such that the *A*'s cannot make the market-sharing arrangement previously discussed.

Suppose, however, that a majority of the combined twelve-person community imposes a governmental restriction on the exchange. Suppose, specifically, that the *B*'s (or at least seven of them), a clear majority, vote in favor of changing the terms of trade so that the Apple price for Bananas is set well above that price observed under the nonrestricted competitive operation of the simple economy. This legislation will insure that the *B*'s secure a larger share of the combined surplus or rent at the expense of a smaller share for the *A*'s. It will also insure that total value in the economy is reduced. Apples and Bananas will not be distributed, after trade, in such a fashion that will maximize total value in the community.

Behind a veil of ignorance and/or uncertainty as to personal identification, no person would allow the constitution to permit majoritarian political action to restrict exchanges in the manner just described. Such restriction is the political equivalent of private agreements in restraint of trade or exchange. The simple analysis here indicates clearly that the simultaneous enforcement of common law or statutory prohibitions on private contracts in restraint of trade and politically orchestrated restrictions on trade is contradictory. Emphasis on the essential similarity between private market-sharing contracts and publicly enacted restrictions on exchange calls direct attention to potential flaws in the policy stances of both the extreme libertarians and those who oppose constitutional protection for economic liberties. The libertarian who defends private, cartel-like agreement among contracting parties on the same side of a market, so long as such agreement is voluntary, must have difficulty arguing against politically orchestrated cartel-like restrictions in particular markets. And those who justify majoritarian political interference with free exchanges should find it difficult to defend common law limits on restraints of trade, along with antitrust institutions.

4. Extensions: Partitionable, Tradeable Goods and Distributional Norms

To this point, the analysis has been limited to very simple exchange models, with almost self-evident results. The contractarian derivation of constitutional protection for the freedom of persons to carry out ordinary exchanges of goods and services is relatively straightforward. But, as the analysis has shown, this protection cannot be extended to freedom of contracts that involve the giving up of liberties to enter the exchange process, in any dimension. These results emerge, however, only in the simple exchange setting that was examined, along with the implied presuppositions that include the partitionability of goods among persons, the moral acceptability of trade in such goods, and the absence of third party or external effects generated by two-person trades. In this section, I want to retain these presuppositions while examining in some detail the distributional implications of free exchange. I want to concentrate exclusively on the effects on the contractarian calculus that distributional considerations may exert.

We may stay with the Apples-Bananas example to illustrate the conditions that must be present if distributional considerations are to be relevant for the results. If, behind the veil of ignorance and/or uncertainty, a person predicts that those who, before exchange, will be endowed with initial stocks of Bananas will be distributionally worse off than those who will have initial endowments of Apples, there may then arise some argument for asymmetrically enforced prohibitions on restraints on trade, whether privately or publicly introduced. If Banana owners (or producers if we extend analysis to a production economy) are predicted systematically to be poor, while Apple owners (producers) are predicted systematically to be rich, the person behind the veil and unable to identify his or her own position, may consider exchange or terms of trade interferences as one means of securing distributional objectives, even in full recognition of the potential loss in total value that any such interference will insure.

As this example suggests, however, to associate distributional positions with the specific ownership and/or production of specific goods and services seems bizarre. Normally, there would be little or no connection between distributional position and the description of the good that is initially owned or produced. Premarket or preexchange endowments may, of course, differ widely but such differences cannot readily be associated with the terms of trade in particular markets. If this is the case, there would be little or no grounds for trying to relate interferences with markets to ultimate distributional norms. This statement does not, of course, imply anything about the appropriateness or inappropriateness or the relevance of distributional objectives in a more general constitutional calculus.

There is one market, however, where distributional elements have allegedly been significant in offering putative justification for restraints on voluntary exchange, both restraints that emerge from privately negotiated agreement to give up liberties to exchange and from publicly imposed constraints on individual freedom of contract. I refer here to the market or markets for labor services, where privately agreed restraints on exchange are widely observed to be publicly enforced, and, further, where governmentally imposed restraints supplement those that are privately sanctioned. It is necessary to examine, with some care, the possible contractarian basis for this apparent exception to the generalized principle of classical liberalism. Can restrictions on voluntary labor exchanges be grounded in any way on the rational choices of persons in a constitutional stage of decision?

Consider a setting most highly favorable to the argument for interferences in voluntary exchange. Assume that persons are, at birth, physically separable into two distinct classes, those who must work for others and those who may fill employer roles. Further assume that all workers are homogeneous and that each worker is location specific, and, hence, unable to negotiate exchanges with alternative employers over space. Employees, as a class, being more numerous relative to their opportunities than employers, as a class, are predicted to earn substantially less, per person, than employers.

In this setting, employees or workers are often said to be at a relative bargaining disadvantage, and this allegation has been used as a justification for either privately organized restraints on voluntary labor contracts, through unions, or for compulsory governmental restrictions on the terms of such contracts. But even in this rarified and highly unreal setting, can such restrictions be derived from a veil of ignorance-uncertainty calculus?

Consider wage negotiations, where the union representing the workers demands, and secures, a wage contract that sets payment above that which would emerge in the absence of the union. Fewer workers than before can secure employment at the higher wage. But, if we assume that the demand for labor is inelastic over the relevant range, the total wage bill may be higher. The total payment to workers, as a class, will then increase. But if this institutional change is to be supported on grounds of distributive justice, the increase in the total wage bill is not sufficient. There must also be some means in insuring that, within the class of worker, the gains are more equally shared. As noted, fewer workers will remain employed, but unless those who lose employment by the wage increase are subsidized by those who remain employed at the increased wage, the institutional change will generate undesirable distributive results, on almost any criterion of distributive justice. It seems clear that wage setting, as such, and without institutional guarantees as to the distribution of benefits from above competitive wage levels, cannot be derived as a consequence of the rational choice calculus of a person behind a veil.

If we introduce more realism into the model and allow for interclass mobility as well as nonlocation specificity and heterogeneity among both workers and employers, any private or public enforcement of wage levels above those attained in the openly competitive market will tend to impose disproportionately greater harm on those potential workers who are precisely the most "distributionally deserving" in any normative sense. The generalized conclusion seems inescapable; the principles of classical liberalism that prohibit enforceable restraints on voluntary exchange, whether privately or publicly implemented, cannot be challenged with a contractarian model of evaluation, even when distributional objectives are fully incorporated into the analysis.

5. Beyond Procedural Norms

To this point my use of the contractarian logic of classical liberalism has relied exclusively on procedural criteria for institutional evaluation. The results appear determinate only because many of the substantive issues have been deliberately avoided by the presuppositions of the analysis. I have simply presumed that all persons, whether located behind the veil or after personal identification, agree on the definitions or classifications of "goods" and "bads." Further, I have presumed that all "goods" and "bads" are fully partitionable in the extreme sense that no person is interested in the production or consumption activity of any other person with respect to any identified "good" or "bad."

It is clear that most of the issues involving the putative legitimacy of private or public restraints on voluntary exchanges arise precisely in those settings where these presuppositions do not describe reality. In the terminology of welfare economics, it is the presence of "externality," whether narrowly or broadly defined, that necessarily introduces indeterminism in any attempted normative justification for a regime of generalized constitutional-legal protection for voluntary exchange. The procedural criteria of contractarianism cannot, in themselves, be extended to the substantive issues of definition and classification, at least not directly. I shall examine the limits of these criteria below. But it remains useful to emphasize the force of the contractarian logic, even within these acknowledged limits.

Empirically, persons are observed to agree on definitions of "goods" and "bads" over wide commodity and service groupings, and, further, persons agree that individual or private preferences with respect to the consumption, production, and exchange of many ordinary goods and services are of little concern to others than those who carry out such activities. Within the domain of social interaction involving the exchange of such ordinary goods and services, the contractarian logic remains unchallengeable. Private or public restraints on voluntary exchanges in these goods and services (bread, clothing, cars, houses, haircuts, consulting) are ruled out by the procedural criteria of contractarianism along with the empirical observation of agreement on spheres of private action.

There exists another domain of activity within which there remains widespread disagreement concerning the appropriateness of privately motivated exchange activity. There are activities that involve what some persons may define to be tradeable or exchangeable goods and services but what other persons do not acknowledge as falling legitimately within the domain of individual choice. Examples abound: slavery, sex, drugs, blood, body organs, babies, guns. There are still other activities that may involve goods and bads that in some circumstances are deemed exchangeable, but which may, in other circumstances, generate third-party or spillover effects. Is an individual to be allowed to produce and market a good, the sale and/or purchase of which is predicted to impact adversely on others than the direct buyer-consumer (alcohol, tobacco, drugs)?

Can individual liberty to enter into voluntary exchanges of goods and bads that fall into the inclusive domain of externality be derived from the contractarian calculus? If not, is there some characteristic feature of such goods and services that we may identify as offering grounds to justify departure from the general norm of protection for voluntary exchange?

It is useful at this point to recall precisely what the individual is presumed to know when he or she makes basic constitutional choices behind the veil of ignorance and/or uncertainty. He or she cannot identify which person in the community he or she will be, what role will be occupied, what endowments will be possessed, or what preferences will be descriptive. On the other hand, the overall or general distribution of these variables among the whole set of persons in the community is presumed to be known, at least within broad limits.

Consider, in particular, the preferences for goods and services, along with the preferences for the activities of others with respect to exchanges of these goods and services. For any one of the potential markets in the domain of externality, the individual behind the veil will predict that there will be a wide range of preference patterns concerning the appropriateness or inappropriateness of entering into unhampered exchange processes. There will be persons whose preferences dictate participation in ordinary exchanges in such markets, without regard to the spillover effects on others in the community. There will be others, however, who will find the existence of such exchanges to be either morally outrageous or economically damaging.

Behind the veil, the chooser cannot predict which one of these preferences will describe his or her utility function. Identification remains impossible on this as on other dimensions. The choice of institutions behind the veil must, therefore, represent some judgment as to the relative significance of the varying preference patterns, along with some estimate of the frequency distribution along the spectrum. The constitutional stage chooser must balance the possible potential gains to those who directly benefit from the exchanges that might take place and the possible potential harms to those who would be damaged by such exchanges. There is no a priori judgment that can be advanced in any particular case here, and, hence, no prediction as to the precise definition of the range of goods and services the voluntary exchanges of which would be constitutionally protected.

This indeterminacy cannot be avoided. We may suggest, however, that rational choice behavior at the constitutional stage must also include some prediction as to the workings of those institutions that might be constitutionally authorized to intervene in the exchange processes for goods and services falling in the domain of relevant externality. In particular, rational choice here would dictate skepticism with regard to the working of politicized majoritarian intervention with voluntary exchange. As it operates ideally, even if not in practice, majority rule tends to allow majorities with relatively mild preferences to overrule minorities that may feel intensely about alternatives. It seems likely that most of the goods and services that fall within any externality domain invoke mildly felt meddlesome negative preferences. Hence, simple majorities would presumably choose to prohibit voluntary exchanges in such goods and services.

These considerations suggest that, if restraints on the voluntary exchanges of goods and services are deemed appropriate, these restraints should take the form of adjustments in the legal structure such as to make contracts of exchange nonenforceable. That is to say, the constitutional-stage decision should delineate carefully those markets that fall within the domain of relevant externality. There seems to be no grounds for allowing the delineation to be made through the operation of ordinary politics. For example, contracts for perpetual servitude should be constitutionally, rather than legislatively, prohibited; contracts for the exchange of sexual services should or should not be constitutionally permissible, independently of the will of particular legislative majorities. The sale and purchase of alcohol was an appropriate constitutional issue, even if the historical experience suggests that the constitutional choice made in the United States was in error. In these cases, as with all tradeable goods and services, there is a prima facie argument against overt politicization of restraint on the exchange process.

6. Contractarianism and Classical Liberalism

There is little that is novel in the preceding analysis. What I have attempted to do is to stay within the contractarian model for evaluation and to examine the possible derivation of constitutional protection of voluntary exchanges between persons or organizations of persons. It seems clear that persons should be allowed, and legally protected, to engage in voluntary exchanges of goods and services that are considered to be appropriate objects for private disposition when such exchanges do not generate significant spillover harms on third parties. This protection cannot be extended to voluntary agreements in restraint of exchanges, at least within any contractarian exercise of justification. For goods and services that are deemed by some persons to be inappropriate for exchanges, or goods and services the exchanges of which are predicted to generate significant spillover damages on third parties, the contractarian model is necessarily indeterminate. No general principle may be laid down for such cases; each market must be treated on its own account, and a constitutional-stage decision must weigh the predicted costs and benefits of the alternative institutional arrangements. This choice calculus must incorporate some recognition of the working properties of those institutions of politics that might be expected to operate in the absence of clearly defined constitutional-legal guidelines. The analysis suggests that a strong argument may often be adduced for locating the critical decision at the constitutional, rather than any postconstitutional, stage of politics.

The contractarian logic may be compared and contrasted with the argument from rights that is often employed for a comparable purpose. In a sense, the whole contractarian evaluation commences from a presumption that individuals possess rights in the initial endowments, including talents, assigned to them. Indeed, without some such presumption, we find it difficult to define what an individual is. I have suggested, however, that the individual's rights to the personal and nonpersonal endowments in initial possession do not include the liberty to offer these rights (to goods and services) in exchange to others, until and unless others grant such liberties. As I have elaborated at length elsewhere,[3] it is in the interest of every potential trader to extend such liberties of entry to all potential traders on opposing sides of markets. The order of "natural liberty" described by Adam Smith suggests that such maximal extensions of liberty be constitutionally protected, and that this protection would emerge from agreement behind a veil of ignorance and/or uncertainty. But restraints or restrictions on the trading process through agreements on market shares, on price setting, or any other of the generalized terms of trade, cannot find support in the contractarian logic.

It is perhaps not surprising that the contractarian exercise yields the essential principles of classical liberalism. These principles may, of course, be justified on general utilitarian as well as contractarian grounds, and, in this application, these two philosophical approaches yield closely similar results. The advantage of the contractarian perspective has always seemed to me to lie in the potential for deriving a logic of institutional structure from the idealized choices of individuals who participate in the structure, as opposed to the equally idealized choice of an external observer, who is presumed omniscient.

---

3. James M. Buchanan, "Towards the Simple Economics of National Liberty: An Exploratory Analysis," *Kyklos* 40, no. 1 (1987): 3–20.

CHAPTER 12

Leadership and Deference
in Constitutional Construction

How do we explain the behavior of James Madison in 1787, along with the behavior of those who followed his intellectual leadership? More generally, we address two questions. First, can models of rational choice be extended to cover the behavior of persons who are observed to invest scarce resources, particularly time and intellectual energy, in becoming more fully informed about constitutional alternatives? Second, can such models of rational choice be extended further to apply to the behavior of persons who are observed to defer to the opinions of those who do choose to become more fully informed?

Our response to the two questions takes the form of developing what we shall call a theory of *rational deference*, a term that we have selected deliberately to suggest parallels with the theory of rational ignorance, which has been introduced in application to individual choice behavior in voting by Anthony Downs[1] and Gordon Tullock.[2]

Our theory of rational deference must, however, embody a second, or additional, behavioral dimension that analogy with the theory of rational ignorance does not suggest. As our second question indicates, we may explain why rational choice behavior on the part of individual participants dictates deference to those persons who do invest resources in becoming informed about constitutional alternatives. But we must then also address the first question. We must explain why some members of the collective group make such investments. This dimension is not paralleled in the theory of rational ignorance, and, indeed, straightforward extension of the familiar theory of voting choice would suggest that no such investment would be made. A comprehensive model of rational choice must explain both why some participants defer to others whom they observe to be relatively better informed and why some others choose to become informed in the first place.

A modified version of this chapter, entitled "A Theory of Leadership and Deference in Constitutional Construction" (with Viktor Vanberg), was published in *Public Choice* 61 (April 1989): 15–27.

1. Anthony Downs, *An Economic Theory of Democracy* (New York: Harper, 1957).

2. Gordon Tullock, *Toward a Mathematics of Politics* (Ann Arbor: University of Michigan Press, 1967).

Our inquiry is narrowly circumscribed and limited to a highly stylized model. Our model is that of a constitutional convention, with a relatively large number of participants, charged with choosing among alternative sets of *general* rules for the political-legal-economic order. In such a setting, the individual is led to deliberate on his or her *constitutional preferences*, that is, he or she is led to array potential constitutional alternatives according to their relative desirability. By the nature of the choice setting, as defined, issues of possible conflicts among individual interests in the *in-period*, *within-rule* choice context do not arise. In particular, the issue of the potential discrepancy between persons' in-period *compliance* or *action* interests and their *constitutional interests* does not arise.[3] The only issue that the constitutional convention model focuses on is that of individuals' preferences over alternative rules for the political-legal-economic order under which they expect to live, and of the kind of behavior that they can be expected to exhibit in the collective choice process by which such rules are adopted.

The particular aspect under which this issue will concern us here is related to the fact that an individual's *constitutional preferences* can be viewed as embodying an *interest component* and a *theory component*.[4] A person's ranking of alternative rules is informed, first, by his or her *interests* in the patterns of outcomes that may result from different rules, and, second, by his or her factual expectations or *theories* about the kinds of outcomes that will result from alternative rules. Potential disagreement in constitutional preferences among participants in a constitutional convention may result from both these sources, from conflicting interests in outcome patterns, from disagreement in theories, or from both.

The central concern of the contractarian approach to the issue of constitutional choice has been with those characteristics of the constitutional choice setting that tend to eliminate potential conflict in constitutional interests, or, more specifically, that tend to translate potential *inter*personal conflicts of interests into *intra*personal ones. The Buchanan-Tullock veil of uncertainty construction,[5] as well as the Rawlsian veil of ignorance construction,[6] both serve the purpose of presupposing a choice context in which interpersonal conflicts in constitutional interests are largely or, in the Rawlsian construction, even perfectly eliminated. If, under such conditions, constitutional agreement is considered unproblematic, an underlying assumption is, of

---

3. For expanded treatment of the second of these issues, see Viktor Vanberg and James M. Buchanan, "Rational Choice and Moral Order," *Analyse & Kritik* 10 (December 1988): 138–60.

4. For a more detailed discussion of this distinction, see chap. 5.

5. James M. Buchanan and Gordon Tullock, *The Calculus of Consent: Logical Foundations of Constitutional Democracy* (Ann Arbor: University of Michigan Press, 1962).

6. John Rawls, *A Theory of Justice* (Cambridge, Mass.: Harvard University Press, 1971).

course, that major obstacles do not result from conflicting constitutional theories, that is, from individuals' different expectations concerning the factual working properties of alternative rules. In fact, in Rawls's construction, such disagreement over theories is excluded by the assumption that each participant is fully informed about the general effects of the alternatives.

The concern of this chapter is the reverse, inquiring into the "information side" of the constitutional choice issue. We explicitly do not assume that the participants in the constitutional convention are perfectly informed about the general working properties of potential alternative rules, but rather, that they have to invest resources, that is, to incur costs, in order to become better informed about what the relevant alternatives are and what outcomes they are likely to produce. Specifically, we want to inquire into the reasons why, as can be observed in real world constitutional choice settings, some persons are willing to make such investments while others choose to remain uninformed and to defer to the constitutional expertise of others.

In order to isolate the informational dimension in constitutional choice we presuppose a choice context in which, due to some sufficiently thick veil of uncertainty, conflicts in constitutional interests are absent. That is, by presupposition, an individual cannot identify, in advance, what rules or set of rules will maximize the furtherance of his or her own interests, or the interests of the group that he or she represents. Under such assumptions, the process of reaching constitutional agreement is not a matter of reconciling potentially conflicting interests but of identifying the set of rules that best serves the participants' commonly shared constitutional interests.

Where participants to a constitutional convention are divided by conflicting interests, the concern for their identifiable interests does, one might be inclined to argue, provide an incentive for individuals to become knowledgeable about constitutional alternatives. The "theory of rational ignorance," however, has pointed to the reasons why, for large electorates, such reasoning may be flawed. The smaller the probability that his or her own vote will be decisive and the larger the subgroup of those voters with whom he or she shares common constitutional interests, the less incentive a person has to incur costs in order to become a better informed voter. Quite obviously, the logic of the rational ignorance argument applies a fortiori if, as in the context of our present analysis, we presuppose the absence of conflicting interests. Under such conditions, constitutional knowledge cannot be employed as a means for protecting or furthering one's differentially identifiable interests. Unable to identify potential differential interests, individuals are induced to favor *fair* rules and they can expect others to be similarly motivated. Given that, in this sense, the issue of fairness is taken care of, the remaining issue for which *constitutional knowledge* would seem to be a relevant concern is that of the overall "quality" of rules, quality in terms of some commonly shared standard for the desirability of patterns of outcomes.[7]

The quality or productivity of rules (in the defined sense) obviously is a genuine public good to the inclusive group of participants in the constitutional convention. Consequently the question arises: Why will any participant, in such a stylized (large-number) setting, supply the genuine "public good" that is presumably involved in becoming informed about the relevant alternatives? Strictly applied, rational choice on the part of participants would seem to dictate relatively little investment in the acquisition of information. And, if all participants act in this fashion, we could predict that the constitutional choices that emerge will exhibit properties of instability, cyclicity, and erratic swings, all of which might be associated with the dominance of expressive voting, as opposed to rationally based interest voting.[8] Or will it be rational for some subset of the participants to make the investment in analysis of the working properties of constitutional alternatives and for other participants to defer to the opinions of those who do make such investment?

1. Rational Deference

Recall that, by presupposition here, the participant who is to vote in the constitutional convention, is assumed to be ignorant in two distinct ways. Each participant, both among those who are passive and among those who might be active in information acquisition, remains, by presupposition, ignorant or uncertain in the Rawlsian sense. Each and every participant remains unable to identify his or her own interest in relation to the working of the choice alternatives in periods after the constitutional choice has been made by the group. This sort of Rawlsian constitutional ignorance may facilitate agreement because it offers a motivation for participants to make choices in terms of generalizable rather than particularized criteria. But the participant also remains ignorant as to the generalized working properties of the alternatives for choice. As mentioned before, this second sort of ignorance is not present in the stylized Rawlsian setting, where each participant is presumed fully informed as to the general patterns of effects of the alternatives. In our setting,

---

7. The implicit assumption here is, of course, that "fairness" and "quality" are attributes of rules that, in some sense, may vary independently of each other: Rules may be *fair*, in the sense of their effects on the distribution of benefits and costs among participants, and at the same time may be *poor* in generating only an inferior level of "welfare." That is to say, for a desirable social order to be generated, it is not only the fairness of rules that is of relevance but their "overall quality" or "productivity" as well.

8. For a treatment of the relevance of expressive voting in large-number electorates, see Geoffrey Brennan and James M. Buchanan, "Voter Choice: Evaluating Political Alternatives," *American Behavioral Scientist* 29 (November/December 1984): 185–201.

not only does the individual participant fail to know what set of rules will further his or her interests; he or she also does not know what sort of rules will maximize the achievement of the generalizable criterion that may be used.

We postulate that the second sort of ignorance can, however, be eliminated by a sufficient investment of resources in the acquisition of knowledge. In this section, we do not examine the choice behavior of the person who might consider such investment. We want, instead, to concentrate attention on the participant who chooses not to make such an investment, who chooses to remain ignorant of the general effects of potential constitutional alternatives. We shall, in section 2, examine the choice behavior of the participant who chooses to make the investment required to become informed about the general working properties of the alternatives. For now, we simply presume that some persons in the group, some participants, are observed to make such an investment. We want to concentrate on the choice behavior of the person who remains outside this informed set, this constitutional illiterate who yet retains a voting power equal to any other member of the constituent assembly or convention.

Such a participant now faces a choice setting that is quite different from that which is faced when all participants are equally ignorant. He or she now is presented with predictions of the working properties of the alternatives as these are advanced by those who claim to have become informed. The "experts" offer their opinions, and the constitutional illiterate can choose among the experts, the intellectual leaders, rather than make some raw choice among the alternatives, as such. That is to say, the uninformed participant may rationally *defer* to the opinion of someone who has gained his or her respect.

In order for deference to the opinion of some selected informed participant to be rational for the participant who remains uninformed, the choice among those informed persons to whom one might offer deference must be less costly in some sense than the raw choice among constitutional alternatives themselves. If the uninformed participant must become informed in order to choose rationally among the informed, then there is nothing to be gained by the additional step. The problem is the familiar one of choosing one's doctor. To choose one's doctor rationally may, in the limiting case, require the acquisition of sufficient information as to make the seeking of the doctor's advice totally unnecessary. By both observation and presumption, the investment required to choose among doctors rationally must be less than that which would be required to make the advice of doctors redundant. Doctors who offer their services exhibit certain readily accessible signs or badges of merit (diplomas, licenses, certificates). Further, both through word and deed, both directly and indirectly observable, doctors present a "sample" that allows a plausibly acceptable generalization to nonobserved and nonobservable areas of potential competence. The individual considers it fully rational to defer to the opinion and advice of the doctor whom he or she selects from among those offering their services.

The analogy with an uninformed individual's choices among constitutional alternatives seems appropriate here. Precepts of rationality need not imply that the individual actually "vote" expressively on the basis of emotional prejudice, on some lotterylike hunches, or cursorily on the basis of the minimal knowledge that is possessed. The uninformed participant, who acknowledges his or her own informational-knowledge status, may rationally defer to a "constitutional doctor," whom he or she deems to be well informed and more competent to array the alternatives. He or she may choose to become a follower of an intellectual "leader," who earns the deference by his or her own differential investment in the acquisition of knowledge, an investment that may be exhibited directly or indirectly, in ways and means fully analogous to those of the physician. In transferring his or her direct influence on the collectively selected outcome to someone considered to be more informed, the uninformed participant is rationally protecting his or her own interests, to the extent that these are known in the constitutional choice setting.

Note that rational deference to the authority of the well-informed "leader" that is chosen is not fully analogous to the delegation of decision-making authority to a selected agent. In the principal-agent relationship, the central issue is one of controlling the agent that is selected to insure that he or she does, indeed, carry out the preferences of the principal. By comparison, in the deference to authority relationship, the problem is not one of keeping the agent under control; the problem is, instead, that of selecting an authority whose superior knowledge allows for an ultimate choice that will more accurately promote the participant's own interests.

2. Rational Leadership

The model of rational deference that has been outlined in the previous section is mainly a variation of the standard theory of rational ignorance. Like the latter, it emphasizes that voters in large-number settings have little incentives to invest in the acquisition of information, and it simply adds the argument that deference to some "authority" may be a lower cost substitute for such investments.

When the theory of rational ignorance is taken as a "reference model," it should be kept in mind that its logic strictly applies only if "casting a better informed vote" is considered the exclusive benefit of being more knowledgeable about the issues at stake. It is only under this assumption that the expected payoffs from informational investments can be said systematically to decrease as the size of the electorate increases, and to be negligibly small in large-number settings. To the extent that there may be other expected payoffs from informational investments—other than the improved "quality" of one's own vote—the theory of rational ignorance has to be reconsidered, in the sense that it becomes an empirical question again whether or not such investments are "rational," measured against whatever benefits knowledgeability may generate. This consideration may be relevant for the calculus of an "ordinary" voter to whom such knowledgeability is a potential asset, for example, in everyday conversation. It is, however, particularly relevant as we approach the issue of how a model of "leadership" may be constructed in the idealized setting for constitutional choice.

By presumption here, it is possible for an individual to remove the non-Rawlsian type of ignorance through an investment of time and intellectual energy. The potential leader can interpret the historical records; he or she can conduct comparative institutional analysis; he or she can simply spend time reflecting on the relevant alternatives; he or she can imaginatively construct and manipulate models; he or she can simulate patterns of behavior under varying constraints and varying assumptions about motivations. Finally, he or she can live through experiences in real time. Deference to elders is one of the traditional conventions.[9] Our concern is not, however, with this last means of acquiring wisdom or knowledge. Our concern is with the acquisition of knowledge or information that becomes possible through the explicitly allocated investment of resources.

Why should any participant undertake such an investment? To the extent that only the effects on his or her voting behavior are considered, such investment would seem beyond the boundaries of a rational calculus. Under the assumptions of our stylized constitutional convention model, there is no source of differential profit from informed voting because of the participant's uncertainty about his or her particularized postconstitutional interests. Further, despite the fact that he or she can, by presumption, make informed choices concerning the choice alternatives, he or she cannot, through his or her individual vote, exert more than a small influence on the outcome that will emerge from the collective choice process.

It is only as we consider other expected benefits from informational investments, benefits that go beyond the negligible potential payoffs from "improved" individual voting behavior, that such investments may be explained in rational choice terms. As we include some other expected benefits from "constitutional knowledgeability" as relevant arguments in utility functions for at least some of the participants in our stylized constitutional convention, we may plausibly explain the investment decisions of those who hope to

---

9. In cultures where communication media are not developed, the veneration of elders seems readily explainable.

assume roles as intellectual leaders. Such other benefits may, for instance, be identified by looking at the demand side of "deference." As noted in section 1, some individuals may supply deference to those whom they consider to be more informed. But, at the same time, those who purport to be relatively better informed "demand" deference in the sense that they place a positive value on having others influenced by their opinions and findings. For such persons, the potentiality that others may be intellectual followers is positively valued—either in and by itself or instrumentally—for example, (but by no means only) because of the directly instrumental effect exerted through enhanced power to determine the ultimate collective result.[10]

The model here may be formalized.[11] The individual, i, has two arguments in his or her utility function, X, a composite bundle of all "goods" of the standard sort, and D, which we describe as deference offered by other persons in the relevant collective group. Hence,

$$U_i = U_i(X,D) \tag{1}$$

where preferences over these two arguments are assumed to exhibit the normal properties.

The individual also confronts a production function that describes the rates at which X may be traded for D and vice versa.

$$F_i = F_i(X,D) \tag{2}$$

By allocating time and other resources away from the "production" of X, the individual can "produce," or anticipates that he or she can produce, D. To attain individual equilibrium, when utility is maximized, the individual must select X and D such that the following familiar condition is satisfied:

$$\frac{U_{ix}}{U_{id}} = \frac{F_{ix}}{F_{id}}, \tag{3}$$

where the second term in the subscript denotes the derivative of the utility and production functions with respect to the arguments designated. Non-

---

10. The ability to influence others is always of this instrumental value to any participant because, probabilistically, any additional voting power increases control over the outcome of collective choice. For a formal analysis of this aspect of the issue in a standard voting model, see James M. Buchanan and Dwight R. Lee, "Vote Buying in a Stylized Setting," *Public Choice* 49, no. 1 (1986): 3–16.

11. The analysis in this section is related to that developed by David Levy in his draft paper, "Fame and the Supply of Heroics" (Center for Study of Public Choice, George Mason University, 1987), mimeograph.

algebraically, utility is maximized when the marginal rate of substitution between X and D in the individual's utility function is brought into equality with the marginal trade-off that he or she confronts in production.

This formal construction is, of course, empty of explanatory content. We need to go further and specify the process through which some persons, but not all, will be led to make the necessary investment of resources in information acquisition, and, further, to examine the process that limits both the amount of investment and the number of those who will seek to fill the roles as intellectual leaders, as demanders of deference.

Interestingly perhaps, and despite the inherent plausibility of assuming inequalities among participants, we need not postulate initial differences among participants, either in utility functions or in production possibilities.[12] That is to say, there need be no differences in preferences for deference relative to other goods, nor need there be differences in the opportunity costs of producing deference relative to other goods. Note that deference cannot be "privately demanded and supplied" within the economy of a single individual. That is to say, the deference relationship exists only in interaction among persons; it cannot exist in a Crusoe setting.

The person who remains uninformed offers deference to *another* person; the person who receives deference does so from *another* person. Note, however, that the simple exchange conceptualization does not apply readily to this interaction. The person who remains uninformed does not supply deference to another "at a price;" they do not "sell their vote" directly for some privately excludable quantity of a numéraire or other partitionable good or service. He or she supplies deference, through following the leadership of another, only in some sort of indirect exchange for the general knowledge of the alternatives that is made available to him, and to all others, as a nonexcludable "public good." The person who undertakes the investment in acquiring knowledge does not use stocks of the goods in X, or his or her capacity to produce such goods, to "purchase" deference directly from others. Instead, he or she uses these stocks or these capacities to produce nonexcludable public goods, namely information about the constitutional alternatives, in anticipation that, indirectly, he or she will secure the deference of others as he or she makes these public goods available to others.[13]

---

12. The emphasis here is on *initial*. An investment in information acquisition, once it is made, is likely to impact on the investor's human capital and, hence, to affect his or her future production possibilities.

13. Obvious indirect benefits can be secured in any setting where the constitutional expert may instrumentally use such deference of others in order to further a professional political career. And, conversely, the competition among candidates in such settings may impose constraints that encourage production of "constitutional knowledge." In other terms, the production of the public good, "constitutional knowledge," may be in part a byproduct of persons' efforts to advance their political career chances.

We do not require initial differentiation among persons in preferences or in opportunity costs because of the inherent extreme or polar-case publicness of that which is produced as a means of earning deference. Both of the qualities that define polar publicness are present here. Once the knowledge about constitutional alternatives is generated and made available to one person, it can, without additional cost, be made available to all persons in the relevant group.[14] Nonrivalry in the "consumption" of this "good" is complete. Also, once made available to one person, others cannot be excluded from the utilization of the same "good."

3. Industry Equilibrium

Let us now examine the process through which the "industry" of information-knowledge acquisition attains equilibrium. Suppose that, in some initial time period, all persons in the stylized constitutional convention are equally ignorant and uninformed. Suppose, now, that by chance, by error, or by some other device, one participant makes a *minimal* resource investment in acquiring information and knowledge. He or she immediately becomes the seer; others defer to his or her demonstrated superior knowledge and others seek and act on his or her advice about the selection of constitutional alternatives. This person, in effect, becomes the lawgiver for the community. As he or she achieves this status, he or she is observed to enjoy the positively valued deference offered by others, as valued either instrumentally or in and by itself.

This situation is clearly not one that describes an industry equilibrium. The supplier of knowledge is using up only a minimal quantity of the composite good, X, while securing a large quantity of deference, D. He or she is shifted to a level of utility well above that attained by his or her fellows, all of whom are here postulated to be his or her equals in all respects. Others will be attracted to enter the knowledge acquisition and promulgation industry. Competition will take the form of differentiation by way of additional investment in knowledge, which may be observed both directly and indirectly. The initial entrant will respond to the threat of his or her competitors by investing more resources in acquiring knowledge about the alternatives.

In equilibrium, the expected utility of any person will be equal between "employment" in the knowledge industry and "employment" exclusively in the production of X. Several interesting aspects of this equilibrium are worthy of attention. First of all, note that the enjoyment of X, the composite bundle of ordinary goods and services, must be higher for those outside the knowledge industry than for those who enter the industry. The member of the latter group

---

14. There may, of course, be costs involved in the process of transmitting whatever constitutional knowledge is generated to other persons in the group.

must sacrifice some potential consumption-enjoyment of X in order to secure the knowledge-information that is expected, indirectly, to allow for the enjoyment of deference. If "incomes" are measured exclusively in X, then incomes of those in the knowledge industry must, in equilibrium, remain below those of persons outside the industry.

Secondly, note that it is expected utility that is relevant in motivating both entry into the industry and the level of investment by those who do enter. Because of the polar publicness of that which is supplied by those within the industry, there need be no equalization of attained levels of utility between employment in and outside the industry by those who actually enter the industry. Deference may actually be offered to, and hence enjoyed by, only a few of those who supply knowledge (at the limit, only one). The successful among those offering leadership in this sense will achieve utility levels superior to that which might have been attained by remaining outside the industry, while those who are unsuccessful will actually achieve utility levels below those that might have been attained by outside employment.

A related feature suggests that, in terms of the orthodox efficiency norm, there may be resource waste in industry equilibrium. There may be excessive investment in the acquisition of knowledge that is closely akin to the rent seeking waste involved when artificial scarcities are introduced. The potential for waste occurs here, not due to artificial restrictions, but due to the peculiar characteristics of the investment required to secure knowledge and information. The hours spent in acquiring knowledge by separate individuals, all of whom are expecting to become leaders, do not generate public goods of an additive nature, at least to the extent that is present in the orthodox case. While it might have been fully rational, for some member of the Philadelphia convention in the expected utility sense, to seek to oust James Madison from his position as intellectual leader, to do so would have required that this person invest time and resources in reviewing constitutional histories that duplicated that already undertaken by Madison. In some communitywide sense, such resource investment must be deemed wasteful.[15]

How many persons will enter the knowledge-information industry and how much investment will be made? The answer to both of these questions will depend on the value placed on D and on the costs, in terms of X, of acquiring the knowledge that, in turn, produces D. If persons, generally, place little or no value on becoming and being leaders of opinion, we should expect relatively little investment in the acquisition of knowledge in our highly restricted model. Similarly, even if deference should be valued highly, if the

---

15. Note that the possible excessive investment in our model does not stem from the same source as that which is central in Earl Thompson's model of competitive supply of *excludable* public goods. See Earl Thompson, "The Perfectly Competitive Production of Collective Goods," *Review of Economics and Statistics* 50, no. 1 (February 1968): 1–12.

costs of securing deference through the acquisition of knowledge are very high, little investment might be predicted to emerge. These costs can be high for two separate reasons. The acquisition of the relevant knowledge may itself require high investment, both in terms of some threshold of achievement and in terms of continued resource outlay. In addition, even when knowledge is acquired, deference may not be forthcoming if the climate of interaction is such that the respect and trust of uninformed participants is difficult to capture.

The converse of these conclusions also follows. If deference is highly valued and if it can be produced at relatively low costs, we should expect a high level of investment, and, possibly, a high level of resource waste in the sense discussed above.

4. Posthumous Deference

The restrictiveness of our basic model should be emphasized. To this point we have worked within the constraining assumptions that all participants are equal, both in preferences and in relevant productive capacities, and that the deference that is valued is *contemporaneous*. That is, the "good" that enters in utility functions as a positively valued argument is measured by the observed patterns of deference offered by persons who exist in the same time period. We have not considered an argument that reflects what we may call posthumous deference, or, more descriptively, fame.[16]

This argument may, nonetheless, be important in explaining why persons invest resources in the acquisition and promulgation of knowledge. Over and beyond, and even quite distinct from, any expected influence on the ideas of contemporaries, individuals may seek to influence those that "live after them," and they may voluntarily make investments for this purpose. It becomes terminologically incongruous to use "expected utility" with reference to this "good," which perhaps calls the whole notion of the expected utility language into question. It is, however, evident that persons do place value on posthumous deference, and we could readily adjust our formal model to include the additional argument. We could, also, extend the statement of the conditions of industry equilibrium to account for this additional element.

If we consider only the behavior of those who make investments in knowledge, any inclusion of valuation for posthumous deference would tend to increase the level of investment, compared with that which would be observed in the presence of only contemporaneous deference. If, however, we

---

16. See David Levy, "Fame and the Supply of Heroics"; see also Douglass Adair, *Fame and the Founding Fathers* (New York: Norton, 1974).

also include the behavior of those uninformed persons who might offer deference, a somewhat different result follows. To the extent that persons, in
periods long past, have been successful in "purchasing" posthumous deference, their influences remain. And persons in the here and now may prefer
to give deference to the ideas of those who lived in earlier periods than
directly to those who offer their current services as potential intellectual or
opinion leaders. To the extent that this residue of past influence remains, to
the extent that James Madison, rather than some contemporary scholar, informs and shapes the attitudes of the commoner today, there is less rational
incentive for the potential investment in knowledge today. Those who seek to
influence and to lead current participants must compete for deference, not
only with their contemporaries who have entered the knowledge industry, but
also with all of those persons who, in past periods, have made such investments and whose ideas have been embodied in documents that are transferable
through time. In a community characterized by stability through time, and
especially a community with a written historical record, this influence seems
likely to dominate the first one noted above. There is, in such a community,
presumably less investment in knowledge than there would be in the total
absence of posthumous deference.

5. The Community of Unequals

As suggested, we have worked within a highly restricted and stylized model.
If we drop the restrictive assumption that persons are equal in preferences
and/or relevant productive capacities, then it becomes much easier, and more
plausible, to develop a general model of rational deference. If we do nothing
more than postulate that, by either preferences or capacities, there are "natural" followers and "natural" leaders, the two patterns of behavior discussed
above fall even more readily within rationality precepts. Further, if, among
those who might possess the capacities to command deference through some
investment in knowledge acquisition, there are discernible differences in the
opportunity costs of making the relevant trade-off between X and D, we can
explain the pattern of entry into the industry that acquires and disseminates
knowledge and information.

   As we indicated at the outset, our inquiry is narrowly focused. We have
sought to use a rational choice model or models to explain the motivation for
genuine constitutional evaluation and, possibly, for constitutional reform. Our
exercise has been one of "extending the limits" of rational choice models. In
so doing, we have not intended to convey the impression that rational choice
models offer the only explanatory tools that are possible. We do not claim to
have offered the explanation for the behavior of either James Madison or that

of those persons who deferred to him in constitutional construction. We have, we think, offered an explanation of this behavior that utilizes the familiar tools of social science. Note, in particular, that we have not advanced the claim that the individual's exercise of rational choice is a sufficient condition for viable constitutional order, an issue that is addressed directly in chapter 13.

Part 3
Ethical Foundations

CHAPTER 13

The Ethics of Constitutional Order

In 1953, Robert Dahl and Charles Lindblom published a challenging book entitled *Politics, Economics, and Welfare.*[1] The central theme or argument in the book was that we, as individual citizens, do not make choices among the grand organizational alternatives; we do not choose between "capitalism" and "socialism." We choose, instead, among the pragmatically defined and highly particularized policy alternatives as these are indirectly presented to us through the political process. And we make our choices on the basis of that combination of ignorance, ideology, and interest that best describes our psychological state.

I distinctly recall that I was somehow quite disturbed by this Dahl-Lindblom argument, but that I could not quite work out for myself a fully satisfactory response or counterargument. Perhaps now, some four decades later, I can make such an effort.

First, let me translate the problem into terminology that is more familiar to me, and also more general. Let me refer to the whole constitutional order, that is, the structure of legal-political rules, within which we act both in our private and our public capacities. The Dahl-Lindblom thesis is that we do not consciously choose this structure. Empirically, they seem to be correct. We go about making our ordinary choices, which involve complex interactions with other persons and groups, within a framework or a structure of rules that we simply take as a part of our environment, a part of the state of nature, so to speak. This descriptive characterization applies equally to ordinary socioeconomic and to political interaction.

If, however, we do not consciously choose, or even think about choosing, among structures or rules, that is, among alternative constitutional orders, how can we be responsible for the very regimes under which we live? And if we are not responsible for the ultimate choice among constitutional alternatives and could not, in fact, choose among them, is it not then meaningless to talk about constitutional change or constitutional reform?

The implication seems clear. We must, willy-nilly, acquiesce in the re-

---

1. Robert A. Dahl and Charles E. Lindblom, *Politics, Economics, and Welfare* (New York: Harper, 1953).

gime under which we live and simply do our best to behave rationally as we confront the pragmatically generated choices that emerge. Something seems wrong with this argument. For most of the time, and for most practical purposes, it is perhaps best that we accept the existing constitutional order as a "relatively absolute absolute." But such acceptance is not equivalent to a denial that change is possible, even for the single person who thinks about, analyzes, evaluates, and proposes alternative structures. I want to suggest here that each one of us, as a citizen, has an *ethical obligation* to enter directly and/or indirectly into an ongoing and continuing constitutional dialogue that is distinct from, but parallel to, the patterns of ordinary activity carried on within those rules that define the existing regime.

Let me illustrate the whole problem here by reference to a poker game example that will be familiar to those of you who have ever had any exposure to my own attempts to present the elements of constitutional political economy. In any observed and ongoing poker game, individuals, as players, abide by the rules that exist and which define the game itself. Players adopt this or that strategy in attempts to win within the existing rules. At the same time, however, the same persons may evaluate the rules themselves, and they may enter into side discussions about possible changes in the rules so as to make for a "better" game. If, as a result of such discussion, agreement is reached, then rules are changed and the regime shifts. A new constitution emerges.

This poker example helps me to make two elementary, but highly important, points. First, the example facilitates the distinction between the choice of strategies within the existing set of rules and the choice among alternative sets of rules, or, more generally, between inconstitutional and constitutional choice. Secondly, the example allows us to see that an individual, as player, may behave responsibly and rationally in choosing and implementing strategies within the rules that define the game, without necessarily concerning himself or herself about changes in the rules themselves. That is to say, the individual player may, but need not, enter into the dialogue and discussion about changes in the rules. To remain as a player in the game, the choice among strategies of play is necessary, but participation in the potential choice among sets of rules is not necessary. The first of these two points has been elaborated at length in modern analyses; the second point has not been fully examined, and it provides the focus of attention in this short chapter.

Let me remain within the more familiar realm of discussion about the first point in order to summarize the now standard argument. The distinction between the levels of choice, between postconstitutional or within-rules choice, and choice among rules has proved helpful in allowing a bridge to be constructed between rational choice behavior by the individual and the emergence of agreement on something that might be called the "general interest."

If persons are unable to identify their own narrowly defined interests, due to the presence of some sufficiently thick veil of uncertainty, they will choose among alternatives in accordance with some generalizable criteria such as fairness. In this setting of constitutional choice, therefore, no need for an explicit ethical norm seems to arise.

The poker game, veil of uncertainty model has proved helpful in introducing the setting for constitutional choice, and it is a model that I have often used. But the model is highly misleading in respects relevant for my purposes here. If we are considering games with effectively *large* numbers of participants, there may exist little or no incentive for any *single* player to participate actively in any serious evaluation of the rules. Each player will, of course, have an incentive to maximize his or her own payoffs within whatever set of rules that exists, and each player may, also, have an interest in the presence of rules that satisfy generalizable criteria when he does not know what his or her own position will be. But having the latter interest is not equivalent to having an interest-based *incentive* to act unless the individual expects that his or her own action will influence the outcome of the collective selection among alternatives. This point will be familiar to those who recognize the elementary public choice logic, especially in application to the theory of rational voter abstention and rational voter ignorance. In a large-number setting, the individual player may not consider himself or herself influential in controlling the ultimate selection among sets of rules; hence, the fully rational player may well refrain from participating in the choice among regimes.

The poker game analogy is misleading in a second respect, especially by extension to politics. A poker game is voluntary; hence, rules must, at least in some sense, be agreed to by all players, because those who are dissatisfied may withdraw from play altogether. In this context, the large-number setting may not be so problematic as it seems, since each player retains a low-cost exit option. But there is no such exit possible in national political regimes. The political game is compulsory, and we all must play. Individually, therefore, we cannot exercise even residual influence over the rules through an effective exit option. The conclusion is clear; if the individual cannot ultimately influence the choice among regimes, it is not rational to participate actively in any discussion of constitutional change or to become informed about constitutional alternatives.

The argument suggests that becoming informed about, and participating in the discussion of, constitutional rules may require the presence of some ethical precept that transcends rational interest for the individual. (The extensions of rational choice behavior, previously traced in chap. 12, may not be sufficient.) The individual who acts on such an ethical precept behaves "as if" his or her own influence on the ultimate selection among regimes is more than that which a rational choice calculus would imply. Behavior in accordance with such a precept embodies an ethical responsibility for the choice among regimes.

Note that this ethic of constitutional citizenship is not directly comparable to ethical behavior in interaction with other persons within the constraints imposed by the rules of an existing regime. An individual may be fully responsible, in the standard ethical sense, and yet fail to meet the ethical requirement of constitutional citizenship. The individual may be truthful, honest, mutually respectful, and tolerant in all dealings with others, yet, at the same time, the same individual may not bother at all with the maintenance and improvement of the constitutional structure.

On many occasions, I have referred to what I have called a loss of constitutional wisdom, especially as observed over the decades of this century. My argument here suggests that this loss of understanding and loss of interest in political structure may reflect the straightforward working out of rationally based individual self-interest, accompanied by an erosion of the ethical principle of constitutional responsibility. To the extent that we, as individuals, do not act "as if" we do, individually, choose among the grand alternatives, then the constitutional regime that we inherit must be vulnerable both to nonprincipled exploitation and to the natural erosion of historical change.

The result is precisely what we seem to have observed over recent decades. The vision of constitutional order that informed the thinking of James Madison and his peers among the Founders was carried forward for more than a century of our national history. This vision embodies both an understanding of the principles of constitutional order and recognition that the individual, as citizen, must accept the ethical responsibility of full and informed participation in a continuing constitutional convention.

The Madisonion vision, with its embodied ethic of constitutional citizenship, is difficult to recapture once it is lost from the public consciousness. The simple, yet subtle, distinction between strategic choices within rules and constitutional choices among sets of rules, the distinction that was illustrated in the poker game example introduced earlier, this distinction must inform all thinking about policy alternatives. The individual, as citizen, cannot restrict his or her attention to policy options within rules; the individual cannot simply reflect on the alternatives that emerge under the operation of a collective decision rule, say, majority voting in a legislature. Choice cannot be limited to a determination of that which is "best," either in terms of the individual's own interest or in terms of the individual's own version of some general interest. Constitutional citizenship requires that the individual also seek to determine the possible consistency between a preferred policy option and a preferred constitutional structure. (This point may be illustrated by a personal choice example. An individual may prefer a dish of ice cream, but eating a dish of ice cream may not be consistent with the furtherance of the rules dictated by a self-imposed diet plan, an eating constitution.)

Much of what we have observed in modern politics is best described as action taken without understanding, or even consideration, of the rules that define the constitutional order. I have referred to this politics as "constitutional anarchy," by which I mean a politics that is almost exclusively dominated by, and derivative from, the strategic choices made by competing interests in disregard for the effects on political structure. This politics has emerged into its current position because we, as citizens, have failed to discharge our ethical obligations. We have behaved as if the very structure of our social order, our constitution defined in the broadest sense, will remain invariant or will, somehow, evolve satisfactorily over time without our own active participation.

Simple observation of the behavior of our political and judicial agents should indicate that such a faith is totally without foundation. We may, of course, continue to default on the ethical obligation of constitutional citizenship. If we do so, however, we leave unchecked the emerging tyranny of the nonconstrained state, a tyranny that can be dislodged only with revolution. Neither such tyranny nor its consequent revolution is necessary if we, as individuals, can recover, even in part, the ethical principle upon which our constitutional order is established.

We must attend to the rules that constrain our rulers, and we must do so even if such attention may not seem to be a part of a rational choice calculus. The amorality of acquiescence generates despair and longing; the morality of constitutional understanding embodies hope as a necessary complement.

CHAPTER 14

Economic Interdependence and the Work Ethic

I commence with a confession of sorts. I have been unable to release myself, intellectually, from a determination to unravel, at least to my own satisfaction, the relationship between the simple choice of an individual, any individual, to work more or less, and the well-being of other persons who interact with the chooser in an extended production-exchange network. I entered this inquiry with a strongly held intuitive hypothesis to the effect that a choice made by anyone to work more, to add value to the economic nexus, generates benefits to others in the interaction, or, to put the hypothesis differently, and more generally, that there is *economic* content in the work *ethic*, that, in this respect as in others, we are ethically as well as economically interdependent.

I have not abandoned my hypothesis, but I have not fully resolved the question in all of its ramifications, even at the minimal levels of meeting my own internal requirements. But I am now able to state my hypothesis more clearly, and to embed it in a plausible analytical account. This chapter presents the argument nonformally, in part to avoid the distraction from the general implications of the hypothesis that formalization might involve.

I shall proceed as follows. In section 1, I shall "purify the model," so to speak, by listing, and describing briefly, the economic-institutional settings within which the ethical interdependence hypothesis clearly holds. Although these settings are intrinsically of some interest and, also, contain implications of important policy relevance, they do not embody my primary concerns. These settings are, therefore, noted in order to get onto the central issues. Section 2 presents these issues full face, in the context of an apparent contradiction, the resolution of which has spurred my interest from the outset. Section 3 represents my best attempt to put the opposition's case, the argument that my hypothesis is simply in error, that there is no economic content in the work ethic under the standard assumptions of economic theory. Section 4 advances my own provisional attempt to modify the received theory to allow my hypothesis to be valid, based on my continuing refusal to bow before the forces of analytic convention. Section 5 extends the analysis, especially as it relates to other elements in the theory of competitive equilibrium. In section 6, the welfare implications of the analysis are examined, with an emphasis on the internalization of externalities through the introduction of ethical constraints. The summary evaluation and extension in section 7 concludes the chapter.

1. Fiscal Interdependence and Team Production

As announced, my purpose in this section is to "cleanse" the analysis, to describe briefly those settings in which the work ethic hypothesis is obviously valid, at least in some respects, but to do so in order to eliminate interference with the later examination of the more interesting question. The first such setting also serves to illustrate, in elementary fashion, the general issues that are to be addressed.

Consider an economy that is organized, and effectively operates, competitively. Rigorous description of the properties of equilibrium is not required at this stage. A public, or collectivized, sector of this economy exists through which collective consumption of public goods and services are financed from revenues collected from a tax that differentially impacts on measured income, as opposed to a benchmark tax on full income. In this regime, *fiscal interdependence* is such as to insure that the work-leisure choice made by any work supplier (or income earner) exerts Pareto relevant external effects, at the margin, on all other persons in the nexus.[1] By a decision to work an extra hour, day, or week, a person increases the effective base of tax which will, in turn, allow others in the nexus to enjoy higher rates of public goods benefits and/or lower tax rates. From the initial position of independent adjustment equilibrium, an agreement (including compensations where required) among all participants that involves input suppliers offering more inputs to the economic nexus must, over some range, promise benefits to everyone. In such a setting, the existence, maintenance, and promotion of an ethical constraint that discourages the consumption of leisure can provide a partial substitute for a potential utility-enhancing general agreement.

I shall neglect further discussion of this sort of fiscal interdependence, although full recognition of the relationship does, indeed, carry obvious implications for the organization of the tax structure. In what follows here, I shall simply assume that any taxes are levied on individuals in such fashion that liabilities for tax (and hence the tax base) cannot be modified by individual behavioral choices.

A second setting in which the validity of the hypothesis cannot be challenged embodies production under conditions where there are genuine advantages from the joint supply of effort by all members of a team. Since, by construction, individuals produce more when they participate jointly than

---

1. For an early analysis see James M. Buchanan, "Externality in Tax Response," *Southern Economic Journal* 33 (July 1966): 35–42.

when they produce separately, there exist genuine technological externalities at the individual work-leisure choice margins under decentralized and nonintegrated competitive adjustment. If, however, the presence of team production or joint supply advantages extend over relatively limited subsets of the total work supply population, entrepreneurs would be predicted to emerge to internalize the relevant externalities among individual members of production teams. If the extent of jointness efficiencies is sufficiently limited to allow these advantages to be internalized within less than industry-sized firms, there need remain no Pareto relevant external effects in full competitive equilibrium.[2]

2. Economic Interdependence and Ethical Independence

The formal model of competitive economic interaction, cleansed of those features that could generate apparent Pareto relevant externalities at the individually defined choice margins between work supply and leisure, is descriptively interesting in its fundamental ethical implications. Despite the acknowledged benefits secured by all participants in an extended network of economic interdependence, there seems to exist no discernible generalized ethical interdependence, at least along the quantitative work-leisure dimension that remains my exclusive concern in this chapter. There is no apparent economic interest, as reflected in expected utility gains and losses, on the part of any one participant in the work-leisure choices made by others in the nexus.

The person who chooses to add a unit of input, who works an extra hour, day, or week, receives a payment (per time unit) that is the precise equivalent to the increment in product value that is generated by the incremental unit of input. Total product value increases by the same amount that the measured income of the person who supplies the incremental input increases. The incomes (and utilities) of others remain unaltered. From this characteristic of competitive equilibrium, it follows that others remain unaffected by, and hence remain uninterested in, the supply of work effort put on the market by the person in question, or indeed, of anyone else. In the formal model of competitive adjustment in equilibrium, individuals do not affect each other. To employ, in a somewhat different sense, the characterization used by David Gauthier, the competitive market in equilibrium is a "morally free zone."[3]

This result seems to be in apparent and blatant contradiction to the elementary principle that is stressed in every economics primer, the principle

2. My colleague, Roger Congleton, with whom I have worked jointly on several aspects of the analysis of the work ethic, has examined the importance and relevance of team production more fully in a draft paper, "The Economics of the Work Ethic," (Center for Study of Public Choice, George Mason University, 1988).

3. David Gauthier, *Morals by Agreement* (Oxford: Oxford University Press, 1985).

that there exist mutual gains from trade, and that all participants gain from the specialization that becomes possible only as trade occurs. How is this apparent contradiction to be reconciled? How is the positive relationship between the utility secured by an individual participant and the size of the inclusive production-exchange nexus ("the market") to be made consistent with the apparent absence of any relationship between any individual's work effort and the utility of others with whom he or she interacts? If an individual's utility does, indeed, depend on the size or the extent of the market, then it would seem to follow that any increase in this size, such as that embodied in the supply of an additional unit of input by any person, must be utility enhancing to others, at least in some potential sense. In this case, however, there must then exist some economic interest on the part of any one participant in the work-leisure choices made by others. Ethical content seems to be restored, despite the implication that is drawn from the conventional model of competitive adjustment.

The intellectual-analytical challenge is evident. What is wrong with the standard model of general equilibrium in an idealized competitive economy that allows the implication of total ethical independence to be derived?

3. The Ethical Irrelevance of Work-Leisure Choice

In this section, I shall present the "opposition's" case. I shall outline, in a nonrigorous way, the formal theory of competitive equilibrium to demonstrate that, under the standard assumptions, there is no ethical content in the work-leisure choices made by individual participants in such an idealized economic interaction setting.

In equilibrium, team production advantages of the ordinary sort are internalized within firms, each one of which operates in the range of constant returns to scale. Entry, actual or potential, insures that no firm receives pure profit. Each firm is small, relative to the industry producing its product, and each firm is a price taker, both as a supplier of product and as a demander of inputs. Each input supplier is also a price taker and freely adjusts quantities supplied to the parametric input price, as dictated by the relative evaluation of earning and nonearning alternatives (work and leisure). Each consumer of final product, or demander, is also a price taker in all markets and freely adjusts quantities purchased in accordance with relative evaluations placed on the different goods that are available. All demanders of final product, all suppliers of inputs, and all decision makers for firms are in positions of optimal adjustment. The necessary conditions for Pareto optimality are satisfied, and, more restrictively, the solution is in the core. There is no economic incentive for any individual, or any coalition of individuals including the all-inclusive coalition, to modify behavior to depart from the equilibrium position as defined.

Let us postulate that this equilibrium is, now, shocked by a single change in behavior. One worker or input supplier, for any reason, increases by one unit the rate of input supplied to the market. This worker supplies one additional hour-per-day, day-per-week, or week-per-year to the production-exchange nexus, which is now larger by precisely the value added by the additional unit of input.

The analytical exercise may be limited to pure comparative statics. We may describe the properties of the ultimate postchange equilibrium and identify the differences between this position and the prechange equilibrium. There will, of course, be transitional shifts in values of the relevant variables, and these shifts will affect utility levels attained by differing groups of market participants during transition periods. These short-run or intermediate-run effects are not of central concern here. I am interested only in the long-run or permanent effects that remain after the idealized system of interaction settles down, conceptually, to its full postchange equilibrium.

Initially it will be expositionally convenient to present the analysis in a single-factor model. We may assume that labor is the only input, or, alternatively, that, as subject to choice by the supplier, "labor" embodies some complementary factor, "capital" in fixed proportions.[4] In this setting, the property that captures my attention here is the identity of both the product price and input price vectors in the prechange and postchange equilibria. And, because these price vectors are not modified, the potential utility levels attained by persons other than the individual who initiated the parametric shift are not changed. Persons do not, therefore, have a long-term economic interest in the supply of inputs put on the market by others. The increase in product value between the two equilibrium positions is precisely measured by the wage, or input price, paid to and received by the individual whose preference shift generated the change in the system.

This result depends, admittedly, on the absence of input specialization, at least over the relevant range of change generated by the shift, in input supply and subsequent output mix. Some units of input must, at the margin, be capable of generating equal increments to value in all uses, although remaining inputs may be allowed to earn genuine rents in specialized uses.

It is perhaps worth noting here that the world of competitive adjustment described in the standard models, at least as I have described it, is in all respects equivalent to the world of classical economics and, indeed, can be

---

4. In this respect the model is similar to that used by Martin Weitzman, "Increasing Returns and the Foundations of Unemployment Theory," *Economic Journal* 92 (December 1982): 787–804.

conceived as only an extension of Adam Smith's deer-beaver model in which relative costs of production determine relative prices to the exclusion of any demand-side or utility influence. Under the defined assumptions of the standard model, any shift in demand, generated by a change in preferences among final products, will, of course, generate shifts in relative supplies, but, unless there exist specialized inputs over the range relevant to the demand shifts, there will be no change in the vector of relative prices.

Dependence of relative prices on demands may, of course, be introduced through some presumption of input specificity, even after full adjustment. But this step would require some relaxation of the standard assumptions of the competitive model, specifically that which embodies constant returns to scale. I do not propose to depart from the input specificity conditions here.[5]

4. Return to Relevance

My hypothesis states that the idealized competitive equilibrium under all of the assumptions embodied in the standard model may *not* be Pareto optimal, which amounts to stating that there may exist nonexploited "gains from trade" remaining to be captured from some potential agreement among all participants. Specifically, my hypothesis is that all participants, as suppliers of inputs and users of outputs, can move to higher levels of utility by modifying behavior to generate an increased supply of work effort to the exchange nexus. I suggest that the error in the received analysis is to be located in an oversight of the full implications of the principle of the division of labor, or, more generally, of specialization. As noted earlier, this principle is recognized generally in the acceptance of Adam Smith's proposition that "division of labor is limited by the extent of the market," but the implications of this familiar proposition for the optimality properties of competitive equilibrium seem to have escaped critical notice, with only few exceptions.

Clearly, any increase in the quantity of any input supplied to the nexus

---

5. The general results are not modified if we drop the single-factor assumption, although there will be net gainers and net losers in the shift between the two competitive equilibria. The postulated increase in the supply of *labor* inputs by the single person will increase the returns to suppliers of the complementary input, "capital," and at the same time reduce returns to suppliers of substitute inputs, "labor." These changes in the input price vector may, in turn, generate changes in the output price vector as differing outputs reflect differing factor proportions.

The relevant result, for my purpose, is that, despite the generated changes in input and output prices, the external beneficiaries of the increase in the supply of the one input cannot, in net, compensate the external losers while retaining gains sufficient to compensate the single-input supplier to modify his or her preferred behavior. In other words, the multifactor model does, indeed, introduce externalities into the choice of any input supplier, but under the standard conditions of competitive equilibrium adjustment, these externalities remain pecuniary and, hence, Pareto irrelevant.

extends the market. Hence, by the Smithean principle, an increased division of labor is made possible. But the defined formal conditions for competitive equilibrium insure that all gains from specialization have been fully exhausted; hence, there are no welfare effects that emerge from the extension in market size. I suggest that this result is artificially produced by the assumptions imposed on the particular model that has come to dominate the neoclassical research program, and that a more acceptable model can be developed that will remove this contradiction. Both models are, of course, analytical idealizations, and neither is designed to reflect reality in any directly descriptive sense.

Let me return to the simple exercise in comparative statics. The economy is in its idealized competitive equilibrium; a single person now works an additional unit of time, reflecting a shift in revealed preference between supplying input to the market and supplying "input" (time) to the production of the person's *own* consumption of leisure. In the latter internalized "exchange," units of time yield utility flows directly; added leisure increases utility, at least over the ranges of choice relevant for analysis. In the external exchange between the person and the market, the converse relationship holds; units of time supplied in exchange for wages reduce utility. It is only indirectly that such exchanges become part of a utility-enhancing behavioral strategy. As the income is spent on the purchase of any valued product, the utility loss incurred in the sacrifice of leisure is offset by the utility gain in product value. Put simply, in the standard model, persons supply inputs to the market nexus for the purpose of being able to purchase output from this nexus. Suppliers are motivated by the prospects of becoming demanders. Say's law is surely valid at this juncture of the analysis. Supply emerges only because it enables its own demand to become possible.

How does this excursion into the elementary behavioral logic of choice in markets relate to my proposed reformulation of the model of competitive equilibrium? The person who supplies the additional unit of work to the nexus receives a wage or income for that unit. This income is returned to the market as an increase in demand for final product. This increase in demand, which is matched by the initiating increase in supply that made it possible, will create the potential for the exploitation of further specialization, *in some production*, that remained just below the margin of economic viability in the prechange equilibrium. The real cost of production (measured in minimally necessary quantities of inputs required for producing given outputs) in the affected industry (or industries) falls. The vector of output prices changes to reflect lower relative prices for the product (or products) now produced at reduced real costs. The vector of input prices will not change, if measured in relative terms, provided that units of input are not product specific over relevant ranges. If measured in terms of an output price index or numéraire, however, the value of inputs increase. For any given quantity of input supplied to the market, the income earned from the sale of that quantity will enable the supplier to purchase a higher index-valued bundle of product value than before the change. For any individual supplier who purchases a product bundle that includes the reduced-cost-price good, there is an increase in utility. The increase in the supply of work by the single person generates external or spillover benefits on all persons in the market nexus who purchase that particular good (or goods), the production costs, and price, of which are reduced due to the exploitation of specialization that is made possible by the market's extension.

5. Competitive Equilibrium, Increasing Returns, and Externalities

The general framework for my argument has been sketched out, but there remains the task of filling in the analytical details. My model violates the generalized constant returns condition imposed for the standard derivation of competitive equilibria. In order for any extension in the size of the production-exchange nexus to generate utility or welfare-enhancing effects, constant returns must be absent in *at least one industry* in the economy. For this industry (or industries), the increase in the demand for product calls forth a supply response that embodies a lowered real cost of producing. For this industry (or industries), the long-run supply-curve slopes downward. The good (or goods) in question is/are produced under conditions of *increasing returns* to size of output for the industry.

This condition need not be inconsistent with competitive organization. Increasing returns to industry output need not imply increasing returns to the output of any single firm within the industry under unchanged conditions of demand. Each single firm may be informed about returns to industry output, but any attempted expansion in isolation would reduce the equilibrium outputs of other firms, making the single firm unable to capture the scale advantages. These gains can be captured only with an increase in demand for the industry's product, which does take place here with the addition of purchasing power to the nexus. For at least one industry, the increment to demand that takes place makes possible a reduction in the average cost of production, thereby generating utility gains to all participants in the nexus who consume the product so affected.

If the industry (or industries) that might be adjusted to take advantage of further specialization could be identified in advance, either by some ideally omniscient centralized economic planner or by decision makers in some idealized collective process, then arrangements might be worked out through subsidization to insure the capture of the potential offered by the new technologies. But, lacking such omniscience and also recognizing the realities of politics, how can the potential advantages of increasing returns be secured?

If the identity of the industry (or industries) that might be the location of the increasing returns is unknown, any reduction in outlay on any industry required to finance the subsidization of other industries might reduce, rather than enhance, the productivity of the economy. There remains, however, one end use of capacity that cannot qualify for the increasing returns characterization due to an extension of specialization. This "industry" is that which is necessarily nonspecialized, namely, that which produces the own-consumption of each person in the economic nexus. From this fact follows the conclusion that any means of reducing the production of a nonmarketable product, mainly leisure, must extend the size of the market for other industries, which must, thereby, include at least some extension of the demand for that industry or industries subject to increasing returns.[6] It is in this sense that the externality discussed here is peculiarly present with the work-leisure margin for individual choice.

In a larger sense, the whole issue of the existence of a competitive equilibrium or some quasi-competitive equilibrium in an industry that operates under increasing returns remains outside my direct interest or concern. Even if the industry (or industries) so described must be organized monopolistically, or, alternatively, if effective competition among firms requires the presence of firm-specific demands thereby generating a monopolistically competitive industry structure, the "externality" stemming from the work-leisure choice will remain.[7]

My emphasis is exclusively microeconomic, but there are analytical affinities between the argument sketched out here and that developed by Martin Weitzman, whose interests and emphases are exclusively macroeconomic.[8] His argument suggests that generalized increasing returns can offer plausible microeconomic foundations for understanding the emergence of quasi-competitive unemployment equilibria. In particular, Weitzman does note the contradiction between the Smithean emphasis on the division of labor as related to market size and the constant returns condition in standard com-

---

6. Only the classic paper on increasing returns by Allyn Young seems to recognize the critical point here; see, "Increasing Returns and Economic Progress," *Economic Journal* 38 (1928): 527–42.

7. A general summary-survey of the whole set of familiar increasing returns controversies, along with appropriate references to the relevant literature, is found in S. Vassilakis, "Increasing Returns to Scale," *The New Palgrave Dictionary of Economics*, ed. J. Eatwell, M. Milgate, and P. Newman (London: MacMillan, 1987), 2:761–65.

8. Martin Weitzman, "Increasing Returns and the Foundations of Unemployment Theory."

petitive theory. Earlier, N. Kaldor stressed the same point in the context of a generalized critique of equilibrium theory.[9]

I have repeatedly referred to the "externality" involved in the behavioral adjustment made by individuals in choosing between work supply to the market and the supply of leisure to themselves. The peculiar nature of this externality warrants more detailed discussion. Note, first of all, that the externality need not be identified by any such attributes as location, occupation, or industry classification. The behavioral margin of relevance involves the supply of productive effort to the production-exchange nexus at any point and at any level of productivity. In particular, note that the operating characteristics of the industry within which the work-leisure choice is made are totally irrelevant. The externality applies to all work-leisure choice margins, whether in increasing, constant, or decreasing returns industries. The increase in value to the overall nexus exerts its external effect only as and when the input supplier returns the added value earned to the market as a consumer-purchaser, thereby generating an increase in effective demand. If the extent of the market limits the potential for deriving the advantages of specialization, at least one industry in the totality that describes the production-exchange nexus must exhibit increasing returns. And the beneficiaries of the externality, stemming from the increase in effective demand initially generated by the person who spends the income from his increased work effort, are those persons who include in their consumption portfolio the good (or goods) produced under conditions of increasing returns. The effects are, of course, reversible; a choice made by an individual to reduce the supply of work to the nexus, with the subsequent decrease in effective demand, will generate a negative externality or diseconomy on all persons who consume the product of the increasing returns industry (or industries).

The externality identified here differs from those that are more often treated in welfare or applied economics and in at least two basic characteristics. There need be no relation of contiguity, locational or otherwise, between the generator of the external effect and the recipients of benefit (or harm). In comparison, consider a few familiar examples. The pollution in the river reduces the fishing and boating opportunities for those who live downriver. The resident who maintains a fine flower garden increases the utility of his neighbors on the street; Coasian cattle invade the land of the neighboring farmers; Marshallian firms are in the same industry. On the other hand, and by contrast, the work-choice externality is potentially economywide, or beyond if the economy is defined to be smaller than the trading nexus.

The individual who supplies additional work in the industry that pro-

---

9. N. Kaldor, "The Irrelevance of Equilibrium Economics," *Economic Journal* 82 (1972): 1237–55.

duces x_i, among the set of final goods denominated: $x_1, x_2, \ldots x_n$, generates value to all persons who consume-purchase x_j, the good produced under increasing returns, who may be "far away" from both producers and consumers of x_i in any and all dimensions.

A second difference between the work-supply externality and others that are more familiar lies in the way in which the benefits (or harms) enter the utility functions of the persons affected externally. In the notation above, the externality affects the utility of the consumer-purchaser of good x_j that is produced under increasing returns through a reduction in the price of x_j. There is no effect on the utility function analogous to the addition of floral splendor by the gardener along the street or on the production function analogous to the pollination of the apple orchard by the neighbor's bees. The consumer-purchaser of the good produced under increasing returns, x_j, finds his or her budget constraint modified by a lowered price for x_j. And this price effect is not, in this case, offset by a compensating price increase elsewhere in the economy, as faced by this or any other consumer-purchaser. The effect emerges as a pure price change made possible by the increase in the aggregate supply of economic value to the economic nexus. The analyst must resist the temptation to disregard the externality because it enters the utility function through price. In the traditional terminology, the externality is "technological," and, hence, Pareto relevant, because it expands the choice-set of some persons in the nexus, without fully offsetting restrictions in the choice-sets of other persons.

Two emendations to the conventional externality analysis can be helpful in facilitating an understanding of the work-supply effect. If we assume that consumption is generalized, in the sense that all final goods are included in each participant's preferred consumption bundle, then every participant in the economic nexus, in his or her role as a final user of the good produced under conditions of increasing returns, becomes a beneficiary of the increase in the work supply of any worker in the whole nexus. If we introduce a model of household production, where Beckerian Z goods are "produced" with the appropriate set of x goods directly purchased from the market, then any reduction in the price of an x good (in this case x_j) modifies the production function for some Z good, making the externality appear analogous to those that are more familiar in orthodox analysis.

6. The Ethical Internalization of Economic Externalities

The precise description of the work-supply externality is helpful in the consideration of possible internalization or correction. In this section, I shall examine four alternatives: (1) intraexchange bargaining, (2) institutional evolution, (3) politicized correction, and (4) ethical norms. I shall try to support the second part of my hypothesis to the effect that, within limits, a culture may internalize the relevant work-supply externality through instillation of a work ethic.

The presence or possible presence of an identified externality suggests directly that "gains from trade" remain to be exploited in some all-inclusive, or economywide, sense. And the recognition of this point provides a precautionary warning to economists who would base their diagnosis of market failure on direct observation by parties external to the potential exchanges or trades that may emerge, or may have emerged, to internalize any relevant externality. This lesson taught by Coase and his followers has been learned.[10] The first question to be asked, therefore, after my putative identification of the work-supply externality, concerns the prospects that this alleged market failure might be or might have been internalized by appropriate intraexchange bargains, agreements, contracts, or trades.

Reference to the Coase literature suggests immediate attention to numbers involved in the relevant interactions. As noted earlier, genuine advantages of team production in the ordinary joint supply sense will tend to be captured through the organization of firms. But for the economywide externality that the work-supply choice embodies, the answer to the question is surely negative. Intraexchange bargains among parties who interact outside ordinary markets can be predicted to emerge in small-number settings, or even in large-number settings if and when affected subsets can be represented as having well-identified joint interests.[11] As the descriptive analysis of section 5 makes clear, however, bargained internalization of the work-supply externality seems beyond the plausible. Consumers, as a group, are beneficiaries of increased work supply, but within the inclusive consumer set there are differentially arrayed benefits depending on relative preferences identified only through conditions of production of goods. It is difficult even to design some imaginary scheme of compensations and payments that could command general agreement.

A second means of internalization that warrants mention is that classified as institutional evolution. As we analyze their workings, markets are idealized, and the institutions that we observe do not seem descriptively close to the analytical idealizations. It may seem plausible to suggest that the institutionalized departures from the analytical idealizations may have evolved and remain viable precisely because they effectively internalize relevant externalities. Examinations of those institutions that seem to affect work supply most directly yield ambiguous results, with perhaps some weighing toward a

---

10. R. H. Coase, "The Problem of Social Cost," *Journal of Law and Economics* 3 (1960): 1–44.

11. James M. Buchanan, "The Institutional Structure of Externality," *Public Choice* 14 (Spring 1973): 69–82.

negative evaluation. Conventions and arrangements, both formal and informal, have emerged over time to place minimal limits on the supply of work, such as the minimal forty-hour week, along with the introduction of differentially higher time rates for overtime work supplied—these arrangements could be rationalized on some implicit "as if" recognition of work-supply externalities. But there exist other developments that seem to reflect adverse effects on work effort. Historically, the length of the workweek has been substantially reduced; the years of working life have been cut, sometimes dramatically, by social retirement programs, some of which are compulsory; there has been almost continuous increase in the number of days of holiday and sickness leave—all of these developments seem opposed to any institutionalized embodiment of directional correction for the external economy in work supply.

In the theoretical welfare economics of midcentury, the mere identification of an externality offered an apparent normative basis for the implementation of politicized correction. The impact of public choice theory has been to destroy this rather simplistic and unexamined argument. Politics, like markets, sometimes fails, and prospects for effective political correction for externalities can be assessed in the same fashion as those for intraexchange corrections discussed briefly above. Even if the importance and relevance of the work supply externality should come to be acknowledged by all economists who proffer advice to practicing politicians, could we predict corrective measures to be taken in the interplay of interest-driven, constituency-based politics?

Reference to the record of political action on the structure of taxation should place an immediate damper on hope for politicized internalization here. The setting of fiscal interdependence sketched out in section 1 is descriptive of real-world fiscal reality in the United States and elsewhere. Fiscal externalities that serve to exacerbate the work supply effects that would remain in a world of fiscal neutrality remain uncorrected. Fiscal examples aside, however, it is not easy to create a model of modern democratic politics that would yield approval for a tax on consumption designed to yield revenues for the payment of generalized wage subsidies, which might be one possible shape of politicized internalization.

We are left with the fourth alternative, that which might internalize the work supply externality through the instillation, maintenance, and transmission of an ethical precept or set of precepts. Before discussing this alternative directly, however, it is necessary to address a possible critical challenge to my whole analysis here, and especially to its welfare implications. If the incentives offered to individual participants who are free to make any sort of contractual agreements they choose, whether through markets, politics, or otherwise, are not sufficient to generate satisfactory internalization, are there justifiable grounds for the claim that the noncorrected solution is nonoptimal in any meaningful sense of the term? If some analogue to transaction costs emerges to prevent the implementation of an enforceable agreement, contract, or trade that will internalize the externality, is not the noncorrected solution optimal, despite the existence of spillover benefits? Is the work supply externality identified in the analysis of this paper Pareto relevant?[12]

In this case, we might acknowledge that there do, indeed, exist external effects from the work-leisure choices made by individuals and that these effects modify the attainable levels of utility by those in the nexus who consume the final products of increasing returns industries in the economy, while, at the same time, we could abandon efforts to construct arrangements that would modify incentives to secure increases in work offered to the market. A policy norm of noninterference or laissez-faire with reference to individualized work-leisure choices would seem to be dictated in this setting.

There is much to be said for this position, and especially if prospects for corrective internalization are limited to the alternatives considered to this point. (If binding contracts are possible, and persons who seem to be caught in apparent Prisoner's Dilemma settings are then observed not to make such contracts, then, through their own behavior, they reveal that the diagnosis of the dilemma was in error.)[13] The very exercise of diagnosis is useful, however, even if, when advanced as hypothesis, it is falsified by an absence of agreement. And it is important at this point to recognize that the impossibility of securing viable and stable agreements through institutional arrangements that rely on the self-interested behavior of individuals tells us little about the prospects for corrective internalization through the introduction of ethical principles.

It is difficult to introduce ethical or moral constraints into the analytical apparatus of the economic theory of choice. The person who supplies work to the market nexus appears simply to adjust quantities to the parametric wage per time unit that he or she confronts. There would seem to be no operational way to determine the extent to which the work-leisure choice actually made embodies the influence of an ethical norm, including the very existence of any such norm. It is possible, however, to depict the constraining force of an ethical standard analytically, provided that we resort to a construction that incorporates internal as well as external constraints on individual choice.

Figure 14.1 illustrates. The indifference contours reflect the relative evaluation of money income and leisure, both of which are "goods." The lines drawn from M, the position of maximal leisure, depict the external constraint

12. James M. Buchanan and W. C. Stubblebine, "Externality," *Economica* 29 (November 1962): 371–84.

13. James M. Buchanan, "Positive Economics, Welfare Economics, and Political Economy," *Journal of Law and Economics* 2 (October 1959): 124–38.

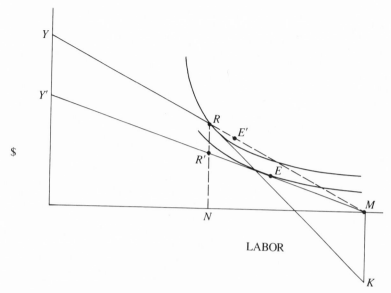

Fig. 14.1

imposed by the market situation, with the slope of these lines measuring the wage rates per unit time (assumed here to be uniform). In the absence of any internal constraint, and with a wage rate shown by the slope of MY', the position of individual equilibrium is reached at E.

We may incorporate a work ethic by treating its presence as an *internal* constraint. If the person locates at M, an internal cost is now assumed to be experienced, a cost that may be evaluated in terms of the money numéraire, and represented in figure 14.1 by the distance MK. As units of work are supplied to the economic nexus, this internal cost (of loafing) is progressively reduced. Note that, as depicted, the individual who faces the wage rate indicated by the slope of MY, and who is also constrained internally over the range NM, will locate at R, which is a corner solution. The segment RM is simply unavailable to the chooser in this modified construction.

Note, however, that the position at R is not attainable by the individual's own effort from the alternative equilibrium at E. The individual is, indeed, "better off" at R than at E, as depicted in figure 14.1. But for the individual located at E, a private decision to work more would simply produce a shift to R' where he or she becomes worse off. It is the presence of a *generalized* work ethic among all or large numbers of participants in the economic nexus, combined with the presence of increasing returns somewhere in the system, that generates the increase in the wage rate. And with the increase in the wage rate, the position attained in the presence of the internal constraint is preferred to that position attainable under the lower wage rate in the absence of the internal constraint.[14]

The construction sketched out above, and depicted in figure 14.1, is misleading, however, because it presumes that the individual who chooses is psychologically aware that the ethical constraint prevents the attainment of what would seem to be an otherwise preferred position (at E'). It seems surely to be more descriptive to suggest that the individual may not be conscious of the ethical norms that guide the choices made in everyday market dealings.[15] As choices are made, the individual senses no constraining influence at all. As felt internally, the individual moves to a most preferred position within the economically feasible set on the utility function that is revealed by his or her choice behavior.

This feature alone suggests that internalization through ethical norms may be more readily accomplished than through any bargained or politicized alternative. In a bargained internalization, those persons and groups that expect to secure benefits must compensate those whose behavior exerts the external benefit or harm. And even if politicization need not encompass the all-inclusive set of participants in an "exchange," there remains a necessity of securing agreement among competing interests, which may also require that expected beneficiaries pay, in some fashion, for the utility gains consequent on the modifications in behavior of those whose choices are to be changed. In comparison and contrast, the ethical constraint, if operative and influential, acts unilaterally on the behavior of the supplier of input to the nexus. The beneficiaries get a "pure play"; they find levels of well-being increased without any necessity of making payment. Bargains, trades, agreements, political compromises—these remain outside the whole calculus.

This nonreciprocal feature of ethical internalization suggests, in turn, two additional, and derivative, aspects that deserve notice. The first relates to the central meaning of Pareto relevance in the theory of externality. An externality is defined to be Pareto relevant if the potential gains (harms) to those who expect to be benefited (harmed) exceed in value the expected losses (gains) that the indicated change in behavior (at the margin or in total) will impose on those who make the change. The classification of externality relationships into Pareto-relevant and Pareto-irrelevant sets requires a benefit-loss

---

14. David Levy has used a related construction to indicate the possible relevance of moral constraints for another purpose. See David Levy, "Utility Enhancing Consumption Constraints," *Economics and Philosophy* 4 (1988): 69–88.

15. F. A. Hayek, especially, has stressed the adherence to codes of conduct in the market that are below the level of individual consciousness. See F. A. Hayek, *Law, Legislation, and Liberty*, (Chicago: University of Chicago Press, 1979), vol. 3, *The Political Order of a Free People*.

comparison, both by the economist observer who makes some initial diagnosis and, finally, by the affected parties on the two sides of the relationship. And the set of externalities that remain Pareto irrelevant is by no means empty; when transaction costs are reckoned, this set may be large indeed. Note that the utility interdependence remains, however. The Pareto-irrelevant classification refers only to the prospects for *economic* internalization.

When we consider internalization through ethical constraints, there is no meaning to the relevant and irrelevant classification scheme, because there is no requirement that the benefits to some potentially affected parties be measured against losses to others. In other words, so long as utility interdependence remains, a potential for ethical internalization is present. For those externality relationships that are Pareto irrelevant, the only means of correction lies in the prospect for some ethically generated modification in choice behavior.

A second characteristic that stems from the nonreciprocality of ethical internalization involves the relative importance of generalization in participation among the whole set of affected parties on one side of the externality relationship. This aspect is closely related to, but seems conceptually separate from, the importance of transaction costs in determining the Pareto relevance or irrelevance of an externality. Consider, again, the work-leisure margin for a single input supplier to the economic nexus. The additional value that might be added to the nexus through an additional time unit generates benefits to all persons who may consume the goods produced under conditions of increasing returns. The input supplier produces a genuine "public good" for members of the consuming group because no single member of this group can secure utility gains separately from others in the set. There is no means, therefore, through which particular benefited parties may effectuate factored down, small-number "trades" with any single-input supplier, or even with all input suppliers treated jointly.

The "publicness" characteristic of increases in input supply does not change under ethical internalization. But because the benefited parties, singly or in total, are not required to "finance" the "public good" that supply increases embody, there is no threshold barrier akin to that imposed by the difficulties of overcoming free riding. Since the "public good" is produced by any increase in input supply, so long as one person modifies his or her behavior due to the presence of a work ethic, some correction for the externality takes place.

7. Work as Benevolent Self-Interest

Perhaps the most familiar statement in *The Wealth of Nations* is that which tells us that "it is not from the benevolence of the butcher, the brewer, or the baker, that we expect our dinner, but from their regard to their own interest."[16] We understand Adam Smith's argument here, but if we take the conventional theory of distribution in the competitive economy seriously, we immediately sense an apparent contradiction. If the butcher, and everyone else, takes from the economy precisely the equivalent of the value added to the economy by his efforts, how do we benefit from individuals' self-interested behavior?

Suppose that the butcher decides to retire early and go fishing, and that he does so out of strict self-interest. How will this change in his behavior affect the rest of us? Not at all in the long-term sense, if we accept the marginal productivity theory of distribution and assume that the economy is effectively competitive. The size of the market will become a mite smaller upon the butcher's retirement, but after other butchers expand their scales of operation, prices will return to the same levels that existed before the butcher ceased to butch.

I have argued that the conventional theory of competitive adjustment must surely be in error in this inference, and that we must look for ways to modify conventional reasoning to allow an accommodation of Smith's central theorem concerning the gains from trade that extended division of labor facilitates. I have sought to show that, in order for the utilities of other participants in the network to be affected by a change in the size of the economic nexus, some relaxation of the constant returns to scale condition for idealized competitive equilibrium must be effected. There must exist increasing returns (decreasing costs) in at least one industry in the all-inclusive production-exchange nexus.

Fortunately for my purposes, I am not required to enter directly into the controversial areas of analysis involving the consistency between increasing returns and competitive equilibrium which, in turn, produce divergent models of industrial organization. Nor is it necessary for me to specify, even conceptually, the relative share of total production that emerges from increasing returns operation, or to distinguish these industries from others (as, for example, between manufacturing, service, and agricultural sectors). For my purposes, I require only that increasing returns characterize operations in at least one industry, which need not be identified. For expositional simplicity, I have tried to present the analysis to minimize the differences with the conventional competitive models. Hence, I developed the argument in the context of an industry characterized by Marshallian external economies, where the advantages of scale cannot be captured by individual firms. But the results are in no way restricted to that setting.

I have tried to show that the characteristics of the work supply externality

16. Adam Smith, *The Wealth of Nations* (Indianapolis: Liberty Classics, 1981), 26–7.

are such that there are severe barriers to either intramarket or politicized correction, leaving the burden of internalization to the possible embodiment of ethical norms in the work choice. To the extent that a work ethic enters the choice calculus of input suppliers, whether or not this be conscious, consumers somewhere in the economy secure spillover benefits. There is economic content in the ethic of work. And because there is this economic content, there is justification for both individualized and collective efforts to promulgate, maintain, and transmit this ethic throughout the culture as well as intergenerationally.

The butcher whose benevolent self-interest dictates work does "good" for others that is lost when he goes fishing. The antiwork ethic of the 1960s summarized in the admonition "take the time to smell the flowers" involves an explicit invitation to destroy economic value for others than the addressee. And, of course, the size of the external effects is directly related to the market value of the input potentially supplied. The radiologist who loafs harms others much more than does comparable behavior by a fast-food employee.

I have deliberately limited discussion in this chapter to the work-leisure choice margin, measured along a time-unit dimension, as the potential source of expansion and contraction in the size of the economic-exchange nexus. The analysis is obviously applicable to qualitative as well as quantitative changes in the values of inputs supplied. The central analysis is, also, readily extendible to sources of change in market size that do not involve behavior of individual input suppliers, *at least directly*. Perhaps the most obvious margin of relevance is that determined by the political-legal constraints that delineate, along several dimensions, the area within which persons are allowed to carry out voluntary exchanges. And specialists in trade theory have long recognized that extensions in the size of the trading network allow for further exploitation of gains from specialization, and increasing returns models have been introduced.

In this literature, however, there seems to have been relatively little attention paid to the inconsistency between nonexhausted gains from specialization and the standard analysis of competitive equilibria. But my suggestion that the work-supply externality is analogous to the "trade extension" externality would surely not be surprising to trade theorists.[17]

The analysis has implications for many other policy areas such as population control, immigration, women's entry into the labor force, work requirements for welfare, and retirement programs, along with those for tax structure already noted. My central concern is, however, not with the derivation of

---

17. See W. J. Ethier for a useful analysis that also contains references to the trade literature, "National and International Returns to Scale in the Modern Theory of Institutional Trade," *American Economic Review* 72 (June 1982): 389–405.

specific policy implications in these areas. My emphasis is limited to an attempt to define the economic basis for an ethic of work. And, if my aim must be generalized, it is to convince fellow economists that we remain ethically as well as economically interdependent, along the work-leisure margin of choice as along so many others. If we, as economists, continue to neglect these ethical interdependencies, even as they embody relevant and important economic content, we stand vulnerable to the accusation that our sometime esoteric analyses become the modern equivalent of the medieval debates about angels dancing on pins.

CHAPTER 15

Economic Origins of Ethical Constraints

Christian churchism (teaches that) thou shalt attend to thy neighbor's business before thou attendest to thine own.

—Ezra Pound

The basic relationships between formal or legal constraints and ethical constraints on human behavior are widely recognized, both in theory and in practice. To the extent that persons in social interaction, one with another, behave in accordance with commonly shared ethical precepts, any rationally based contractual justification for generalized legal constraints becomes weaker. Common public awareness tells us that if relatively few persons steal, and/or if these few steal relatively little, fewer and less restrictive laws against stealing are needed, along with fewer policemen.

It is relatively straightforward to locate the logical origins of formal constraints in a calculus of individual self-interest.[1] To my knowledge, there exists no comparable explanatory exercise with respect to the origins of ethical constraints. This chapter is a preliminary attempt to fill this gap.[2]

From an individualist perspective, a person involved in social interaction seeks to constrain the behavior of others, either through contractually derived legal rules or through the nonformal operation of ethical norms, only if and when nonconstrained behavior is predicted to impose damages, as measured in anticipated utility losses, at least in some opportunity cost sense. The existence of *externality* is necessary for the initiation of any effort aimed at constraining behavior. And, in this setting, legal and ethical constraints become alternative institutions of internalization.

Section 1 sets out the analytical framework through the introduction of familiar two-by-two matrix illustrations, which are, in each case, generalizable to the many-person setting by designating one player to be "all others."

---

1. James M. Buchanan, *The Limits of Liberty: Between Anarchy and Leviathan* (Chicago: University of Chicago Press, 1975).

2. For a more extended treatment that emerged from discussions of a preliminary draft of this chapter, see Hartmut Kliemt, "Moral Externalities," in *Papers on Buchanan and Related Subjects*, 37–60 (Munich: Accedo Verlagsgesellschaft, 1990).

Emphasis is placed on the distinction between economic and ethical interdependence. Section 2 identifies the direct relationship between economic self-interest and investment in the ethical internalization of externalities. Section 3 examines the productivity of investments in persuasion. Section 4 extends the analysis and addresses the issues of comparability under modified preference orderings. In section 5, the discussion is related to the Hayekian theory of the evolution of moral order. The analysis is then summarized in section 6 through a comparison of the ethical constraints derived here with both legal-formal constraints and ethical constraints derived in alternative constructions.

I advance no claim of explanatory inclusiveness here; I suggest only that an understanding and appreciation of the economic origins of the ethical constraints on behavior move us somewhat closer to a match between our models of behavior and observed empirical reality. That is to say, the analysis here adds a hitherto missing element in our general understanding of why persons behave as they are observed to behave in social interaction.

1. Relevance and Irrelevance in Contractual (Economic) and Ethical Internalization of Externalities

The simple two-by-two matrix illustration in figure 15.1 will be readily identified by the cognoscenti as the standard Prisoner's Dilemma, with the numerical payoffs representing ordinal utility indicators for the two players. Almost all of the analysis and discussion in modern social contract theory, inclusively defined to cover applications that range from the origins of private property and the state, to public goods, environmental cleanups, through to matters of social etiquette have been (or could have been) put in this highly abstracted setting. The central result leaps out upon elementary observation. The self-interested, own-utility maximizing behavior of each of the two players generates a result or outcome that neither desires nor would have independently chosen. The choice setting is such that separate and noncoordinated behavior on the part of each player produces a solution that violates the Pareto criterion for efficiency or optimality. Both players could be made better off, as measured by each player's own-utility indicator, in an alternative cell in the matrix, a cell that would reflect a different pattern of behavior but one that remains within the set of feasible options.

Attention is immediately focused on prospects for a coordinated or cooperative strategy, one that would represent agreement by the actors on a jointly chosen, two-element behavioral set that would shift the outcome to cell I, which would be preferred by each player to the noncoordinated outcome in cell IV. In the terminology of welfare economics, cell I is Pareto-preferred to cell IV. The indicated joint or cooperative behavior becomes possible, however, only if a binding agreement or enforceable contract between the players

B

A		b_1	b_2
	a_1	I 3,3	II 1,4
	a_2	III 4,1	IV 2,2

Fig. 15.1

is possible. And an institutional change that would be represented by such a contract would act to modify the utility payoffs faced by each player.

In such a potential contract, note that each player trades or exchanges his or her own freedom to act independently for the reciprocal constraint accepted by his or her partner to the deal. Each player agrees to bind himself, not for the purpose of placing limits on his or her own behavior for his or her own benefit (not for self-control, à la Ulysses) but because only an acceptance of such constraint can secure the reciprocal constraint on the behavior of another party or parties to the agreement. And such an agreement-contract becomes possible without any requirement that either of the parties express concern for the well-being or utility of the other person or persons in the nexus.

In the setting depicted in figure 15.1, the two players are economically interdependent. Neither person, acting on his or her own and independently, can do as well as he or she could do by engaging the other in exchange or trade. This interdependence is reflected in the relative utility payoffs in cells I and IV. But note that the two players are also ethically interdependent. The separate behavior of one person outside or apart from any agreement on a coordinated strategy, affects the utility of the other person unilaterally. This sort of interdependence is reflected in the relationship between the ordinal utility payoffs in cell IV (the independent adjustment solution) and either cell II or cell III, each of which would represent a shift to cooperative behavior by only one of the two actors.

In the restricted setting of figure 15.1, the contractual and the ethical means toward internalization of the reciprocal externality are substitutes in a straightforward sense. If both parties can be converted to behave in accordance with an ethical precept that dictates cooperation (a_1 and b_1 in fig. 15.1), there is no need for an explicit contractual agreement.

In a paper written jointly with W. C. Stubblebine three decades ago,[3] we introduced the distinction between Pareto-relevant and Pareto-irrelevant externalities. A Pareto-relevant externality exists when the behavior of one or both parties in an interaction affects the utility levels of other parties, *and* there exist potential arrangements through which the behavior can be modified to the benefit of *all* parties. That is to say, Pareto-superior corrective changes are possible, by definition, when Pareto-relevant externalities exist. In the standard Prisoner's Dilemma case depicted in figure 15.1, the reciprocal externality is clearly Pareto relevant. Either contractual or ethical internalization can shift the solution to the Pareto-preferred cell I.

An externality is defined to be Pareto irrelevant if the behavior of one or all parties to the interaction continues to affect the utility levels of other parties but there exist no alternative arrangements through which this behavior can be modified to the expressed mutual benefit of all parties. The payoff matrix of figure 15.2 illustrates this case, again under the symmetry assumptions consequent on the use of ordinal utility indicators.

The economist will directly observe that, despite the continued presence of row and column dominance that describes the payoff matrix, no potential for corrective adjustment appears. In the choice setting depicted in figure 15.2, independent behavior on the part of each of the two players will generate the cell IV solution, as before, but this solution is now Pareto optimal. No further gains from trade, no matter how complex, are possible. Hence, the economist, who concentrates his or her attention almost exclusively on trade, exchange, and contract, will not be concerned with such interactions. There is no economic interdependence that remains for further exploitation in the independent adjustment solution in figure 15.2.

Note, however, that the reciprocal externality relationship remains. The two persons remain ethically interdependent in the sense used earlier, in that each person's utility can be affected by a unilateral shift in the behavior of the other. To the economist, the externality that remains is Pareto irrelevant.

What, precisely, does Pareto irrelevance mean in this setting? The shift on the part of A from the a_2 to the a_1 strategy will, as in figure 15.1, exert spillover benefits on B (and vice versa for a behavioral shift by B in affecting A). But B remains unwilling to accept constraints on his or her own behavior that require a shift from b_2 to b_1, if this should be required. The spillover benefits to B, from A's shift from a_2 to a_1, are less than the internal utility loss that B expects to suffer in modifying his or her own behavior from b_2 to b_1. The potential losses from the potential behavioral "exchange" exceed the gains; hence, the reciprocal externality, though it remains, is Pareto irrelevant.

3. James M. Buchanan and W. C. Stubblebine, "Externality," *Economica* 29(November 1962): 371–84.

B

	b_1	b_2
A a_1	2,2	1,4
a_2	4,1	3,3

Fig. 15.2

As a simple comparison suggests, there is a categorical difference in the *economic* characteristics of the two choice settings depicted in figures 15.1 and 15.2. However, the comparison also reveals that there is essentially no difference in the *ethical* content of the interaction. That is to say, the distinction between the Pareto-relevant reciprocal externality (fig. 15.1) and the Pareto-irrelevant reciprocal externality (fig. 15.2) does not, in itself, carry ethical implications.

This result is not, of course, surprising when it is recognized that the utility dimension is not the same in the economic and the ethical relationship. Any economic evaluation of a choice setting involves some assessment of the potential gains and losses from a change for *both* (or all) parties. Exchange is necessarily reciprocal; each trader gives up something of value in exchange for something of value given up by the other trader. In the universe of social interactions, it seems clear that the set of possible mutually beneficial exchanges will be small relative to the set of unilaterally beneficial gifts. (The Christmas tie would never have been purchased; yet it remains undiscarded on the tie rack in the closet.)

2. Ethics and Economic Self-Interest

The absence of an ethical distinction between the two types of interaction analyzed in section 1 suggests that the motivation behind efforts to seek out ethical internalization is more general than that behind efforts to organize trades or contractual agreements. As a glance at figures 15.1 and 15.2 indicate, each party will, in either setting, place a value on unilateral action by the other party that is higher than that placed on any two-party behavioral shift. Each person, in each setting, will find it advantageous that the other person in the interaction choose a cooperative strategy on the basis of ethical or moral principle. The "ideal" arrangement for any person is located when he or she remains at liberty to act as his or her raw utility indicator dictates while the other party acts cooperatively.[4]

In either of the two settings depicted, each person has a direct economic interest in the ethical or moral characteristics of the behavior of the other. Hence, unless this latter behavior is assumed to be wholly beyond the possibility of change, each person finds it privately rational to invest at least some resources in efforts to modify the behavior of the other unilaterally in the direction of enhanced cooperation. If, at the same time, the technology involved in "producing" any such desired behavioral shift embodies publicness of the classical variety, the result is that generalized investment in the promulgation of moral norms will be observed, with all parties being subjected to essays in persuasion carried out by specialists, whom we may call "the preachers."

Note that this result is described by the provision of privately costly inputs by all parties, but with this provision being accompanied by no conscious sense that any explicit exchange of inputs is taking place. Each party considers the return on his or her investment to be measured by the potential change in the behavior of the other party (parties). Each party gives up some valued resource in exchange for some prospect of a change in the other party's behavior. But there is no agreement, either explicit or implicit, that involves either party's willingness to constrain his or her own behavior, which represents potential value loss, in exchange for reciprocal constraints.

It is helpful to compare and/or contrast the economic analysis approach to ethics advanced here with its familiar alternatives. In each of these, the origin of the constraint that is expected to modify individual behavior is *internal* to the calculus of the actor. Attention is exclusively focused on answering the question: *Why* might the choosing-acting person behave cooperatively, when opportunistic utility maximization indicates noncooperation? The first, and most familiar, alternative invokes the dominance of learned and self-imposed moral norms, which are quite consciously allowed to supervene a sensed loss of utility in directing behavior. The individual follows the moral norm in an expressed departure from that course of action that would maximize his or her expected utility. The second alternative simply redefines utility maximization in such a way that the acting-choosing individual fully takes into account the long-range consequences of his or her behavior, and particularly as it may motivate, at least probabilistically, reciprocating behavior on the part of others in the relevant social interaction. The third, and closely related, alternative incorporates a disposition to cooper-

---

4. See James M. Buchanan, "Ethical Rules, Expected Values and Large Numbers," *Ethics* 76 (October 1965): 1–13; reprinted in idem, *Freedom in Constitutional Contract: Perspective of a Political Economist* (College Station: Texas A & M University Press, 1978), 151–68.

ate more directly into the meaning of rationality and does not require reckoning of long-range consequences.[5] In one sense, of course, the second and third alternatives here do not seek to explain the origins of ethical constraints; instead, these approaches involve attempted demonstrations that behavior normally considered to be ethical or moral follows from properly conceived self-interest on the part of persons caught in dilemma-type interactions, one with another.

By contrast with these alternative means of incorporating something like cooperative behavior internally into the individual's choice calculus, the model presented here does not require either that moral norms override utility maximization or that utility maximization be reinterpreted to generate behavior that looks like it is motivated by moral concerns. My approach in this chapter does not seek an *internal* origin for the modified set of constraints that may be required to resolve, in whole or in part, the generalized social dilemma. Note that, in the settings depicted both in figures 15.1 and 15.2, I have emphasized only that parties in the interactions retain an economic self-interest in modifying the behavior of others, and that they will seek to further this interest by investment in "behavior modification" if this prospect is technically feasible. To the extent that the result of such investment embodies more cooperative behavior on the part of one, or all, parties, the origins of the behavioral changes are *external* to the choosing-acting participants. Neither some self-imposed ethical limit nor some heightened awareness of "true" self-interest is called on to generate the escape, partial or total, from the utility losses produced by ethical interdependencies.

3. The Productivity of Preachers

As noted, straightforward utility maximization on the part of persons who recognize the existence of ethical interdependency dictates some investment of resources in efforts to secure unilateral behavioral changes by others in the social interaction, provided only that such an investment, over some range, yields a return over and above opportunity costs. And, of course, rationality norms would suggest that the extent of such an investment would be determined when expected marginal yield here is equalized with other investments.

Economists, in particular, have tended to neglect analysis of this sort of investment because their disciplinary toolkit embodies the fixity of utility or preference functions. If individuals' preferences are indeed rigid, and hence immune to change, any investment in efforts aimed to modify behavior through inducing preference shifts must remain totally unproductive. In this setting, persons who recognize the presence of ethical interdependence have

---

5. David Gauthier, *Morals by Agreement* (Oxford: Oxford University Press, 1985).

no recourse other than exchange or contract, which is, as indicated above, viable only for the Pareto-relevant subset.

For many purposes, the economists' working hypothesis of fixed preferences is useful, but surely any rigid advocacy of this hypothesis as descriptive of behavioral reality makes the economic enterprise vulnerable to the familiar communitarian criticism which is then extended to any and all efforts to derive characteristics of social interaction from individual choices. The methodological individualist must, it seems to me, acknowledge the relationships between individual utility functions and the socioeconomic-legal-political-cultural setting within which evaluations are made. But such acknowledgment carries with it, almost as a matter of course, the possible productivity of investment in the promulgation of moral norms. The relative efficacy of such investment will, of course, vary among the several targets of effort. Persons who are hardwired into the set of preferences that dictate strictly opportunistic behavior, as defined by the observing economist, will represent less productive yields to the "preachers" than the persons whose preferences are less firmly anchored.

To be productive, investments in the promulgation of moral norms must change behavior through a shift in utility functions. But return to the internal-external distinction emphasized earlier. The analysis here does not require that persons seek to change *their own* preferences. While it may be empirically descriptive to say, with Frank Knight, that persons really "want better wants," we do not need to take this additional step here. We need no such bootstrap ethics. Individuals may or may not seek to modify their own preferences. My model suggests, much more restrictively, that persons rationally will "want others to want better wants," or, specifically, that others behave more cooperatively toward themselves in social intercourse.

4. Internalization by Ethics

The next stage in the argument is to demonstrate precisely how ethical interdependence is internalized by rationally selected, and, hence, successful investment in the promulgation of moral norms. As the simple two-by-two matrices of figures 15.1 and 15.2 indicate, each person faces a rational incentive to undertake an investment in modifying the preference ordering of the other. Let us suppose that, for the discrete, two-element behavioral set of each person, the investment of each participant is successful in changing the behavior of the other. As mentioned, however, this result can take place only if preference orderings over the relevant outcomes are shifted. If we remain within the discrete two-by-two matrices, successful two-way promulgation of the cooperative behavioral norm must modify the preference orderings to those embodied in figure 15.3.

B

		b₁	b₂
A	a₁	4,4	2,3
	a₂	3,2	1,1

or

B

		b₁	b₂
A	a₁	4,4	3,2
	a₂	2,3	1,1

Fig. 15.3

The combined orderings in figure 15.3 continue to exhibit both row and column dominance for players in their choices. The solution in cell I is preferred by both parties to any other outcome that is attainable by either individual or joint action. Note that the presumed successful effort on the part of each party to modify the preference ordering of the other internalizes the externalities that were present in both the settings of figures 15.1 and 15.2. There is no problem with the dilemma-type setting of figure 15.1; the shift in utility functions has been such as to enable the interacting parties to shift to the cooperative solution, which is Pareto optimal, under *either* configuration of preferences.

But what conclusion can be drawn when we compare figure 15.3 to figure 15.2? By having their preference orderings modified so as to induce cooperative behavior, a solution in cell I is insured. But this outcome is not Pareto optimal if evaluation is carried out in terms of the nonmodified, or "raw," preference orderings of figure 15.2. Does the internalization of the externality represent an improvement in the well-being of the parties in this case, or the reverse? Or is there, here, a welfare theory example of an index number problem?

In one sense, of course, the two solutions remain noncomparable, since for analytical purposes we define an individual by a preference ordering over alternative outcomes. Hence, a shift in the ordering redefines the person; evaluative comparisons become empty. But we may, to some extent at least, overcome this personal identity problem (so dear to philosophers), by looking more carefully at the payoff matrices of figures 15.2 and 15.3. The independent adjustment, or Nash equilibrium, in each of these cases is Pareto optimal if evaluated in terms of the preference orderings that generated the equilibrium. But there is an element of social stability present in the equilibrium of figure 15.3 that is absent in that of figure 15.2. As previously noted, in the cell IV solution of figure 15.2, each party continues to have an incentive to invest in changing the behavior of the other in the direction of inducing more cooperation. And, as discussed above, if these investments succeed, a shift of orderings to those shown in figure 15.3 becomes possible. In the solution of figure 15.3, however, no comparable externality remains. Each party now has an incentive to insure that the other party's behavior remains unchanged, and, hence, that there be no shift in utility functions. To the extent that some slacking off of the morally induced behavioral pattern is anticipated, investment in moral suasion may continue, but now this investment will be directed toward maintenance of the ethical status quo. The solution in figure 15.3 can be described as an *ethical equilibrium* as well as an exchange or economic equilibrium. The second characterization tells us that players have no further incentive to initiate trades, contracts, or agreements. The first tells us that the players have no incentive to initiate efforts to change the behavior of others, a feature that is absent from the equilibrium of figure 15.2.

The highly simplified and abstracted models introduced here are useful in allowing the central features of personal interaction to be identified, but the possible extension to more complex interaction settings would be recognized. The two-element behavioral set of alternatives faced by each player (cooperate-defect) can, of course, be replaced by a multielement set which might approach continuous variation in some limit. And the symmetry between players emerges from the use of ordinal utility indicators and need not be a condition of interaction. More importantly, the two-person interaction can be generalized to cover individual behavior in n-person settings, where each player confronts "all others" in some relevant sense. While this change in the models leaves the logical structure of the analysis in place, it does reduce the possible direct incentive that each person has to invest privately in the promulgation of moral norms designed to affect the behavior of others. The results of such investment become genuinely public goods in large-number settings, and each individual will have familiar free-rider incentives to hold back on his or her own contribution. Collective organization of the moral persuasion enterprise may be necessary. These free-rider difficulties are, of course, equally severe in securing support for enforcement outlays required for contractually agreed schemes of cooperation, that is, for ordinary laws against defection. Since, however, contractually agreed schemes are, ideally, limited to those interactions that exhibit potential economic interdependence when uncorrected, while ethical interdependencies are more inclusive, we should predict that there will exist an inverse relationship between the size of the relevant interacting community and the amount of investment (per person) in the promulgation, transmission, and maintenance of moral norms.

5. The Evolution of Moral Order

F. A. Hayek, particularly in his later works,[6] has emphasized the cultural evolution of the norms of a moral order, norms that are quite distinct from those of a moral community, and he has persuasively argued that some emergence of culturally evolved norms was a necessary condition for the modern leap into what he calls the "great society," where social interaction is extended to include persons who do not share membership in genetically derived groupings, those that describe moral communities.[7] Hayek has stressed that individuals who behave in accordance with the norms of a moral order are not conscious of, and do not understand, the origins of such norms.

For my purposes, it is noteworthy that the norms stressed by Hayek are roughly those that we have concentrated on in the game-theoretic settings of this chapter. These norms do not, in any case, require explicit concern for the utility of others; altruism does not enter the calculus. They include, instead, such moral precepts as promise keeping and respect for personal and property rights. Again roughly, the ethics is that which is appropriate for sportsmanship; the norms embody playing by the rules; they exclude cheating.

The analysis in this chapter offers a possible understanding of *why* the behavioral rules necessary for the functioning of a moral order emerged. By drawing attention to the economic interest that each person has in the behavior of others with whom he or she interacts, or may interact, we have located a

---

6. F. A. Hayek, *The Political Order of a Free People*, vol. 3 of *Law, Legislation, and Liberty* (Chicago: University of Chicago Press, 1979).

7. I have elaborated the differences between membership in, and individual behavior within, moral community and a moral order in James M. Buchanan, *Moral Community, Moral Order, or Moral Anarchy*, Abbott Memorial Lecture Monograph no. 17 (Colorado Springs: Colorado College, 1981); reprinted in idem, *Liberty, Market, and State: Political Economy in the 1980s* (Great Britain: Wheatsheaf Books, 1986), 108–20.

source for efforts directed toward a modification of preference orderings that may, ultimately, generate the behavioral changes desired. We need add only the presumption that such investment is, to some extent and over some range, productive in order to "explain" the process through which preference orderings, generally, come to be changed.

The emergence of the minimally cooperative norms that are necessary for the effective functioning of the extended economic nexus offers a good example of "order without design," again stressed by Hayek and attributed to the insights of the eighteenth-century Scots moral philosophers. In the scenario suggested here, each individual who anticipates participation in social interaction with others will have a direct, and continuing, incentive to take action to insure that others with whom he or she may interact "play by the rules." There need be no consciousness of the generalized importance of an inclusive economic-political-legal nexus characterized by such behavior, and there is no sense of submission, personally, to some agreed upon set of rule following constraints. Because, however, all participants are roughly symmetrical, or may be, in their incentives here, persons will necessarily find themselves subjected to external persuasive pressures that may succeed in modifying their own orderings, with no internally generated conscious shift. Ultimately, all participants may find themselves "wanting to play by the rules," even if they have no sense of being coerced to choose and act other than in their own interests, while, at the same time, they do not trust others to behave similarly without continued efforts at persuasion.

6. Summary and Comparison

Why do individuals in socioeconomic relationships, one with another, behave in ways that seem to be contrary to their own economic interest, as such interest may be assessed by an external observer? This question is of especial importance to the economist because the empirical evidence seems to place limits on the explanatory range of his or her basic behavioral hypothesis, despite the empirical support for this hypothesis over an extensive domain of human action. How can the economist draw the distinction between these choice settings in which operationally meaningful utility maximization hypotheses apply and those settings in which some emendation of these hypotheses are required for explaining the choice behavior that is observed?

Let me be more specific. Why do individuals play by the rules of the socioeconomic game? Why do they often seem to shun and to pass by opportunities that would, if expediently seized, further their own apparent self-interest? The argument that I have developed in this chapter can be adequately summarized in a comparison with different responses to these questions.

The Costs of Violating Rules

The standard economists' response to the question invokes the presence of collectively enforced rules that insure the imposition of costs on violators sufficient to change the ordinal payoffs from those that describe the no-rule setting. In this model, individuals act always to maximize measured self-interest, and they would not refrain from cheating in the absence of formal rules when such behavior is anticipated to advance their interests. The dilemma-type choice settings of figure 15.1 are used to justify contractual-collective agreements that effectively enforce cooperative behavior on the part of all parties. The agreement itself, "the law," will and must include penalties sufficient to shift the original utility payoffs to those of figure 15.3.

This model leaves no space for that realm of social intercourse that is ordered voluntarily by nonopportunistic behavior. Simple empirical observation suggests that this realm of "orderly anarchy" may be large, relative to that which is described by the existence of formal rules. The economists' response must be judged incomplete.

Overriding Transcendental Norms

The responses that depend on some internally generated motivation of behavior that departs from the strictly interpreted homo economicus hypothesis have been already introduced in section 2 and may be briefly summarized here. In the most traditional of these models, advanced by ethical philosophers through the ages, "higher values" derived from sources external to the individual are allowed to become compelling in some choice settings, even when they conflict with the actor's preference orderings. "Values" trump "tastes." The opportunity cost, measured in utility sacrificed, from behaving in accordance with moral precepts is acutely sensed by the chooser-actor.

The problem with this essentially Augustinian model lies, first, in locating the source of the external values, and, second, in the articulation of a choice calculus that would require action contrary to preference.

Enlightened Self-Interest

David Hume's response relies on a redefinition of individual self-interest rather than on any behavioral departure from utility maximization.[8] An indi-

---

8. For modern variants of Hume's argument, see Robert Axelrod, *The Evolution of Cooperation* (New York: Basic Books, 1984); and Robert Sugden, *The Economics of Rights, Co-operation, and Welfare* (Oxford: Basil Blackwell, 1986).

vidual's interest, properly defined, embodies predictions about the generalized consequences of departures from broadly cooperative interactive strategies, especially in settings characterized by repeated or continuous dealings. An individual's choice to play beyond, or in violation of, established rules, that is to cheat, even when it may seem expedient to do so, must reckon on the potential for reciprocating behavior on the part of others in subsequent rounds of play. Full recognition of such feedback effects may, for many choice settings, suggest that rule following remains privately rational.

The limits of the Humean argument are evident. There remain many choice settings in which individual defection or violation promises to yield utility gains with little or no prospect for subsequent losses.

Extended Rationality

David Gauthier has mounted a valiant modern effort to extend the very meaning of rational choice to include cooperative, rather than noncooperative, behavior in all dilemma-like settings.[9] If the individual recognizes the mutual destructiveness involved in following straightforward utility maximization strategies, he or she will find it rational to take on a "disposition to cooperate" when he or she identifies others like himself or herself in social interaction. Morality in the form of cooperative behavior will emerge from the implicit agreement of the parties, and need not call on anticipations of repeated encounters or on transcendental norms. The Gauthier enterprise, like the others, requires that the individual choose and act, at least on occasion, contrary to the predictions implicit in preference functions.[10]

Economically Motivated Production Shifts

In one sense, the analysis developed in this chapter is simpler and more straightforward than any of the alternatives sketched out above. Individuals behave in accordance with norms of cooperation in social interaction because of the dictates of their preference orderings. They "do not want to steal," even when opportunities exist. This behavior is differently motivated from that which relies on expected losses upon probable apprehension and punishment for formal rules violations, from that which expresses the overriding of temptation by a conscious inner morality, from that which represents generalized adherence to the furtherance of enlightened self-interest, and from that reflecting acceptance of the extended rationality of provisional cooperative dispositions.

---

9. David Gauthier, *Morals By Agreement*.
10. For an extended treatment, see chap. 16.

The construction here does not require that the individual sense that he or she behaves differently than he or she might have behaved if the investment of others had not been successful in shifting his or her preference ordering toward cooperation. There is no consciousness of coercion, whether legal or ethical; there is no psychological tension of the sort that is present in any of the other models.

The analysis is consistent with the sociologists' criticism of the economists' hypothesis of operationally meaningful utility maximization. The preference orderings of individuals are subject to change brought about by the sociocultural environment within which choices are made and action taken. "Social norms" do, indeed, determine individual choice behavior, at least within limits. But the model supplies operational content to the sociologists' criticism; the origin of and the direction of the effects of social norms are themselves grounded in a calculus of self-interest.

As suggested initially, I do not claim inclusive explanatory power for the model of economically motivated, externally influenced shifts in preference orderings. Each of the several alternatives, including, perhaps, others than those discussed briefly above, may be helpful in explaining behavioral departures from opportunistically calculated self-interest in social intercourse. I suggest only that a person does not steal, in part, simply because he or she does not want to steal, and that the preference ordering that reflects this stance may have been, again in part, "produced" by the moral suasion undertaken by others, in furtherance of their own economic self-interest.

CHAPTER 16

The Gauthier Enterprise

I take it as my assignment to criticize the Gauthier enterprise. At the outset, however, I should express my general agreement with David Gauthier's normative vision of a liberal social order, including the place that individual principles of morality hold in such an order. Whether the enterprise is, ultimately, judged to have succeeded or to have failed depends on the standards applied. Considered as a coherent grounding of such a social order in the rational choice behavior of persons, the enterprise fails. Considered as an extended argument implying that persons should (and possibly must) adopt the moral stance embodied in the Gauthier structure, the enterprise is, I think, largely successful. Considered as a set of empirically falsifiable propositions suggesting that persons do, indeed, choose as the Gauthier precepts dictate, the enterprise offers Humean hope rather than Hobbesian despair.

Morals by Agreement[1] is developed in conceptually separate parts that are made to seem more integrated than they need be. The first, and most extensive, part of the book involves Gauthier's attempt to ground cooperative behavior in rational choice. In strategic interactions between persons *who possess defined and mutually respected initial rights*, the argument is that it becomes rational for each person to adopt a cooperative strategy. This part of the analysis falls within the theory of bargaining, and it is presented as such. The second part of the book, and much the more difficult part, attempts to extend aspects of the same argument to the *definition and assignment of initial rights* to persons.

I shall discuss the first of these two parts of Gauthier's argument in sections 1, 2, and 3, with each section devoted to elaboration of a separate criticism. In section 4, I shall discuss the second part of the Gauthier enterprise involving the definition of rights. In section 5, I shall present particularized criticism of the whole analysis that emerges from my disciplinary location as an economist. This section is included largely because of my expectation that, among the several critical evaluations of the Gauthier enter-

A modified version of this chapter, entitled "The Gauthier Enterprise," was published in *Social Philosophy and Policy* 5 (Spring 1988): 75–94.

1. David Gauthier, *Morals by Agreement* (Oxford: Oxford University Press, 1985).

prise, mine may be the only one by an economist. Finally, in section 6, I shall discuss Gauthier's general perspective on social order.

1. Cooperation and the Definition of Community

As noted, Gauthier presents his analysis of rational cooperation in the first part of his book as a contribution to the theory of bargaining. He seeks to demonstrate that the individual, who recognizes himself or herself to be in a strategic interaction, will rationally choose that pattern of behavior that generates a cooperative outcome or solution. This demonstration is opposed to that which suggests that cooperative behavior in dilemma-like settings must exhibit a departure from individual rationality, defined as individualized utility maximization. Gauthier does not, of course, question the straightforward analytics of nonzero-sum games and the translation of objectified payoffs into their utility equivalents. His criticism is more general, and it does carry considerable appeal as carefully developed in his argumentation. The individual, when placed in such an interaction setting, will exclude the off-diagonal or behaviorally asymmetric cells from his or her realm of feasible solutions. He or she will do so, not out of any altruistic concern for his or her counterpart in the interaction, and not out of any expectation of repeated plays, but out of his or her rationally grounded interest in his or her own payoff. The temptation to "take advantage" that emerges as the motivating force in orthodox treatments of dilemma-setting behavior is suppressed in an extended rational choice structure that embodies adherence to cooperative strategies as utility enhancing. Morals by agreement do not require other-regardingness or resort to supraindividualistic norms.

Descriptively, the Gauthier analysis applies to many areas of human interaction. I have often referred to the ordered anarchy that seems to define behavior in ordinary informal social relationships. We do not, as individuals, take advantage of each other each and every time that the occasion warrants. We do behave in accordance with precepts of mutual respect, and we brand as deviant the person who violates the mutuality norm.

There exist alternatives to the Gauthier enterprise that offer explanations for this behavior. Hayek suggests that we tend to behave in accord with certain codes of conduct, certain rules, that have emerged in a long process of cultural evolution, and that these codes or rules for behavior cannot be interpreted as products of any rational calculus.[2] These rules evolve spontaneously and direct our actions even though we cannot, consciously, understand them. I shall not discuss the Hayekian argument further here; I shall say only that in

---

2. See F. A. Hayek, *Law, Legislation, and Liberty* (Chicago: University of Chicago Press, 1979), esp. vol. 3, *The Political Order of a Free People*.

any relevant comparison, my own sympathies lie with Gauthier. Generally, I applaud rational choice reductionism, especially in its promise for ultimate institutional reform. Acquiescence before the inevitability of spontaneous evolution is a stance that holds, for me, little appeal.

My first, and most fundamental, criticism of the whole Gauthier enterprise lies, therefore, *within* the postulated structure of the argument.[3] I shall leave to the game theorists any dispute concerning the appropriate definition of technical rationality. In the setting of *Morals by Agreement*, and for purposes of my argument here, I shall accept the essential elements in the Gauthier demonstration. My concern is nontechnically definitional. What does cooperative behavior mean in complex interaction settings that involve several possible interpretations of the set of players in the game, several, and competing, interpretations of the relevant community of persons within the strategic interaction, members of which might be "taken advantage of" by departures from cooperative strategies of behavior?

My point may be illustrated most directly with reference to the Prisoner's Dilemma in its classic exemplary formulation where two prisoners are apprehended and suspected of a crime but where there exists no hard evidence. The prisoners are led by the structure of the payoff matrix to confess to the crime. They do so, in the familiar argument, because they adopt individualized utility maximizing strategies. The Gauthier enterprise seeks to supplant the elementary logic here and to suggest that the prisoners will not confess, but that they will, instead, act on a rationally generated disposition to cooperate.

Or so it would seem. But does the Gauthier enterprise really imply a nonconfessing strategy on the part of the individual prisoner in a literally interpreted version of the classic dilemma? The relevance of this question is immediately obvious when we observe that the "Confess-Confess" cell of the payoff matrix is presumed to be the *socially optimal* solution. The payoff structure with which the two prisoners are confronted is deliberately designed to offer incentives to the prisoners, who are presumed to have committed the crime for which they are charged, such that their predicted behavior becomes compatible with the socially desired outcome. The inclusive community, which includes those who are potential victims of crime as well as those who are potential criminals (partially intersecting sets) presumably selects an

3. There are, of course, other approaches at explanation that do not rely on evolutionary processes and that do not involve incorporating behavior within the rational choice framework, as this is normally defined. These approaches usually involve redefinitions of the arguments in individual utility functions. For one such recent effort in this direction, see Dennis Mueller, "Rational Egoism versus Adaptive Egoism as a Fundamental Postulate for a Descriptive Theory of Human Behavior," Presidential Address, Public Choice Society, Baltimore, Md., (University of Maryland, 1986), mimeograph.

		Firm 2	
		Produce $1/2$ profit-maximizing output	Adjust output independently (Cournot)
Firm 1	Produce $1/2$ profit-maximizing output	$4050, $4050	$3375, $4500
	Adjust output independently (Cournot)	$4500, $3375	$3600, $3600

Fig. 16.1. Two-firm, two-strategy interaction (profits in dollars; industry demand function: $p = 200 - q_1 - q_2$; firm cost function: $c_i = 20q_i$, where $i = 1,2$).

institutional-constitutional structure that imposes the dilemma on those apprehended upon the commission of crimes. If the Gauthier precepts for rationality are generalized over the whole community, should the individual prisoner confess?

The point can be clarified with a numerical illustration developed for instructional purposes by my colleague Charles Rowley, an illustration that will also prove useful in the analysis of section 2. In figures 16.1 and 16.2, payoff matrices are presented for two identical firms that produce-sell a single product. The algebraically defined cost and demand functions that generate these payoffs are specified in the footnote accompanying figure 16.1.

In the two-by-two matrix of figure 16.1, each firm has available two courses of action. A firm may behave cooperatively vis-à-vis the other firm or it may act independently. If both firms adopt the cooperative strategy, the joint profit is maximized, as shown in cell I of the matrix.

Is such cooperative strategy dictated by the Gauthier norm? If the firms cooperate one with another, joint profits are maximized, but consumers of the product suffer. Price is higher because output is restricted. Consumers are, in this setting, being "taken advantage of" by the colluding duopolists. The Gauthier argument, to the effect that cooperative behavior emerges from a rationally generated disposition based on a recognition of the strategic setting, seems highly plausible when the interaction between the two firms, taken in isolation, is examined. The same argument, however, becomes implausible in the extreme when the community of interaction is extended to include consumers as well as the two firms. The same behavior that is defined to be cooperative in the one community becomes noncooperative in the differently defined community.[4]

---

4. Only after I completed a draft of this chapter did my colleague, Viktor Vanberg, point

Firm 2

	Produce $1/2$ profit-maximizing output	Adjust output independently (Cournot)	Produce $1/2$ competitive output
Produce $1/2$ profit-maximizing output	I $4050, $4050	II $3375, $4500	III $2025, $4050
Adjust output independently	IV $4500, $3375	V $3600, $3600	VI $1800, $2700
Produce $1/2$ competitive output	VII $4050, $2025	VIII $2700, $1800	IX $0, $0

Firm 1 (row label, left of table)

Fig. 16.2. Two-firm, three-stragegy interaction.

This is not a minor difficulty with the Gauthier construction. The problem of definition of the community of strategic interaction is a general one that cannot be readily avoided. There is no "natural community" for the application of the rationally generated morality by agreement. Anthropologists and moral philosophers have long recognized the distinction between the norms for behavior of individuals toward members of the tribe and those for behavior toward strangers. The shift into what Hayek has called the "great society" and what I have called "moral order" require behavioral traits that are close cousins of those emerging from the Gauthier analysis.[5] My concern is with his attempted derivation of these norms from game theoretic or bargaining interactions in which the cooperative solutions are perhaps too readily identified. I have the same concern with the attempts to derive the evolution of cooperation from gamelike settings.[6]

---

out to me that an earlier criticism of a paper by Gauthier contains essentially the same argument that I have presented in this section, even to the extent of utilizing the same examples. See E. Ullman-Margalit, *The Emergence of Norms* (Oxford: Clarendon Press, 1977), 41–45.

5. See James M. Buchanan, "Moral Community, Moral Order, or Moral Anarchy," in idem, *Liberty, Market and State: Political Economy in the 1980s* (Brighton, England: Wheatsheaf Books, 1985), 108–20.

6. See Robert Axelrod, *The Evolution of Cooperation* (New York: Basic Books, 1984). Some critics have suggested that a disposition toward cooperative behavior, whether rationally or evolutionarily grounded, describes the behavior of persons generally, quite independently of the setting of interaction. The prisoners do not confess; the duopolists maximize joint profits. In this view, it becomes inappropriate to evaluate the results of such behavior against any notion of generalized "optimality" of "efficiency" for a more inclusive group. If this line of defense is taken, however, "cooperation," as such, may or may not be judged a character trait deserving of positive evaluation in all settings. Resolution of the dilemma present in subgames may create a dilemma in more inclusive games.

2. Cooperation and the Size of Community

A closely related but conceptually distinct criticism involves the prospects for cooperative behavior on the part of an individual in a setting where the interaction clearly involves more than a critically small number of actors. Assume that there is no problem of subgroup versus inclusive-group cooperation, as discussed in section 1.

Here, the methodological constraints imposed by the analytical setting of elementary game theory should be emphasized. Simple, two-person games can, at best, offer insights into sources of behavior that may be generalized to large-number settings. The interaction of persons in two-person settings, taken literally, remains of relatively little interest. As the number of choosing-behaving units in an interaction increases, there is an exponential increase in the prospects for noncooperative behavior on the part of at least one of the parties. The relationship between the selection of cooperative strategies and the size of the group does not emerge from Gauthier's analysis.

Gauthier's prescriptive rule is that a player should adopt a cooperative strategy if his or her expected payoff from this pattern of behavior is higher than his or her expected payoff from the solution that embodies independent, utility-maximizing behavior by all parties.[7] The rule does require that the probabilities of other players' choices of strategies be considered, but only for purposes of avoiding being "taken advantage of" rather than for those of "taking advantage." The prospects for attaining the off-diagonal cells in the simple two-person matrix are reckoned with, but only with reference to the lower of the paired payoffs in these cells.

The application of the Gauthier rule, as well as the dependence of the strategy choice on numbers, may be illustrated in the numerical example of figure 16.1. (And, for present purposes, consider the firms in isolation from other possible players in the more inclusive economic game.) The Gauthier rule is that a firm should adopt the cooperative strategy if the expected value of the payoff is greater than that indicated in cell IV, where all parties adjust behavior independently. Suppose that, in the two-firm model depicted, Firm 1 expects cooperative behavior on the part of Firm 2 with a probability coefficient of one-half. In this case, the Gauthier rule would dictate cooperation because $4050 plus $3375 divided by 2 exceeds $3600. The expected value from cooperation is $3718; that from independent adjustment is $3600.

Suppose, however, that there are three identical firms rather than two, with product demand and firm cost functions unchanged. In this setting, even if the expectation remains that each firm will behave cooperatively with the *same* probability coefficient of one-half, the Gauthier rule will dictate adop-

---

7. David Gauthier, *Morals by Agreement*, 166.

tion of a noncooperative strategy. The computations yield an expected value of $1950 from cooperation against an expected value of $2025 from independent adjustment behavior (details of the computations are provided in the appendix). In order for the Gauthier rule to dictate continued adherence to a cooperative strategy as numbers in the interaction increase, the probability of any one player adopting the cooperative strategy must *increase*, which seems to counter commonsense notions about the way persons behave.

The numerical example extends the numbers only from a two-party to a three-party interaction; as numbers increase beyond small-number limits, the prospects for cooperative behavior, even on the part of those persons who try to behave in accordance with Gauthier's rational morality, will disappear in many situations. This apparent flaw is critical to the Gauthier enterprise, because it is the potential breakdown of the ordinary, two-person relationships of the competitive market that gives rise to the necessity of some morality that exhibits comparable properties of reciprocation without concern. Coase-like bargaining can be depended on in small-number spillover relationships; it is precisely the difficulties of marketlike bargaining that create the problem in large-number settings.

3. The Rationality of Retribution

A third criticism is closely related to those discussed in sections 1 and 2. In the Gauthier idealization of society, individuals rationally take on a disposition that prompts them to refrain from taking strategic advantage of others when such advantage seems profitable in the orthodox utility maximization sense. The functioning of this social order requires general adherence to such rational morality by a sufficiently large number of the community's members to make both free riding and parasitic behavior the exception rather than the norm.

In this construction there is no room for whom we may call the moral entrepreneur; there is no means through which the individual, acting singly, can enforce the precepts of rational morality on others. The whole enterprise would seem to be more promising if it incorporated some role for individual entrepreneurship.

If we are willing, with Gauthier, to jettison orthodox utility maximization as a necessary and central feature of the very definition of rational behavior, we may ask why the extension of rationality need stop at the point where the individual takes on the disposition not to take advantage of others in strategic interactions. Could not argument be advanced on Gauthier-like bases for the possible development of a rationally generated disposition to behave *retributively* toward those persons who violate the contractarian precepts? Why not punish those who depart from the cooperative norms?

The virtue of this extension of something akin to the Gauthier enterprise lies in its ability to incorporate a role for the individual as moral entrepreneur, as enforcer of cooperative norms for behavior on the part of others. The attainment and maintenance of the cooperative solutions to strategic interactions can be guaranteed by adherence to rationality by a much smaller set of the community's overall membership than that required under Gauthier's more limited model.

The point may be illustrated in the matrix of figure 16.2, which adds a row and column to the matrix employed in figure 16.1. The example is identical with that of figure 16.1; there are two identical firms producing a homogeneous good. For present purposes, I shall ignore any concern about consumers, as expressed in section 1. The row and column additions indicate the payoffs to the two firms when one or the other firm, or both, adopt what we may call a retributive strategy. In this case, we define such a strategy to be production of one-half of the industry output that will satisfy the marginal cost equals price requirement. When both firms adopt this strategy, profits fall to zero, which is the competitive solution where the benefits to consumers are maximal.

Is it not as plausible to impute, as rational, a strategy that dictates such retributive behavior to the firm upon observance of noncooperative behavior on the part of the other party as it is to impute comparison with the independent adjustment position as the benchmark or fallback option? Look carefully at the numbers in the matrix cells of figure 16.2. Suppose that the two firms are initially in the cooperative solution of cell I, but that Firm 2 tries to take advantage and shifts the outcome to cell II. If Firm 1 recognizes this potential for deviance on the part of Firm 2, it may have built into its response pattern a disposition to impose punishment; it shifts the solution to cell VIII, where the payoff to Firm 2 is reduced considerably below that attainable in independent adjustment (cell V).

By comparison with the simple tit-for-tat sequence confined to the four upper left cells of the matrix, the potentially deviant party, in this case Firm 2, is guaranteed a net loss in the sequence of plays. By contrast, and ignoring discounting, Firm 2 breaks even in the tit-for-tat sequence, as does Firm 1, the enforcer. By communicating that it has rationally disposed itself to behave retributively, and making this strategy-set credible to Firm 2, the enforcing firm has established an incentive structure such that the cooperative solution will tend to be maintained without explicit adherence to any cooperative strategy on the part of Firm 2. The latter knows that it must lose in the sequence to be played out if it departs from cooperation; it also knows that it loses relatively to Firm 1 in the process, although Firm 1 will also incur losses.

I shall not extend the argument further since I have discussed this sort of strategic behavior elsewhere under the labels "samaritan's dilemma" and "punishment dilemma."[8] My reason for bringing this discussion to bear on the Gauthier enterprise is to suggest that, once the model extends rationality beyond the limits of orthodox utility maximization, there seems no reason why rationality may not be attributed to retributive strategy as well as to the more restricted reciprocal strategy advanced by Gauthier.

I am not clear concerning Gauthier's possible response to this third criticism of his argument. He may well accept, in certain cases, the extension of the rationality norm to retribution. He does suggest that deterrence is rational, and that it remains rational to carry out even a failed threat. I agree. But he does not sufficiently emphasize that a retributive strategy is not an initiating threat strategy. The enforcer does not threaten others so long as they behave cooperatively. To communicate a strategy that will punish those who might take advantage is quite different from a strategy that employs threats as a means of taking advantage. Nor does Gauthier recognize that the retributive strategy, in comparison with his strategy of reciprocation, can produce social stability without the necessity of general adherence on the part of most parties to interaction.[9]

4. The Definition of a Person

The criticisms advanced in sections 1, 2, and 3 are independent of any derivation of a theory of rights. So long as there exists some mutually acknowledged set of initial positions from which social interaction commences, precepts for individual behavior within this interaction may be analyzed. The Gauthier enterprise would, indeed, have been ambitious even if it had been limited to this extent. The enterprise goes much further, however, and includes the effort to outline a normative theory of rights, a theory that derives the definition of the initial positions from which rational bargainers start.

I find this part of Gauthier's work to be basically incoherent. My criticism can best be discussed with reference to Gauthier's treatment of my own argument as developed in my book, *The Limits of Liberty*. I employed the concept of the "natural equilibrium" distribution in Hobbesian anarchy. This distribution is that which tends to emerge in the total absence of agreed upon

---

8. See James M. Buchanan, "The Samaritan's Dilemma," in idem, *Freedom in Constitutional Contract: Perspective of a Political Economist* (College Station: Texas A & M University Press, 1977), 169–80; see also idem, "The Punishment Dilemma," in idem, *The Limits of Liberty: Between Anarchy and Leviathan* (Chicago: University of Chicago Press, 1975), 130–46.

9. I have limited the discussion to behavior that involves threat of punishment for individual departure from a pattern of cooperative behavior. A more inclusive treatment would, of course, include moral indoctrination of the ordinary sort, designed to instill feelings of guilt and shame in those persons who might be otherwise inclined to defect.

or accepted rules defining individuals' rights, endowments, or boundaries. I argued that this distributional equilibrium offered the only basis upon which conceptual agreement among persons on some delineation of rights, some assignment of things and acts to "mine and thine" categories, could be grounded. Such agreement emerges because parties recognize that there are gains to be secured from a cessation of investment of resources in predation and defense. A set of rights comes to be established prior to the emergence of exchanges of these rights among holders, a second stage of contract that will further increase expected utilities.

David Gauthier fully understands and appreciates my analysis, including its purpose in my enterprise. For his own enterprise, however, he is critical of my construction because of its alleged failure to incorporate some recognition of the illegitimacy of coercion in the preagreement, or Hobbesian, setting. Gauthier's criticism is superficially appealing, and I should acknowledge here that it is probably shared by most of the philosophers who have examined my argument.

Why should the slave, who is coerced by the master in the preagreement equilibrium, agree on terms of a contract that will permanently preserve the preagreement advantage of the master? Despite the fact that both master and slave improve their positions by a removal of restrictions in exchange for continued work for the master on the part of the slave, Gauthier argues that no such agreement could be justified from a rationally based morality.

The Gauthier criticism fails because, in my view, it does not account for the basis of the alleged coercion in the anarchistic setting. Why should the slave be in the master's chains? Clearly, he or she is enslaved only because of some inability to enforce more favorable terms of existence. The slave does not, presumably, possess a viable exit option, one that would allow him or her to carry on with an independent and isolated existence. There is no independent existence benchmark that will define the presence or absence of coercion. If the slave cannot survive independently, can he or she be said to be coerced? Suppose, however, that the slave could have lived independently, but that he or she has been captured against his or her will. Despite our civilized sense that the master's act of enslavement is unjust, hardheaded analysis here must conclude that an independent existence for the slave was not feasible, and that any such existence was fantasy, given the presence of the potential master.

Gauthier's reluctance to accept the preagreement base for the measure of cooperative surplus stems, in part, from his desire to make his precept of rational morality extend to include compliance with agreement or contracts once made. The slave who had been captured against his or her will in the preagreement setting would never, rationally, comply with the terms of an agreement that would preserve the advantages of the master. Note, however, that the extension of rationality discussed in section 3 can extend to compliance. Recognizing the prospect that the slave might not rationally comply with an agreement, the master, before agreeing to terms, can communicate to the slave that any departure from the terms will bring punishment. And, indeed, the agreement itself may include the establishment of an effective enforcement agency.

I acknowledge that my own construction is conceptually *explanatory* in a sense that Gauthier may not intend for his justificatory alternative. For his purposes, the independent existence of the individual provides the normative benchmark from which cooperative gains are counted. In my enterprise, in contrast, parties to a potential contract commence from some status quo definition of initial positions because, quite simply, there is no other place from which to start. This existential acceptance of the status quo, of that which is, has no explicit normative content and implies neither approbation nor condemnation by any criterion of distributive justice. My contractarian explanation allows me to justify the emergence of institutions of cooperation and, with respect to the constraints on individual behavior within these institutions, I should find some Gauthier-like rule to be necessary, whether this rule be adhered to voluntarily or enforced by the sovereign. My analysis embodies the justice of natural liberty, to employ Adam Smith's fine terminology, and at some levels there are parallels with the apparently more inclusive and more ambitious Gauthier enterprise. I commence from the status quo distribution of rights, and I do not apply criteria of justice to this distribution. My emphasis is almost exclusively placed on the *process* through which potential changes may be made, rather than on either the starting point or the end point of change. Gauthier extends his justificatory analysis to the initial distribution from which cooperation commences, and he seeks to establish that the distribution qualifying as "just" is only indirectly related to that which may exist. Although his enterprise here does not require rectification as extensive as that of Robert Nozick (see below), the definitional problems raised by the Lockean proviso in Gauthier's usage are more serious than those required by Nozick. Past injustice must remain potentially relevant in both enterprises.

How is past injustice defined? For present purposes, let me address this question within Gauthier's justificatory framework. A person has been unjustly treated if he or she has been taken advantage of, if his or her well-being has been reduced below that level which he or she might have attained in an independent and isolated existence totally apart from those persons with whom he or she has been forced to interact. Some version of a secession criterion for exploitation is useful, and, indeed, it is one that I have also invoked in recent papers.[10] But it is surely heroic to imply that the individu-

---

10. See James M. Buchanan, "The Ethical Limits of Taxation," *Scandinavian Journal of Economics* 86 (1984): 102–14; see also James M. Buchanan with Roger Faith, "Secession and the Sharing of Surplus: Towards a Theory of Internal Exit" (Center for Study of Public Choice, George Mason University, 1985), mimeograph.

ally attainable level of well-being in isolation from social interaction is more than a tiny fraction of that which is secured by almost anyone in complex modern society. The secession criterion, even if it extended to apply to groups rather than to individuals singly, may offer little or no support to those critics of the existing distribution of rights among persons, and hence, little or no warrant for differential bias in the sharing of cooperative gains to rectify past injustice.

In concrete application, the Gauthier version of the Lockean proviso may be empty in the sense that it generates results equivalent to those that emerge, much more simply, in my own existential usage of the status quo. Consider an example. *Neither* the relatively rich man *nor* the relatively poor man could earn more than a pittance in isolation from the social exchange nexus. Individuals' "natural talents" are specific to the social exchange nexus in which they find themselves. Almost all of the income enjoyed by any person stems from the cooperative surplus produced by social interaction. Despite observed wide disparity in levels of well-being in the status quo, the observed distribution falls well within the inclusive bargaining-set outlined from the initial positions defined by Gauthier's proviso.

If we seek to go behind "the justice of natural liberty," it is necessary squarely to face up to the distribution of rights and endowments, as such. It is, of course, legitimate to inquire into the separate stages in the historical process through which the status quo distribution has been generated. And contractarian criteria of fairness may be applied to any or all of such stages. To label a single stage of development in the historical process as "unfair" (for example, the capture and bondage of slaves), may imply some noncontractarian attribution of "unfairness" to the end state defined by *that which exists*. But such an attribution does not, in any way, remove the normative legitimacy of evaluating potential changes from *that which exists* in terms of procedural criteria for fairness, actual or hypothetical agreement, that are equivalent to those procedures that may have applied historically to earlier stages in the process. Rectificatory redistribution, if effectuated, must, as a process, involve violation of the contractarian or agreement criteria for fairness, and it is on this process that my own emphasis lies.

As observed, the status quo distribution has been generated through a complex process of political-legal evolution, deliberative political action, preference shifts, economic development, and social change. It is appropriate to ask to what extent does the observed pattern embody precepts of fairness? And if fairness criteria have been violated at earlier stages of the process that generated that which exists, do these historical violations in themselves offer justification for violations in some process of rectification? Or is it best to concentrate on the process as it operates from the here and now?

I submit that the contractarian exercise does not require rectification of prior injustices before application to relevant forward-looking questions. The relevant questions must, ultimately, be answered empirically, with reference to the general attitudes expressed by the community's members. "Equal chances," "fair shakes," "equal treatment for equals," "play by the same rules," "equality before the law," "careers open to talents"—these seem to me to be principles of process fairness that find widespread acceptance. They are fully consistent with, and indeed are required by, the Gauthier enterprise, including the appended Lockean proviso.

As noted earlier, rectificatory redistribution may be nonexistent even on full acceptance of the Gauthier argument. By contrast, Gauthier's characterization of the market as a morally free zone may be misinterpreted as an indirect defense of the distributive patterns emergent from market interactions. Close examination of his argument reveals that persons are to be justified (by the proviso) in receiving only the values of their external marginal product, values that exclude rents.[11] As his discussion makes clear, the baseball free agent who may earn $500,000 from each of several major league clubs is not "entitled" to this total.[12] If his nonbaseball alternative is the $20,000 salary of a truck driver, the $480,000 is rent that emerges only from the exchange nexus and is, therefore, subject to sharing in accordance with the Gauthier bargaining norm, minimax relative concession. If, in turn, the genuinely isolated prospect for the person is $5,000, not $20,000, the inclusive measure of rent increases to $495,000. As this numerical example suggests, application of the Gauthier norm may require very substantial distributive departures from those patterns that are emergent from the market process as it operates.

If rents assume major quantitative significance in the reward structure of the market, the Gauthier precept for the sharing of the overall cooperative surplus may seem both to be equally arbitrary with, and not too different from, the familiar difference principle advanced by Rawls. Implicitly, Rawls assumes that the isolated individual can produce no value and that all observed income is "social rent." In the absence of incentive-induced feedbacks on production of value, the Rawlsian principle generates equality. The Gauthier principle generates inequality only as related to differentials in the capacities of persons to produce values in isolation one from another. In practical application, the two positions seem much closer than Gauthier's discussion might suggest.

Although they disagree on the specific sharing principle, both David Gauthier and John Rawls seek to go beyond the criterial usage of contractual

---

11. For related discussion, see James M. Buchanan and Robert Tollison, "The Homogenization of Heterogeneous Inputs," *American Economic Review* 71 (March 1981): 23–30; see also idem, "Coercive Taxation in Constitutional Contract" (Center for Study of Public Choice, George Mason University, 1985), mimeograph.

12. David Gauthier, *Morals by Agreement*, 276.

agreement as the test for distributive fairness. Both philosophers seek to define "that principle upon which contractors will agree," a step that I have tried consistently to avoid. My own contractarianism is, therefore, more limited; it enables me to acknowledge that any one of several sharing principles may emerge from an ideally conceptualized agreement, including those of Rawls, Gauthier, and others that embody much less redistributive thrust.

5. The Market as a Morally Free Zone

The idealized relationship between the individual buyer and the individual seller in competitive market exchange is a cornerstone of the Gauthier enterprise. In this relationship, mutual gains from trade (cooperation) are realized, and these gains are shared between the parties in a determinate manner, without other-regardingness on the part of either party, without resort to transcendental moral norms, and without costly investment in bargaining. As so idealized, it is not surprising that this basic market relationship appeals to David Gauthier, the modern moral philosopher, in much the same way that it appealed to Adam Smith, the moral philosopher of the eighteenth century. (A damning indictment of twentieth-century moral philosophy emerges when we recognize that David Gauthier's appreciation of the moral content of the exchange relationship is the exception, rather than rule, within the set of his disciplinary peers.)

The crowning discovery of the eighteenth century lay in the recognition that the spontaneous coordination properties of the market remove dilemma-like opposition of interests among persons from wide areas of social interaction, thereby eliminating the necessity of pervasive and overriding political direction of individual activity. Adam Smith stressed, however, that these properties of the market, properties that allow for the self-interested behavior of persons yet generate socially beneficial results, require an environmental setting of the appropriate "laws and institutions." Individual rights must be guaranteed; contracts must be enforced; fraud in exchange must be prevented. There need be no inconsistency between the enterprise of Adam Smith and that of David Gauthier. Smith might well agree with Gauthier's implied inference that the formal structure of law must be complemented by a rational morality that incorporates reciprocal respect among persons in the relevant nexus. Adam Smith, along with most of the economists who have followed him, might be more skeptical than Gauthier concerning the relative importance of the two influences. We recall Smith's differentiation between the behavior of the Dutch merchant constrained by the discipline of continuous dealing and that of the once-encountered, rude Scots highlander.[13]

---

13. See Adam Smith, *Lectures on Jurisprudence* (Oxford: Clarendon Press, 1978), 538.

Although he does not make the point directly, Gauthier's analysis implies that the set of social relationships classified as "the market" will more or less emerge naturally from the self-interested behavior of participants and, further, that within this set of relationships there arises no possible conflict between the precepts for rational morality and straightforward utility maximization. A participant in exchange will refrain from taking advantage, from cheating on the agreed upon terms of trade. If, however, we should remove the protective legal umbrella, Adam Smith's "laws and institutions," the basic elements of the Prisoner's Dilemma appear in even the simplest of exchange relationships. The whole of the Gauthier enterprise would have been strengthened by an explicit recognition that the market relationship offers the exemplar of rational morality rather than a "morally free zone." As Adam Smith emphasized, men *trade*; animals do not, despite recent empirical evidence demonstrating that animals have well-ordered utility functions and that they exhibit some sense of property rights. Is not the very existence of exchange the best proof that something like Gauthier's rational morality applies to normal behavior within market relationships?[14]

There is, of course, a major difference between the idealized market relationship in which each participant is a price taker and those relationships characterized by the absence of exogenously determined terms of trade. In the competitive setting, the dilemma-like elements of potential conflict arise only with respect to the prospects for gains from cheating in carrying out the terms of contract, the type of cheating that cannot be wholly prevented except in the imagined abstractions of the general equilibrium economists, abstractions that Gauthier seems to have imbibed somewhat too uncritically. In general equilibrium, producers' rents are absent and all owners of inputs secure returns equal to opportunity costs. But, as the discussion of rents indicated in section 4, opportunity cost *within* the market nexus is far removed from opportunity cost outside the nexus. As presented, Gauthier's argument suggests that distributional conflicts arise only in noncompetitive settings where prices are indeterminate. In any less abstracted conceptualization of market process, both producers' and consumers' rents are ubiquitous, and the apparent distributive neutrality of markets emergent from Gauthier's sharing norm disappears.

For basically the same reasons, Gauthier is too enthusiastic about the properties of the market in its institutional role as the eliminator of externalities *in the sense required by his enterprise.* So long as the inclusive economic nexus can be factored down into simple two-person or two-unit buyer-seller deals, there is no requirement that the rational morality of the two parties do more than secure some sharing of the cooperative surplus. The

---

14. I am indebted to my colleague, David Levy, for discussion on these points.

morality must extend to take on a heavier burden only in those settings where "markets fail" in the sense that such a factoring down cannot take place, or where there are external effects on persons who are not primary participants in the simple exchange processes.

The examples are familiar. The discharge of toxic waste into the stream kills the fish. The person who takes such action is "taking advantage" of others with whom he or she is not primarily dealing, and he or she must refrain from taking such action by some explicit resort to the rational morality of Gauthier. To the extent that rights are exhaustively assigned, however, the need to call on such an explicit sharing norm is not required. The implication is clear that such externalities are relatively rare.

The market does allow persons to act without direct regard for the interests of others, and, over very extensive areas of interaction, this process does generate results that are welfare maximizing for the whole community of persons. The market process fails in this respect only in the presence of relevant externalities. But these are only a small subset of the set of all externalities, if this term is defined simply as the imposition of noncompensated harm or benefits on parties who are not primary participants in exchanges. The conventional distinction in theoretical welfare economics is that between *technological* and *pecuniary* externalities, that is, between those actions that directly affect the utility or production functions of parties outside the exchange, and those actions that affect such parties only through changes in terms of trade, or prices. This distinction is also broadly recognized in the traditions of the common law. The market fails in the standard sense when the first sort of externalities are present; the market works only because the second sort of externalities can be disregarded.

The question for moral theory is whether or not there exists a means of making this distinction. The point is closely related to that which has already been discussed in section 1. How can a person know the difference between the two sorts of noncompensated harms or benefits that his or her behavior imposes on third parties? An example may be helpful here. Suppose that I enter into simple exchange dealings with construction firms, with wholesale grocers, with employees, and others and open up a hamburger stand on the corner of Main and Broad streets. In so doing, I impose noncompensated capital losses on the existing owner-operator of the Burger King franchise on the opposite corner. This person is a third party to my transactions, and this third party is harmed by my behavior. This is clearly a *pecuniary* externality. But am I taking advantage of the Burger King franchisee in any sense that would require me either to refrain from acting, or to share the cooperative surplus in accordance with some norm? Economic theory tells us that I need not do so, and that any attempt to force me to do so, either in formal law or in a derived morality, would be harmful to the welfare of the community as a whole. To be able to make the required distinction between noncompensated harms and benefits that would, and those that would not, invoke the application of some rational morality seems beyond the limits of the plausible, even within the acknowledged confines of the Gauthier enterprise.

6. The Enterprise Assessed

I have advanced several fundamental criticisms of the Gauthier enterprise, based on my understanding of it. These criticisms are intended to be relevant primarily, if not exclusively, to the interpretation of the enterprise as an effort to ground the morality necessary for orderly social interaction in precepts of rational choice behavior. Recall, however, that this was only one among three sets of standards for evaluating the Gauthier effort that I enunciated in the first paragraph of this chapter. By the second set of standards, my judgment of the inclusive enterprise is favorable. I shall defend this judgment in this section, and I shall make a few comments on the third set of standards suggested.

Considered in the large, the Gauthier enterprise represents an attempt to fill a major gap in our understanding and explanation of how we act and how we should act in social relationships, one with another. I am convinced that social order, as we know it, would collapse overnight if all persons, or even a large share of persons, should suddenly commence to behave strictly in accordance with the utility-maximizing models of orthodox choice theory and within the constraints only of formal legal enforcement structures. We need only refer to the statistics of crime and punishment. It is much easier for our formal models to explain why persons commit crimes than it is to explain why persons do not do so.

By comparison with David Gauthier, I am much less concerned with whether or not the behavioral norms required for what I have called the "moral order" can or cannot be grounded in some extension of rational choice. As I have indicated, I am skeptical of his success in this respect. I am concerned, however, with the presence of such norms in the behavior of persons with whom I must interact in the complex social-political-economic nexus of modern life. Gauthier shares my conviction that the norms emergent from his enterprise, or some that are roughly similar, are necessary for the liberal social order. If his effort is reinterpreted as offering an argument, even if oblique, in support of this proposition it should carry much more weight, even to those who remain highly skeptical of his more ambitious enterprise. Clearly, we must understand (to the extent that is possible) the sources of the moral norms that provide the cement of liberal society if we are to think about constructive improvement or even constructive prevention of further erosion.

So interpreted, Gauthier is a *moral* constructivist, whose enterprise is distinguishable from many other moral philosophers by its individualist-contractarian foundations. By way of comparison, my own position is that of a *constitutional* constructivist, whose enterprise builds on the same individualist-contractarian foundations. But my emphasis is placed on the rules that constrain behavior rather than on the norms for behavior itself. In this rough classificatory schemata, Rawls combines elements of both moral and constitutional constructivism, still within the contractarian framework. The three of us, Rawls, Gauthier, and Buchanan, seem clearly to be closer to each other than any of us is to the nonconstructivism of Nozick or Hayek.

By my third set of standards, I suggest that the Gauthier enterprise offers Humean hope rather than Hobbesian despair. Recall that Hobbes wrote amid the turbulence of revolutionary mid-seventeenth-century England; Hume worked out his ideas in the relatively well-ordered Scotland of the eighteenth century. It is far easier to imagine the empirical reality of a rational morality in the Scotland of David Hume and Adam Smith than it is to model Puritans and Cavaliers as agreeing on precepts for sharing the cooperative surplus. Both Hobbes and Hume were individualist in their rejection of supraindividualist sources of value; one offers reasons for constraints, the other offers reasons for abiding with those that exist.

The enterprise of David Gauthier has both Hobbesian and Humean elements. Does the enterprise presuppose that we live in a social environment nearer to the Scotland of Hume than to the England of Hobbes? Is the community of social interactors sufficiently well defined to make any system of morals by agreement viable? Is a rational morality independent of history, of culture, of institutional-constitutional structure? Perhaps we do have a *moral* obligation to answer these three questions affirmatively.

Arithmetical Appendix

In a shift from the two-firm to the three-firm interaction with product demand and firm cost functions unchanged from the example in figure 16.1, joint profit-maximizing industry output will, of course, remain unchanged at ninety units. In the three-firm setting, this output will be shared equally among the three identical firms, with each firm producing thirty units. The price remains at $110 per unit, and each firm's profit becomes $2700 [(30 × $110) − (30 × $20)]. This is compared with the $4050 profit in the two-firm setting. In considering whether to adopt a cooperative strategy by the Gauthier rule, the firm must compare the expected payoff under this strategy with that which is predicted under fully independent adjustment by each of the three firms.

Consider, first, the prospects if Firm 1 cooperates, which, in this case, means setting the output rate at thirty, which is one-third of the joint profit-maximizing output. The firm expects that each one of the other two firms will behave cooperatively with a probability of one-half. There are four possibilities, with probabilities indicated below, with C and N referring to cooperative and noncooperative strategy choices.

Payoff for Firm 1
if it adopts cooperative
strategy

Behavior of Firm 2	Behavior of Firm 3	Prob.	Profit to Firm 1
C	C	1/4	$2700
C	N	1/4	$1800
N	C	1/4	$1800
N	N	1/4	$1500

Expected value of payoff $1950

Values for the profit for Firm 1 are computed by postulating that all firms with N strategies maximize profits subject to the C firm's retention of joint profit-maximizing output.

Payoff to Firm 1 if it adopts
independent adjustment strategy,
and same strategy is adopted by
other two firms $2025

Value computed by postulating that each of three firms adjusts output independently to outputs of other firms.

Part 4
Science, Philosophy, and Politics

CHAPTER 17

Shackle and a Lecture in Pittsburgh

It is both intellectually and emotionally stimulating to be drawn back to the radical subjectivism of G. L. S. Shackle, who has consistently exhibited the courage to state the implications of his perspective for the whole realm of scientific inquiry in economics. Along with many others among my disciplinary peers, I have found it too easy to slip into orthodox methodology when its applicability beckons, thereby implicitly expressing a lack of concern with the apparent logical incoherence that describes my work upon any inclusive evaluation. This chapter provides me with an opportunity to reevaluate my own position specifically as it relates to that taken by Shackle, which is restated severally in his new book, *Business, Time, and Thought*. This book collects twenty papers, most of them short, almost all of which have been quite recently written and published, well beyond the productive years of most economists. But, as we have long been aware, George Shackle is no ordinary economist, and his ability to present even familiar ideas in a prose that sparkles with enthusiasm remains characteristic of this new volume.

I can commence my reevaluation by a direct citation.

> The elemental thing we study is *choice*. If choice means anything, it means *origination*. The making of history (on however small a scale) is the making possible one path of affairs rather than another. By origination, I would say (and here take a decisive step outside all orthodoxy, even the Austrian) we ought to mean an act of thought that is a *first cause*, so that choice in its essential nature is unpredictable in its effects, its sequel. Many "choices" are of course mere response or obedience to habit or simple reckoning. By choice we ought to mean a *momentous* act of thought. If such an act is truly originative, it cannot be foreknown in character or timing, and thus we are essentially denied the power to specify the sequel of any present choice as a singular path.[1]

This chapter is a slightly modified version of James M. Buchanan, "Shackle and a Lecture in Pittsburgh," *Market Process* 7 (Spring 1989): 2–3, which is a review article of G. L. S. Shackle, *Business, Time, and Thought*, ed. Stephen F. Frowen (New York: New York University Press, 1988).

1. G. L. S. Shackle, *Business, Time, and Thought*, 206f; italics in original.

I want to suggest that Shackle's definition of choice, expressed here and elsewhere, tends to conflate two distinguishable mental events, both of which can, with qualifications, be brought within his definition but which remain categorically different in their implications for both economic theory and the whole scientific enterprise of economists.

I propose to introduce a personal, autobiographical example to develop the distinction between the two quite separate conceptions of choice, and I hope, in so doing, to construct a bridge of sorts between the implied scientific nihilism in Shackle's position and the positivism that describes orthodox neoclassical economics.

In late 1987, an officer-agent for the National Association of Business Economists invited me to deliver the annual Adam Smith Lecture at the association's scheduled meeting in Pittsburgh in September 1988. This lecture, as delivered by me, involved two quite distinct choices that illustrate the category differences I want to emphasize. There was, first of all, a decision, a choice, made by some officer, officers, or committee on behalf of the association. This choice was expressed by the sending of the initial invitation to me. This choice was *creative* in that a sequence of events was made possible, a sequence that did not exist prior to choice and that was brought into being, literally, by the choice itself. This creative choice seems to be the sort that occupies Shackle's attention almost exclusively and, by inference, his treatment relegates all other "choices" to the status of behavioral responses.

I suggest, however, that the lecture, as delivered, involved a second genuine choice, this time a choice on my part concerning acceptance or rejection of the invitation. In one basic sense, my choice in this instance was not creative; it was, instead, *reactive*. I found myself confronted with a modified set of environmental alternatives, but I had done nothing directly or indirectly to create the change in conditions that had brought the new opportunity into realization. Clearly, however, I did face a genuine choice that fits within the inclusive Shackle definition. I was not merely responding to a stimulus in my act of acceptance.

There is a categorical difference between *creative* and *reactive* choice when we come to the realm of predictability, the domain of scientific inquiry. My reactive choice could have been, probabilistically, predicted by those who advanced the association's invitation. By contrast, there was no way that I could have, even probabilistically, predicted that such an invitation would have been forthcoming. The matching of the name *Buchanan* with the *1988 Adam Smith Lecture* was creative in a Kirznerian entrepreneurial sense.

I need not push the personal illustration too far. But it does allow me to clarify my own position, as expressed variously, which may have seemed to embody inconsistency by my acceptance of much of the Shackle critique while continuing to use the neoclassical framework of analysis. Neoclassical analysis is, and must be, restricted entirely to the domain of *reactive* choice, which is always predictable, at least within probabilistic limits. A genuine science of reactive choice is possible, and patterns of order can be predicted to emerge, even if each choosing participant retains the fullest Shacklian freedom to originate his or her own sequence of future events. The domain of reactive choice extends over a wide spectrum of possible choice settings. At the one extreme, the individual actor is genetically programmed to respond uniquely and predictably to the alternatives that are confronted; in this limit, "choice" in any meaningful sense disappears. As we move beyond this limit, *individual choice* becomes possible, and indeterminacy replaces determinacy in any attempt to predict individual behavior. Such indeterminacy need not, however, extend to *patterns* of behavior that describe the choices made by many persons, comparably situated in at least some respects, or, alternatively, the choices made by a single person over a whole series of comparably defined circumstances.

I should stress that the *reactive* choice of an individual may meet the Shacklian criterion for *originative* choice, when examined from the perspective of the individual who chooses. Such a person does, indeed, originate the particular sequence of events that can only come into existence, *for him or her*, after genuine choice is exercised. In my acceptance of the invitation to deliver the Adam Smith Lecture in Pittsburgh, I originated a sequence of events, for myself and others, that would not have been within the possible had my choice been rejection. I suggest, however, that my choice in this instance was not itself *creative* because it was at least probabilistically predictable, as indeed all reactive choices must be. The *pattern* of response might have been such as to allow for my private choice to have been either one of the alternatives that I faced, while retaining some appropriate appellation of stochastic determinacy. And, of course, as we move back along the spectrum of reactive choice toward generalization over persons and over time sequences, the determinacy of reactive choice patterns increases and with this comes enhanced productivity of scientific inquiry.

All such reactive choices are, however, categorically distinct from genuinely creative choice, which does indeed bring into being a sequence of events that remains indeterminate, not only at the level of individual action but also at the level of any conceivable pattern of behavior generalized over many persons and many periods. In creative choice, the behavior of the individual is not probabilistically predictable because such choice, in itself, *creates* alternatives from which the other individuals choose. The creative chooser does not select from among competing "forks in the road" that remain "out there," thrown up to him or her either by natural circumstance or by the action of others, privately or collectively. The reactive choice I faced in accepting or rejecting the invitation to deliver the Adam Smith Lecture came into being by the creative decision of the agents who acted on behalf of the association. This choice was dimensionally different from that which I faced in reacting to the modified opportunity that I found.

The essential contribution of G. L. S. Shackle, who is surely one of the most neglected economists of this century, lies in his emphasis and insistence on the indeterminacy of choice. And the related emphasis of modern Austrian economists, notably that of Israel Kirzner, on the necessary role of entrepreneurial choice in the dynamic operation of any economy, deserves our praise. Understanding how the economic order works requires that we give due attention to both dimensions for choice, and neoclassical orthodoxy has surely neglected creative choice as the necessary complement to the reactive choice that must be its central focus. But all "choice" that deserves to be so labeled is originative, while not all "choice" is creative (entrepreneurial).

In this short chapter, stimulated again by reading Shackle, I have shifted my own position toward a more catholic and less critical attitude on the orthodoxy of neoclassical economics than that expressed in separate essays published in celebratory volumes in honor of Hayek and Mises.[2] I remain a Shacklian, but I now recognize, more than before, the essential distinction between individual and pattern indeterminacy.

---

2. See James M. Buchanan, "Is Economics the Science of Choice?" in *Roads to Freedom: Essays in Honor of F. A. Hayek*, ed. Erich Streissler (London: Routledge and Kegan Paul, 1969); reprinted in idem, *What Should Economists Do?* (Indianapolis: Liberty Press, 1979), 39–63. Also see James M. Buchanan, "The Domain of Subjective Economics: Between Predictive Science and Moral Philosophy," in *Method, Process, and Austrian Economics: Essays in Honor of Ludwig Von Mises*, ed. Israel Kirzner (Lexington, Mass.: Lexington Books, 1982); reprinted in idem, *Economics: Between Predictive Science and Moral Philosophy* (College Station: Texas A & M University Press, 1987), 67–82.

CHAPTER 18

The Foundations for Normative Individualism

What is the ultimate justification for regimes of social interaction that allow biologically defined members of the human species to choose separately among locational, occupational, associational, evaluational, life-style, production, and consumption alternatives? Why are such regimes deemed superior, in some relevant normative sense, to others that restrict, in some relative degree, the choice options of separate persons? Why is a liberal social order that is descriptively permissive of individual migration among many interlinked communities preferred to an order that defines and enforces the status of each person within the many communitarian dimensions? Social philosophers who are, at the same time, advocates of a liberal or free society embodying the maximal exercise of individual liberties have often neglected these basic questions, perhaps in some misguided presumption that answers are as unnecessary as they are obvious.

1. Epistemic Individualism

It is to Douglas Rae's credit that he has forced a consideration of such questions. At a June 1988 conference in Santa Cruz, California, Rae presented a paper entitled "Epistemic Individualism, Unanimity, and the Ideology of Liberty."[1] The subject matter of the first part of the three-part title, and the paper, directly addresses the justificatory questions and offers a provisional answer. Rae's claim is that the liberal tradition, from which *The Calculus of Consent*[2] emerges, rests upon what he calls *epistemic individualism* as its fundamental justification principle. The claim is that the liberal advocacy of free institutions, notably those of the market economy, find normative justification in epistemological considerations. In Rae's account, the epistemic individualism claim is that the individual is privileged as a

---

1. Douglas Rae, "Epistemic Individualism, Unanimity, and the Ideology of Liberty: The Calculus of Consent Revisited" (paper presented at the Liberty Fund Conference, Santa Cruz, California, June 1988).

2. James M. Buchanan and Gordon Tullock, *The Calculus of Consent: Logical Foundations of Constitutional Democracy* (Ann Arbor: University of Michigan Press, 1962).

choice maker because he or she knows better than anyone else what is "best" for his or her own well-being.

I do not challenge the descriptive relevance of Rae's presentation, and implied criticism, in so far as it applies to the normative justification for individualism, along with its institutional consequences, that informs the attitudes of many of my peers in economics and political economy. I want to reject, however, the descriptive accuracy of Rae's thesis in application to my own underlying philosophical perspective. My conceptual starting point, as expressed in *The Calculus of Consent* and other writings, is not based on the individualism that Rae labels to be "epistemic," either in its descriptive or its normative components.[3] In the discussion below I shall attempt to explain in some detail the fundamental ontological and normative assumptions that inform my position and also discuss how these differ categorically from the epistemic individualism attributed to me.

Although economists rarely pause to think about the philosophical foundations of their own constructions, when and if forced to explicit commitment most of them would accept the qualified utilitarian designation that their models descriptively incorporate. In these models, individual choosers-actors maximize utility by selecting a preferred combination of the feasible alternatives available, with the feasibility-set being determined by both natural and institutional limits. In these constructions, "utility," or more generally "that which is maximized" has a presumptive existence that is independent of any exercise of choice itself. An individual's utility function is described as a complete ordinal array of all potential alternatives, both those within and without the feasible set. There exists a unique utility-maximizing choice that can be located once the utility or preference function is specified along with the appropriate constraints.

As noted, implicit in this whole construction is the ontological assumption that there is "something"—whether called a utility function or not—that exists and can, at least conceptually, be objectified and separated from individual choice. If this assumption is made, then the relation between an individual's choice behavior and his or her utility function becomes a matter of fact. That is, there arises a factual question open to investigation concerning the correspondence between the choices made and the change in the individual's position as measured on the independent scalar. It becomes appropriate to classify certain choices as appropriate or even maximizing, as applied against the criteria provided by the utility function.

Only if this ontology—which I *do not* accept—is adopted, do the questions supposedly faced by epistemic individualism arise. And only within this ontology does the conflict between epistemic individualism and its potential

---

3. I make no claim concerning the position of my coauthor, Gordon Tullock.

alternatives assume relevance. Only if it is presumed that an individual's choice behavior and the utility function exist as conceptually separate things does it make sense to raise the question as to whether the individual or some third party or parties can most reliably identify the choices that are defined as "best" in terms of the given utility function.

If the well-being or welfare of the individual is equivalent to utility and is accepted as the ultimate normative objective, and if, further, the individual is presumed to possess superior knowledge of his or her own utility or preference function, there is an epistemic basis upon which arguments for extending the range of voluntary individual choices can be constructed, along with consequential arguments for the establishment and maintenance of institutions that maximally allow such choices. Conversely, there is a basis for arguments that call into question the normative legitimacy of institutions that restrict individual freedom of choice. Those institutions of an individualistic social order, and notably those of market exchange, derive their normative justification from the relative efficacy of these institutions in exploiting this epistemological privilege granted to participants. Conversely, those institutions that limit individual choice, and notably those of the state, derive their possible normative justification only upon the emergence of some effective demonstration that the epistemic privilege of participants is somehow more than offset by other considerations, or that, in other settings, participants do not enjoy such privileges at all.

2. Challenges to Epistemic Privilege

I propose to examine briefly three separate but related challenges to the legitimacy of social arrangements that embody maximal dependence upon individual choice, each one of which reflects an attempt to deny the epistemic privilege of individuals who participate in such arrangements.

Benevolent Paternalism

Welfare economists often refer pejoratively to those persons who seek to impose their own "meddlesome preferences" on others whose conflicting preferences reflect differing life-styles. And the difficulty of separating attempted intrusions of genuinely meddlesome preferences from the attempted exercise of benevolent paternalism must be acknowledged. The existence of benevolent paternalism on the part of some persons cannot, however, be denied. Such persons genuinely seek to insure that others than themselves secure the highest level of well-being or utility that feasibility limits allow. The paternalists reject only the claim of epistemic privilege; they do not think that individuals know what is best or good for them. The paternalists advance the counter claim that they, as outsiders, as informed experts, know more about the ability of the relevant choice options to satisfy the ultimately desired objectives of the persons affected than those persons themselves who might otherwise make the choices in question. The paternalistic claim is that, in some final or ex-post reckoning, individuals must acknowledge their own initial unknowledge or tendency to err, and, thereby, must validate, ex-post, the limits that are imposed on their ability to make the "right" choices.

Note that the paternalists' claim can be exclusively epistemic. They need not replace individual utility maximization as the normative goal. And they need not introduce arguments reflecting some supraindividualistic "social" or "public" interest into the relevant functions. The claim is, quite simply, that someone knows better than the individuals themselves how to secure their own well-being.

"Scientific" Socialism

Quite a different sort of challenge to the epistemic privilege of the individual under liberalism is mounted by the "scientific" socialists, especially of the classical Marxist-Leninist tradition. That which is "good" for individuals is to be determined by the objective laws of historical development. Mankind, rather than existing, empirically identifiable individuals, is the normatively relevant unit. Neither the voluntary participation of individuals, even as members of the proletariat, nor their ex-post approval, is required as any part of the justificatory exercise. "Social choices," in this construction, are not derived from "individual values" but are, instead, the implementation of mankind's recognized destiny.

The challenge of the "scientific" socialists to individualism remains epistemic, but in a much more intrusive sense than that of the paternalists. The ultimate objective, at least rhetorically, remains the welfare of individual participants in the political community, but this welfare is not measured, even conceptually, by individually separable indicators of utility. Individuals themselves are defined only as members of the community; they cannot, in principle, conceive of, much less have knowledge of, their separably identifiable well-beings.

Political idealism

A third criticism of the liberal social order in which persons are allowed wide scope for voluntary choice, particularly through the institutions of a market economy, can be interpreted in epistemic terms, although here it is the object of knowledge rather than the means of its attainment that assumes center stage in the argument. This criticism, which I call "political idealism," does not embody a conception of individuals seeking out or aiming for separately identifiable goals or objectives that assume meaning in other than communitarian terms. This feature is shared with the scientific socialists. But the goals or objectives of persons-in-community are now to be sought, not in some pretense of scientific inquiry, but rather in the Platonic summum bonum—the good, the true, and the beautiful—that can be defined for us by the philosophers. In this strand of criticism, those institutions that allow individuals to exercise private choices over wide ranges of action may tend to promote the vulgar and animalistic desires of ordinary humankind which then take priority over those higher values that can be revealed only to the select few who hold access to the founts of wisdom.

The three criticisms of the liberal order sketched here along with other variants, for example, technocracy, intersect, one with another, and each incorporates different epistemological presuppositions concerning both the inner knowledge of the means possessed by individuals and the "outer" knowledge of the ends that "should" provide the ultimate motivations for action. My purpose in this section has not been to examine any of these, or other, criticisms of liberalism in detail; my purpose is, instead, to suggest the potential vulnerability of any pure epistemic defense, whether to the arguments noted here or to others. A liberal order that is founded on epistemic justification remains open both to analytical and empirical deconstruction of its essential proposition.

3. Subjectivism: Epistemic Limitation and Normative Implications

My purpose in this short chapter is to suggest that the foundation for a normative individualism is not epistemic. In addition, I suggest that the criticisms of the liberal order that seek to exploit the vulnerability of the epistemic argument are not pertinent to the alternative justificatory argument that best describes my own position.

My own ontological presuppositions do not allow any conceptual separation or distinction between an individual's choice behavior and his or her utility function. My position is sometimes classified to be one of strict *subjectivism*, applications of which have been discussed in my book, *Cost and Choice* and other works.[4] From a subjectivist perspective, a "utility function," as such, does not exist which, even conceptually, could be observed and recognized independently of an individual's choice behavior. All there is are individual choices, and it is about these choices, not about some alleged

---

4. James M. Buchanan, *Cost and Choice: An Inquiry in Economic Theory* (Chicago: Markham Press, 1969).

relationship to some utility function, that we develop theories. We may, for example, observe that persons sometimes regret choices that have been made, and we may conjecture that some third person might have been able to predict that such regret would occur, post choice. And we may then hypothesize that this third person might have been able to offer "good" advice to the chooser, pre choice. But none of these theories about choices require the introduction of a choice-independent utility scalar.

The modern economist who models the individual as choosing among feasibly alternative bundles of goods to maximize a utility function that does exist independently of choice itself presents no evidence that such functions actually exist, and, if pushed, the economist would agree that "utility" is little more than a rhetorical artifice that is introduced as an aid in explaining choice behavior within an imposed rational choice reconstruction. While the issue of epistemic individualism is of relevance for this conception, it has no bearing on my ontological perspective; the individual chooses that which he chooses, and there need exist neither prior nor posterior "knowledge" that enables any choice to be classified as "correct" or "incorrect" against some criterion of well-being. At the moment of choice itself, the individual selects the alternative that is preferred, but this tautological proposition embodies no presumption about epistemic privilege.

Choice exercised by an individual involves self-creation along with the creation of constraints imposed on the choices of others. This reciprocal interaction takes place over a whole temporal sequence. The "individual," as described by a snapshot at any moment, is an artifactual product of choices that have been made in prior periods, both by himself or herself and others. If it is acknowledged that any person, post choice, is necessarily different from the person that made the choice, and that the difference is produced, in part, by the act of choice itself, it becomes absurd to apply criteria of "correctness" directly to choice, as such, including epistemic criteria.[5]

Knowledge concerns that which is, or that which is potentially knowable, by someone. Knowledge cannot, therefore, extend to the unknowable, which must contain *all* that takes place in the future, *including* choices that will be made. Neither the individual who may choose internally nor the paternalist who may impose a selected alternative externally can claim epistemic privilege, since the selection among alternatives at t_0 will itself *create* a setting at t_1, from within which any evaluation of the t_0 choice must be made.

The distinction between the two ontological conceptions that I have tried

---

5. For an elaboration of my position here, see James M. Buchanan, "Natural and Artifactual Man," in idem, *What Should Economists Do?* (Indianapolis: Liberty Press, 1979), 93–114. I have been influenced by the work of G. L. S. Shackle. For the most complete statement of his position, see G. L. S. Shackle, *Epistemics and Economics* (Cambridge: Cambridge University Press, 1972).

to contrast has implications for justificatory arguments advanced in support or opposition to alternative social-organizational arrangements. As I have noted, epistemic individualism plays no role in my own ontological presuppositions, but this statement implies nothing directly about the justificatory argument.

The justificatory foundation for a liberal social order lies, in my understanding, in the normative premise that individuals are the ultimate *sovereigns* in matters of social organization, that individuals are the beings who are entitled to choose the organizational-institutional structures under which they will live. In accordance with this premise, the legitimacy of social-organizational structures is to be judged against the voluntary agreement of those who are to live or are living under the arrangements that are judged. The central premise of *individuals as sovereigns* does allow for delegation of decision-making authority to agents, so long as it remains understood that individuals remain as *principals*. The premise denies legitimacy to all social-organizational arrangements that negate the role of individuals as either sovereigns or as principals. On the other hand, the normative premise of individuals as sovereigns does not provide exclusive normative legitimacy to organizational structures that—as, in particular, market institutions—allow internally for the most extensive range of separate individual choice. Legitimacy must also be extended to "choice-restricting" institutions so long as the participating individuals voluntarily choose to live under such regimes.

For the justificatory construction here, epistemic features of choice are simply irrelevant. Individuals are to be allowed to choose among potentially available alternatives simply because they are the ultimate sovereigns. And this conclusion holds independently of the state of knowledge possessed about either means or ends. If individuals are considered the ultimate sovereigns, it follows directly that they are the *addressees* of all proposals and arguments concerning constitutional-institutional issues. Arguments that involve reliance on experts in certain areas of choice must be addressed to individuals, as sovereigns, and it is individuals' choice in deferring to experts-agents that legitimizes the potential role of the latter, not some external assessment of epistemic competence, as such.

4. Application

I have opposed a subjectivist to an epistemic foundation for normative individualism. The discussion has indicated the central differences between these two philosophical frameworks. I have not yet examined the implications of the two foundations in any practical application. It is, I think, relatively easy to show that the social philosopher who relies on epistemic privilege to defend individual freedom of choice and the institutions that allow this freedom to be exercised maximally faces a much more difficult burden of proof than the philosopher who rests his or her argument squarely on a subjectivist interpretation.

Consider the eighteenth- and early-nineteenth-century argument in defense of the institution of human slavery. Intellectually honest philosophers, from Plato through the nineteenth century, supported the institution of human slavery on epistemic grounds. Commencing from the presupposition that persons differ in their intrinsic epistemic capabilities, a presupposition that carries solid empirical support, even if not in terms of distinct groupings of persons, these philosophers, both classical and modern, support attempts to construct and to maintain an institutional correspondence between epistemic capabilities and the ranges of voluntary choices allowed to individuals. These institutions are explicitly designed to allow those who are more capable epistemically to impose their will coercively upon those who are considered less capable. And this institutional correspondence is not, of course, limited to the explicit institution of slavery; it applies equally to all institutions that allow for differential access to the exercise of individual choice.

How does the epistemic individualist counter the sometimes persuasive argument of the elitist, which itself evokes epistemic standards? The response that the individual really does "know best" what is "good" for him or her may seem quite empty, and especially when the individual is observed to make choices that seem to guarantee hunger, deprivation, myopic prodigality, and addiction. Is it not preferred, on epistemic grounds, that the homeless alcoholic in the streets be made a slave (under the auspices of the modern state) for "his or her own good"?

The burden of argument placed on the epistemic individualist in all such cases may be contrasted sharply with that which the subjectivist confronts. The latter can remain appropriately deaf and blind to the entreaties of the elitist who claims supraindividualist status. The biological dividing line that separates members of the human species from other animals is surely easier to draw than any within-species line (even the no line limit) that the epistemic defense of individuality must trace out. I am not suggesting that all problems of identification disappear; qualification for membership as individuals in the human species that is relevant for the free exercise of choice cannot be met by children and the mentally incompetent. These problems seem, however, minuscule in comparison with those that arise in the alternative framework.

If "that which is best" for an individual exists independently of choice by that individual, the institutional arrangements within which choice may be exercised are not directly related to the definition of the objective. The problem for institutional-constitutional design is one of achieving "efficiency" in the attainment of the defined state of the world. By contrast, if "that which is best" for an individual does not exist independently of choice by that individual, the institutional structure must, at some level, facilitate such choice if, indeed, "that which is best" is accepted as the ultimate normative objective. "That which is best" is objectively meaningful only at the moment of choice itself. In the observed context of the institution of human slavery, it becomes absurd to refer, as Plato, to the superior knowledge of the master concerning "that which is best" for the individual slave. In directing the activity of the slave, the master is, at the moment of choice, selecting "that which is best for the master"; he or she could do nothing other than this.

The subjectivist argument requires, however, much more attention to the level of choice than the epistemic argument. As noted it is ontologically absurd to define the master's choice as selecting among alternatives "that which is best for the slave." On the other hand, "that which is best for the *individual* as slave," determined only by the individual in question, may possibly involve voluntary agreement, as some level of contractual choice, to submit to the coercive authority of another person. Slavery, as an institutional arrangement, cannot be condemned as "not best" independently of its observed coercive establishment.

The alternative philosophical foundations for normative individualism, and for the structure of institutions that allow the exercise of voluntary choice, carry quite different implications for individual responsibility. The vulnerability of the epistemic defense of individualism to demonstration of incompetence on the part of some members of the political community lends itself readily to politicized corrections for such incompetence. Regardless of the institutional structure, which may itself reflect a generalized acceptance of normative individualism, the elite may express concern for those who do not demonstrate the capability of knowing what is really best for themselves, in the selection of either means or ends. The way is open for the modern welfare states, which combine elements of epistemic individualism with the elitism of those who defend the institution of human slavery. The normative individualist whose ontology is subjectivist operates on the presumption that, by their very being as individuals, members of humankind are and must be treated as responsible for their own choices. Individuals are not to be "protected from their own folly," even if this basic stance is tempered with ordinary compassion.

CHAPTER 19

Constructivism, Cognition, and Value

This chapter addresses the general theme of the 1987 Alpbach European Forum, which was "Cognition and Decision." It is, of course, appropriate that this theme be sufficiently comprehensive to incorporate many variations of emphases. I could not, even if I tried to do so, incorporate all elements of such a general theme in a single chapter. I shall make no such attempt here. Instead, I shall try to develop some elements of subject matter that fall within the general theme.

As some of you who may know my work will have anticipated, I shall concentrate on the choices that we make among rules or institutions that enable us to live in *social order* without conflict while at the same time achieving tolerably acceptable levels of well-being. More specifically, I shall examine the linkage between the knowledge that we possess or may possess about the predicted working properties of alternative sets of rules and the choices that we may make among these sets.

The first step involves the supposition that we do, in fact, choose the constraints within which we carry out our everyday activities, both private and public. That is to say, the rules for social order are not exclusively the product of some process of cultural evolution, rules that we have inherited and that we abide by without understanding their purpose or function. At least within limits, the supposition here is that rules are deliberately "constructed" from the choices of those persons who are to be subject to the constraints that these rules embody.

In channeling the discourse toward constructive choice among sets of rules, I am, as you will recognize, both modifying and going beyond emphasis on cultural evolution associated with the work of F. A. Hayek. I accept, of course, the importance of cultural evolution in the establishment of the rules of social order, and I need not assign weights to the relative significance of evolved and constructed rules. I want only to suggest that, at least

---

A modified version of this chapter was presented as the opening plenary lecture at the Alpbach European Forum, Alpbach, Austria, in September 1987. It was published in the Forum's proceedings, Otto Molden, ed. *Erkenntnis und Entscheidung* (Vienna: Europaisches Forum Alpbach, 1987).

along some relevant margins, we can deliberately modify the institutions that constrain our interaction, one with another.

1. Moral Constructivism

The next step in my argument involves a distinction between moral and constitutional constructivism. We have long recognized that constraints on behavior may be moral or extramoral, or, to put the point differently, may be internal to the psyche of the potential actor or externally imposed. A person may not steal because of an internal moral imperative—"it is wrong to steal"; or because of an external sanction—"if I steal I shall suffer punishment."

A moral constructivist seeks to modify behavior by changing the morality of the potential actor. Traditionally, the moralist has sought to urge upon us ethical precepts that are presumably derived from some external source of knowledge—from God, from reason, from natural law. And such precepts have often been introduced explicitly as constraints upon the rationally derived self-interests of actors. I am not a moral philosopher in the sense that I can claim any competence in the derivation of moral or ethical precepts from transcendent sources of knowledge about values. Indeed, I remain highly skeptical about the very existence of such sources of moral values.

I am much more sympathetic to a quite different sort of moral constructivism, one that seeks to ground moral precepts for behavior within the rational self-interest of individuals, in the cognition and preferences that exist, rather than in some extraindividualistic sources. We find elements of this second sort of moral constructivism in David Hume and in other leaders of the eighteenth-century school of Scots moral philosophers. Some elements are also present in Kant's whole enterprise. But I want to concentrate my remarks here on an important book, *Morals By Agreement*, by an American philosopher, David Gauthier.[1] In *Morals By Agreement*, Gauthier seeks to demonstrate that a cooperative morality is an essential part of rational choice. In his construction, moral rules do not constrain choices that would otherwise be dictated from considerations of rational utility maximization. Instead, it becomes rational to be moral in dealing with others in settings where the reciprocal behavior of others can be anticipated.

Gauthier generalizes the setting described in the classical Prisoner's Dilemma of modern game theory, and he argues that the choice of a disposition to behave cooperatively is rationally grounded. Despite the existence of several problematic aspects of his technical construction, it does seem to me that

---

1. David Gauthier, *Morals by Agreement* (Oxford: Oxford University Press, 1986). For an extended discussion of Gauthier's work, see chap. 16.

Gauthier has moved the argument one stage beyond that at which Hayek's argument finishes. If we acknowledge, as I think we must, that we do, indeed, behave in accordance with rules of conduct that makes order in a "great society" possible, we are left with the unanswered question, "Why?" Gauthier's construction offers an explanatory answer that does not require the altruism of the moral community, an altruism that is appropriate only to the small-number setting descriptive of our tribal heritage.

In a very real sense, Gauthier is arguing that individuals choose dispositions or personal behavioral rules for themselves that will direct their patterns of choice behavior in a sequence of interactions with others. In my own terms, individuals choose among alternative "moral constitutions"; they choose among alternative constraints rather than among alternative end states available to them in particularized situations. A reconciliation, of sorts, may be effected between Gauthier and traditional moralists by noting that the rational morality of an individual does require constraints on the open-ended choice options that seem to describe particularized situations. But these constraints are themselves a product of, and are chosen by, a rationally based choice calculus at the "higher" level of dispositional alternatives.

The classical dilemma setting may then be misleading. If the payoff matrix is interpreted to reflect the utility payoffs that the individuals actually confront in a single interaction, it cannot be descriptive of that faced by Gauthier's rationally moral person. Having rationally chosen a disposition to cooperate, as a binding element of a moral constitution, the individual does not, and cannot, confront the ordinally arrayed payoff structure of the classical dilemma. The off-diagonal cells do not contain the ordinal utility numbers that generate the familiar dominance.

Gauthier's construction is explicitly contractarian, and he suggests that individuals will agree generally on the adoption of dispositions to cooperate reciprocally in interactions that contain the potential for a cooperative surplus. These dispositions will not, however, include the extension of comparable treatment to others who are not similarly disposed. Gauthier's enterprise requires an ability to recognize, within probabilistic limits, those who are free riders and/or parasites, along with a willingness to initiate appropriate noncooperative behavior toward such persons, from ostracism to retribution.

The cognitive requirements placed on the individual in Gauthier's construction are immense. The individual must, first of all, recognize the potential for cooperative surplus, and he or she must projectively measure this surplus in a quasi-objectifiable way necessary to allow for shared agreement with other parties to interaction. Further, he or she must identify the limits of the relevant community of potential cooperators. Even if, as Gauthier acknowledges, the exercise is carried out in "ideal theory," as opposed to explanatory analysis, the observed limits on the cognitive capacities of persons as they exist may raise issues of relevance. The ambitious nature of Gauthier's enterprise must be stressed.

Nonetheless, his effort is unique among modern social philosophers in that he does advance a conceptually explanatory framework that allows us to understand how persons might survive and prosper in an "orderly anarchy." I have long argued that much of the observed interaction in western liberal settings does proceed without formal legalized-politicized constraints. Gauthier's analysis contains elements of explanation, and, because it does so, I welcome it as a contribution that deserves careful attention.

2. Constitutional Constructivism

If we interpret David Gauthier's enterprise as an analysis of the rational bases for the individual's choice of a "moral constitution," a choice that will constrain his noncooperative proclivities in dilemma-like particular interactions, there is a direct linkage with the "constitutional constructivism" that has, directly or indirectly, occupied much of my own attention for many years, and which is ultimately derivative from the construction of Thomas Hobbes.

Recognizing that we must, as members of a society, interact variously and continuously with others, we may rationally choose to impose constraints upon our own behavior along with that of others, constraints that will operate externally to our own volition, constraints that will be imposed coercively. We may voluntarily and deliberately choose to restrict our own freedom of action, to close off choice options, so long as we are insured that the choices of others are similarly constrained. In choosing such constraints, we are seeking to secure the expected benefits to be derived from the assurance that other persons will, reciprocally, be restricted in their freedom of action. Civic order becomes possible as individual behavior is confined within appropriately defined limits, whether these be internally imposed, à la Gauthier, or externally operative. Law and morals are both complements and substitutes, one for the other. And a rationally based logic of law becomes fully analogous to a rationally based logic of morality in some Gauthier-like framework of analysis.

We have, therefore, three sources of constraints, one of which is nonrational, and two of which have rational choice foundations.

1. "It is wrong to steal."
2. "It is rational to choose a disposition not to steal from persons who reciprocate in their moral attitudes."
3. "It is rational to choose an enforceable law against stealing applicable for the whole community of persons."

These alternatives need not, of course, be mutually exclusive.

I have discussed the second of these sets of constraints at some length in section 1, in the context of the work of David Gauthier. I want to discuss the third set of constraints in more detail here, and to compare and contrast this alternative with the second. That is to say, I want to compare Gauthier's rational morality with the more familiar rationally derived constitutional contract for political order that embodies coercion of persons in postconstitutional actions.

The critical difference between the two sets of rationally based constraints on individual choice lies in the necessary "externality" that is embodied in any Hobbes-like structure of civil order. The initial compact or covenant, real or imagined, with the "sovereign" involves the agreed upon submission of the individual, as subject, to the dictates of that person or agency charged with the task of enforcing the agreed upon rules. This subjection of the individual to potential coercive force beyond his own internal precommitments must be present, regardless of the possible predictability and controllability of the agent or agency that might exercise such force. Even if technology should permit the ultimate rule enforcer to take the form of some impersonal robot, the individual, as subject, remains bound by the external constraints programmed in the structure. And, more familiarly, if the ultimate rule enforcer necessarily embodies human agency, the potential for exploitative behavior that extends beyond the limits of consensually based law must be recognized.

"How may the controllers be controlled?" Hobbes responded with despair. But historical experience suggests that, in some times and some places and under some circumstances, constitutions can, themselves, bind sovereign governments. Nonetheless, the attention of the constitutional constructivists must be primarily focused on the effective implementation of constraints on the operations of constitutionally authorized and established governments. The protection of individuals from the state, the very agency that he employs to protect him from other persons and to provide collective goods and services, becomes the critical challenge for the political philosopher. Even at a level of "ideal theory," there is no satisfactory resolution of this issue.

Unfortunately, this issue is less widely understood today than it was in the seventeenth or the eighteenth century. Discussion over two centuries has been plagued by acceptance of what I have elsewhere called "the electoral fallacy," the idea that so long as governments act "democratically" in accordance with decisions made by duly elected representatives in parliamentary or legislative assemblies, the individual is sufficiently protected against the overreaching of the State. So long as the individual remains at liberty to participate freely in the electoral process, there need be no cause for the traditional concern over the state's limits. So long as legislative bodies reflect genuine majoritarian preferences, any constitutional constraints on their exercise of authority are unnecessary and may, indeed, be undesirable. I suggest that this whole set of related ideas and attitudes reflects monumental confusion that produces possibly tragic consequences.

As modern public choice theory has demonstrated, the linkage between the individual's participation in the electoral process and insurance against exploitation by the agency of governance is tenuous at best. The individual in a large-number electorate has little or no rationally based interest in the act of participation, in voting, and he or she has no rational motive for seeking to become informed as to the consequences of alternatives presented for collective choice. Moreover, the potential for majoritarian exploitation of minority interests may well exceed that which is possible in nonmajoritarian settings. A practical consequence of the electoral fallacy has been to lend an artificial legitimacy to the overreaching of modern states into spheres of activity that would never have been contractually or consensually ceded to any sovereign.

As I have suggested elsewhere, there is a pressing need for a requisite understanding of the central issues involved in man's relationship to and with the state. This understanding does not emerge "naturally" in the thought processes of modern Western culture, as it seemed to emerge in the political philosophy of the eighteenth century.

3. Knowledge, Understanding, and Value

In a very real sense, there has been a loss of wisdom between the late eighteenth and late twentieth centuries. We seem to know and to understand *less* now than we did when David Hume, Adam Smith, Wilhelm Von Humboldt, and James Madison lived and worked. But what is it that we know less about? Scientifically, we have, of course, made dramatic progress over the two centuries. The frontiers of knowledge about the physical-natural universe have been enormously expanded. We know much more about almost all aspects of our universe. How is it, then, possible to suggest that we know less, about anything, than we did then?

Lest we presume an unwarranted arrogance, even about matters of pure "science," it is useful to remind ourselves that knowledge about the natural universe has been lost in earlier epochs. The late Roman empire was characterized by less knowledge about many things than the level of cognition attained during Rome's grandeur. Applied to modern times, however, there is no evidence to suggest a loss of technical and scientific knowledge. My reference is to the loss of knowledge about man's relationship to man in organized social community and particularly about man's relationships to the institutions of the state.

There is an ontological difference between the object of knowledge in the two cases. The natural universe exists, independently of that which man creates. By contrast, the institutions of order may, themselves, be constructed or created by man himself. The difference in "that which we know about" categorically separates the physical from the social scientist. For the former, for the natural scientist, there is, at base, only *one reality*, a reality that may, of course, be viewed from differing perceptions, but which, nonetheless, is characterized by an exogeneity that is acknowledged to be present by all who claim license as scientists. This reality need not be static, and its formal laws need not imply reversibility, even in some ideal sense. But the exogeneity of the physical universe remains. In social science, by contrast, the institutional-organizational reality that can be observed empirically is only one among a large set of possible alternatives. Because the institutional-organizational reality is not, and cannot be, exogenous to the choices of those who are constrained by this reality, we have a source of cognitive differences that cannot arise in natural science. Not only can different scientists view reality from differing perspectives, but, also, different scientists impose differing attributes of exogeneity on the reality itself. The social scientist is almost necessarily a cognitive constructivist in a sense over and beyond the enterprise of the natural scientist. The social scientist would violate the canon of responsibility if he or she remains quiescent and refuses to consider alternatives to that structure that exists.

The social scientist faces a continuing choice among institutional-organizational arrangements, alternatives to those that exist, to be subjected to scientific and analytical scrutiny. The inclusive research program, which incorporates the extension of one central analytical model to existing and alternative structures cannot, almost by definition, be "scientific" in a strict sense analogous to the natural sciences. Man's actions are not limited to those observed in the existing institutional-organizational setting.

The loss of wisdom between the eighteenth century and modern times can be located in a general failure to recognize the limits of the feasible sets of institutional-organizational arrangements, limits that are imposed by those elements of stability in "human nature" that so excited the minds of the philosophers of the eighteenth century. Precisely because they were not bound to that which exists in observed patterns of social relationships, social reformers sought to move structures beyond the realm of the feasible, as dictated by characteristics of natural man. Neither the "new Soviet man" nor the ideally benevolent despot is a resident of any feasible structure of social interaction. The "fatal conceit" (Hayek's term) that was socialism has been revealed for all to see.

Developments in academic discourse since the 1960s offer grounds for hope. Public choice theory's extension of utility-maximizing models of behavior to politics has exposed the romantic illusion of governmental benevolence as well as the electoral fallacy noted above. Critical works by F. A. Hayek, John Passmore, Thomas Sowell, and others have exposed the terrible vulnerability of structures that are based on presumptions of human perfectibility. The time is ripe to examine institutional-organizational alternatives that embody an updated eighteenth-century wisdom or knowledge about the limits of human nature, while remaining cognizant of the dramatic advances in ordinary science. It is time to dream realistic dreams rather than fantasy.

David Gauthier's major effort to ground cooperative morality in a rational choice calculus may be a significant step. A resurgence of interest in and on the Hobbesian issue of controlling the sovereign may offer a productive complementary program. Both "moral constructivism" and "institutional constructivism" may be informed by an understanding and knowledge of the limits of human potential.

CHAPTER 20

The Potential and the Limits of Socially Organized Humankind

I shall commence this chapter with some notes of caution, especially as I examine the contribution that academic-scientific practitioners from my own discipline, political economy or economics, have made, are making, and can make to the solution of ongoing social problems of social interaction, both within and among nations. I shall follow this cautionary warning with a more positive discussion (sec. 2) that sets out a role for the social scientist and philosopher. And, acting within this role, I shall (sec. 3) proceed to outline specific steps that can be taken toward insuring that we can enter the twenty-first century with hope, without which there can be no creativity. In section 4, I shall then try to relate the discussion to the historical setting with some projections of alternative futures.

To an extent, we live, in Western countries, with a modern achievement described by the simultaneous presence of widespread individual liberty, economic prosperity, and both domestic and international order. This modern achievement is, however, fragile in the extreme, and its fragility must be recognized. It is vulnerable to destruction and erosion, both from deliberately fostered attacks and from nonattended historical evolutionary drift. This vulnerability increases as the philosophical underpinnings of the achievement come to be increasingly forgotten, neglected, and misunderstood. In summary (sec. 5), this chapter is a plea for simultaneous recognition both of the *potential* for deliberately organized change in institutional order and of the *limits* that history, human nature, science, technology, and resource capacity impose on efforts to move toward the betterment of humankind.

1. Science, Understanding, and Control

It is critically important that we emphasize both the potential benefits of scientific discovery and the potential damages that might be caused by misunderstanding and misapplication of that which might be alleged to be scientific

A modified version of this chapter was published as "The Potential and the Limits of Socially Organized Humankind," in *Nobel Laureates Forum in Japan, 1988* (Tokyo: Yomiuri Shimbun, 1989), 85–94.

findings. It is perhaps incumbent on me, as a beyond ordinary science scholar, to stress the negative here, at least in the sense of issuing a cautionary warning. Many modern scientists, secure in their own achievement of genuine discovery of new laws of the workings of the physical universe, and observing firsthand the extension of humankind's mastery as these laws are applied, exhibit a natural proclivity to attribute what seem to be flaws in the structure of social interaction to "scientific" backwardness, and to expect improvements from inappropriate extensions of science's domain into the realm of social control.

Let me be precise. I do not suggest that there is no "science" of economics, or of human behavior more generally considered. We have, indeed, made major progress in the development and testing of falsifiable hypotheses concerning how persons behave under specified sets of constraints, and these hypotheses enable us to make predictions concerning the effects of changes in constraints on human behavior patterns. The activity of those who derive, test, and extend these hypotheses in the human sciences is not different, in kind, from the activity of their counterparts in the ordinary hard sciences.

A categorical difference emerges, however, from what I can call the *public artifactuality* of the constraints that we observe as the domain for inquiry in the human sciences. There is no *natural* order within which we, as human animals, must confine our activities, one with another. We remain, necessarily, in a set of artificially constructed, or historically evolved, "zoos." There exists no natural habitat, no "jungle" to which we can return specimens for scientifically antiseptic observation. Neither the ethnologists nor the anthropologists are of much assistance.

Just as there is no natural order that confines our social interaction, there is no *ideal* order that is revealed to us transcendentally, revealed to us as if it embodies the truth of scientific discovery. The set of constraints that define the limits on human interaction in society must be chosen from among a subinfinity of alternatives. And there is no external standard—either embodied in "nature" or transcendentally revealed—that would single out one alternative as "objectively" best. If the image of scientific discovery and technological application by *experts* can be assumed to be characteristic of the perceived role of modern science, the closest analogy in the sociopolitical arena is the totalitarian regime where an elite separates itself from the others in the society and applies its scientific findings to control and direct human behavior toward a furtherance of the elite's own self-selected purposes. As modern history has surely told us emphatically, all such efforts aimed at scientific control of human beings tend to fail, even to accomplish that which the masters seek.

As soon as one steps outside the mind-set of the totalitarian model of social engineering, one cannot avoid recognition that the problems of social organization in nontotalitarian regimes are vastly more complex, and that the scope for any direct applications of the findings of science, in the standard sense, remains limited. If there is no expert-elite that can legitimately claim to know what, in some objective sense, is the ideal social arrangement, and, further, if individuals who participate in social interaction are acknowledged to be the ultimate judges, then, even with major advances in our understanding of human choice behavior, there remains the problem of securing *agreement* among those who participate in the complex network of human social interaction. There are important implications if the problem of social organization is analyzed as one of securing agreement on the self-imposed set of constraints within which we engage with one another, from war to trade to love. Agreement on the rules by which we shall live, one with another, domestically and internationally, is, of course, informed by scientific inquiry and understanding. But, at base, the problem is not one involving technological application of scientific discoveries, and it seems a mark of folly to treat it as such, that is, as an engineering problem.

2. The Role of the Social Philosopher

I have suggested that scientific inquiry into human behavior, as such, is not different, in kind, from the activity that describes the working of ordinary scientists. Discoveries are made, and these add incrementally to a stock of knowledge that, presumably, will prove helpful in some ultimate improvement in the human condition. For the physical scientist, as such, the task is done when a discovery is made. The results of inquiry are published, and there is left to the engineer the assignment of translating these results into valued practical applications.

Things seem quite different with the sciences of human behavior. In nontotalitarian societies, there is no proper role for the "social engineer," for the expert who takes the results of scientific inquiry and applies these results in the furtherance of the specific end objectives either desired by the engineer or dictated by a master elite. Who, then, is to make use of the findings that emerge from the sciences of human behavior? Who can assume the task of "constitutional design," the task of setting up or of modifying institutional rules so as to "improve" predicted patterns of results?

There is a subtle but vitally important distinction between the social philosopher, who may assume the role of leader in discussions of constitutional design, and the social engineer. By inference from the very word *engineer* there is implied some more or less direct translation of scientific findings into end objects. Such an inference becomes misleading as applied to the social philosopher, who may make himself or herself fully aware of the scientific laws, but who then takes on the role of persuading others in the body politic to reach agreement on principles of design that will further *commonly shared* objectives.

In the necessary dialogue on constitutional design, involving the continuing evaluation of the workings of existing rules of social order along with an evaluation of the working properties of potential alternative rules, two distinct elements must be separated. Persons may differ both in their *theories* of how institutions work and in their *interests*, against which the expected workings of institutions are measured.[1] The conceptual separation of these two potential sources of disagreement in matters of social organization is of basic importance, even if, in reality, a clear distinction between the theory and interest components is rarely present. The principal task of the social philosopher who assumes any leadership role in the discussion is to facilitate the initial distinction between these two elements, and to bring the fruits of scientific inquiry to bear on securing a reconciliation of conflicting theories. Beyond this basically scientific task, the philosopher can also assist in facilitating agreement among participants by reducing or dispelling bases for conflicts among identifiable interests.

This second assignment is less difficult than it may initially appear if emphasis is placed on the potential for agreement on the set of rules-constraints within which persons interact, and from which, indirectly, patterns of outcomes or end states will emerge, rather than on problems of securing agreement on desired end states, as such. The identification of individual or group interests becomes more difficult as attention comes to be centered on rules, constraints, constitutions, and general principles of order. When choosing among potential alternative rules of the "social game" they are to play, individuals must, to an extent, choose from behind a veil of ignorance[2] or uncertainty.[3] That is to say, individuals must choose without being able to predict perfectly how they will be specifically affected by the expected workings of these rules. The less transparent the veil from behind which choices are made, the more the precepts for rationality dictate the use of generalizable criteria, tending thereby to reduce or eliminate conflicts based on interest.

I do not want to suggest that agreement or consensus on the set of rules within which we interact to generate complex patterns of outcomes (allocations, distributions, scales of value, growth rates, etc.) will somehow emerge spontaneously as if by some invisible hand. The social philosopher must, indeed, engage actively in the whole dialogue, analysis, and discussion. And, to the extent that his or her scientific competence and integrity are acknowl-

---

1. See chap. 5.
2. See John Rawls, *A Theory of Justice* (Cambridge: Harvard University Press, 1971).
3. See James M. Buchanan and Gordon Tullock, *The Calculus of Consent* (Ann Arbor: University of Michigan Press, 1962).

edged, others may defer to his or her authority in the array of the alternatives of structural change.[4] But the social philosopher cannot assume the arrogance of the social engineer, and, ultimately, those changes in the rules that he or she proposes must be presented as hypotheses, the test for which is the generation of agreement among those who are to act within the chosen structure.[5]

3. Liberty, Prosperity, Peace—And Justice

All of the discussion to this point is preliminary to any suggestion or proposal on my part as to specific steps that might be taken, by socially organized groups, from local communities to nation-states to international organizations, with a purpose of insuring a "better" twenty-first century. The precautions were necessary. It would have been arrogant folly to parade my own privately derived preferences for social change under some guise of scientific validity. At best, the suggestions that I advance must be treated as hypotheses about the working properties of certain rules as well as about what persons may consider preferable, hypotheses to be tested in the continuing dialogue in which all persons participate under self-imposed limits of reciprocity and mutuality of respect. My suggestions emerge out of my own generalized knowledge of the findings of the human sciences and out of my application of these findings in the context of comparative institutional analysis.

I suggest that there does exist general agreement on some of the ultimate objectives to be sought in socially organized communities. As individuals, we place a value on liberty, on the freedom to make choices for ourselves over a broadly defined private space. As individuals, we also place a value on the attainability of a sufficiently high level of primary goods and services without undue hardship and suffering. And finally, as individuals, we place a value on the existence and maintenance of peace or order, both within local communities as among persons and groups, and between separately organized communities, including nation-states. Individual liberty, prosperity, peace—these are universally acclaimed values. But can these values be secured in the complex interaction processes that describe modern sociopolitical arrangements?

The central problem is, of course, that liberty, prosperity, and peace are sensed as *individualized* values, independently of any generalization to a social context. As an individual, I value *my own* liberty, *my own* economic well-being, *my own* peace, and it is only when I am forced to acknowledge that these values cannot differentially or discriminatorily be made available to

---

4 See chap. 12.

5. See James M. Buchanan, "Postive Economics, Welfare Economics, and Political Economy," *Journal of Law and Economics* 2 (October 1959): 124–38.

me, individually, that I shift my attention to the generalization of these values to all persons involved with me in the institutions of social interaction.

How can social interaction be organized to allow all persons, simultaneously, to enjoy the values of liberty, prosperity, and peace? What are the limits that political equality, economic reciprocity, and mutuality of respect impose on the attainment of any or all of these values?

Historical experience offers empirical evidence demonstrating the necessary complementarity between individual liberty and economic prosperity. Experiments in which liberties have been suppressed under centralized political direction allegedly aimed at expanding economic product, whether enjoyed by the exploited or the exploiters, are now acknowledged to have failed, universally so. Institutional reform now taking place, on what is literally a worldwide scale, is based on the developing recognition of this complementarity between individual liberty and economic prosperity.

There is an analogous complementarity between peace on the one hand and both prosperity and liberty on the other. Resources are wasted in negative-sum conflicts among persons, groups, and nation-states, and individuals find themselves deprived of liberties when their energies are coercively mobilized in the furtherance of communitarian objectives in social conflicts.

The great scientific discovery of the eighteenth century, out of which political economy (economics) emerged as an independent academic discipline, embodies the recognition that the complementary values of liberty, prosperity, and peace can be attained. It is not surprising that my eighteenth- and early nineteenth-century counterparts were so enthusiastic in their advocacy of market organization. So long as the state provides and maintains the appropriate structural constraints (the "laws and institutions," the rules of the game), individuals, as economic actors, can be left alone to pursue their own privately determined purposes, and in so doing enjoy the values of liberty, prosperity, and peace in reciprocal and mutual respect, one for another. The role of the state is critically important in maintaining and enforcing the rules that define the limits of the economic game, but the role is also minimal in that there is no place for detailed politicized intervention with the liberties of persons and groups to enter into voluntary exchanges. Policy reforms are to be concentrated exclusively on the rules, the structural framework, the constitution broadly defined.

This ideal of the great classical economists was never fully realized. There was a failure to understand the separation between political attention to structure, attention that is both necessary and appropriate, and political intervention into the socioeconomic game itself. As a result, states rarely, if ever, offered a satisfactorily supportive structure for the economy, most notably as regards the monetary unit. And, as we know all too well, states failed everywhere to limit political manipulation to structure alone.

Why did the vision of classical political economy fail to capture the imagination of more than a few generations of intellectual leaders? Why did social philosophers from the middle of the nineteenth century forward lose interest in the classical teachings? Why did the socialist century emerge, and with the active support of social philosophers?

These questions admit of relatively easy answers once we recognize that my earlier listing of the universally desired objectives or values of liberty, prosperity, and peace is not complete. The listing omits *justice* which is also a value, in both Aristotelian senses, *commutative* justice, an attribute of a system of rules, and *distributive* justice, an attribute of patterns of distributive outcomes that are generated in an economy. The vision of classical political economists of a regime that meets the norm of equal liberty implies nothing directly about access to primary goods, which depends upon the distribution of endowments and talents among participants.

The distributional experiments of the socialist century, many residues of which remain in the 1990s, long after the socialist god has been declared dead, were and are charged with an elevated moral purpose, that of furthering distributional norms as measured by enhanced equality. But these experiments have been generally characterized by an apparent incongruity between declared purpose and observed results, an incongruity that can and must be subjected to the scrutiny of scientific analysis. The failures of the explicitly totalitarian experiments in achieving distributive justice are now widely acknowledged. What is not yet generally realized are the threats that are inherent in the ordinary mechanisms of majoritarian democratic politics. The traditional perception of democratic politics has been characterized by an implicit acceptance of the post-Hegelian romantic image or model of politics and the state, based on the surprisingly unchallenged presumption that persons who assume roles as political agents shed off all individualized interests and behave both benevolently and omnisciently in their assigned public duties.

The incongruity between the justice-driven moral purpose and the realities of interest-motivated constituents and agents has produced results that surely could have been predicted with more careful scientific scrutiny. When the political dynamics that describe modern democracy come into force, it is not surprising that efforts to redress economic results toward enhanced distributional equality should have become the cover for interest-driven efforts to gain distributional advantage. Under the aegis of welfare state redistributionism, the interest-driven politics of modern democracy has given us the "churning state"[6] which does, indeed, involve redistribution, but which is, to a large extent, unrelated to "legitimate" welfare state objectives, and which has more or less openly been transformed into a negative-sum game among

---

6. Anthony de Jasay, *The State* (Oxford: Blackwell, 1985).

competing interest groups. Whether or not the redistributive activity of the modern state, constrained only within majoritarian electoral limits, "improves" at all upon the nondisturbed patterns that might be generated by the market remains an open issue, one that cries out for both analytical and empirical research.[7] We do know that the redistributional game that we observe in the churning state motivates a very substantial wastage of valued production due to the investment in rent seeking by competing groups seeking to curry political favor. And this waste appears to be growing exponentially as we enter the last decade of the twentieth century, at least in my own country.

I do not suggest quiescence before the very real issues of distributive justice, and I surely do not claim ethical legitimacy for the distributional patterns that the historically evolved distribution of premarket endowments along with the workings of the market itself might generate. I should, nonetheless, argue that, pragmatically considered, these patterns may well be preferred, *on agreed upon criteria of equality*, to those that are being generated in the rent-seeking politics of the churning state, as observed. But such politics is not the only institutional route toward the attainment of distributional norms. Once again, it becomes necessary to hold fast to the distinction between potential reform in the structure of an economic order and activity that is allowed to take place within that structure. There are prospects for building redistributional elements into constitutional regimes, elements that can be effectively insulated from the machinations of interest group politics.

The demands of justice require, first of all, constitutional articulation and implementation of the rule of law, which itself embodies the principle of equality before the law. This basic precept must be extended to insure that all "play by the same rules," that differentiation or discrimination in political treatment is strictly out of bounds. Second, the demands of justice require that, upon entry into the "game" itself, players face opportunities that are equalized to the extent institutionally feasible. I have often suggested that this principle implies equal access to, and state financing of, education at all levels. Beyond these constitutionally implemented steps, some rectification in the intergenerational transmission of asset accumulation may be dictated, again to be secured only via constitutional procedures rather than through ordinary politics.

If we use the analytical and empirical results of the social sciences to evaluate the prospects of politics realistically rather than romantically, we have good reasons to think that, beyond these limits of constitutional justice, the siren songs of the churning state masquerading under welfare state arguments should be resisted. Submission to the false prophets of welfare state

7. See Geoffrey Brennan and James M. Buchanan, *The Reason of Rules—Constitutional Political Economy* (Cambridge: Cambridge University Press, 1985).

expansion promises only the further sacrifice of liberty, prosperity, and, possibly, domestic peace, and *without* substantial gains, if any at all, toward the agreed upon norms of justice.

In a single chapter, I cannot describe in detail the political economy that would be both institutionally feasible and normatively preferred by citizens at the turn of the next century. I have suggested that, building on the insights of the great classical economists of the eighteenth century, as appropriately modernized for the technology, resources, human capacities, and scientific advances that describe the late twentieth century, we can secure a social-economic-political order that would allow individual liberty, economic prosperity, peace, and justice to be achieved. This order is possible only if political activity is largely confined to structural reform and if politicized intrusions into the privately chosen lives of persons are severely limited by effective constitutional prohibitions.

This emphasis on the limits to collective activity should not, of course, be taken to imply that individuals, as members of organized political units, may not share common objectives that can be best secured through collectively organized effort. There is a legitimate range of action for the "productive state"[8] but this action must remain within the limits defined by the evaluations of individuals. In the appropriately derived classically liberal conception, there is no place for, or meaning to, such terms as *national purpose*, *social interest*, or *social welfare*, unless, of course, we define these terms by genuine agreement among interacting persons.

My suggestions apply directly to the internal structure of a national economy, but the same principles lend themselves to ready extension to the increasingly interdependent international community of states. Interest-driven politicizations of voluntary exchanges between citizens and associations of separate states reduces the economic well being and the liberty of all members of the international nexus. And constitutional sanctions against politicized interferences should extend equally in application to both domestic and international markets.

4. After Socialism, What?

I have referred earlier to the end of the socialist century, and to the death of the socialist god. These statements are based on my reading of the history of this century. The romantic faith in the state and in politics that emerged and blossomed in the late nineteenth century and the twentieth century no longer exists, and, once lost, such faith does not seem likely to reappear. In the

---

8. James M. Buchanan, *The Limits of Liberty: Between Anarchy and Leviathan* (Chicago: University of Chicago Press, 1975).

preceding section, I tried to outline the features of the "good society" that could emerge in our post-Hegelian epoch. However, as I stated before, this normative structure is advanced only as a set of hypotheses, the test for which becomes generalized agreement on the changes that are therein implied.

There are two complementary elements in the argument, or two sides of the coin, both of which are necessary for consensus to emerge. There must first be some convergence of opinion on the relative inefficacy of politics (including the bureaucracy) as it is observed to work. The romantic blinders must come off; persons must learn to view ordinary politics as it is, not as it might be if all actors were saints. Public choice, the new subdiscipline with which I have been associated, has done much to dispel the romance here, although direct observation of program failures of the agencies of the over-reaching modern state has perhaps been of much greater significance than any scientific demonstration.

But this shedding off of the romantic image is not sufficient unto itself. It must be accompanied by an understanding and appreciation of what Adam Smith called the simple system of natural liberty, by a generalized willingness to leave things alone, to let the economy work in its own way, and outside of politicized interference. I am by no means convinced that this second element for constructing the "good society" is present. We seem, instead, to be left with a generalized public skepticism about the efficacy of ordinary politics to accomplish much of anything, but, at the same time, we seem publicly unwilling to allow the forces of voluntary agreement and association to work themselves out. We have, indeed, lost faith in the socialist god, but we are a long way from regaining any faith in the laissez-faire principle of the classical economists.

The combination of attitudes on the part of the citizenry, at least in my own country, lends itself to exploitation by those interest groups that have their own ready-made agenda for state action designed to yield these groups differentially high rents or profits. Building on the public's unwillingness to act on principle in support of market solutions to apparent problems, whether real or imagined, these interest groups secure arbitrary restrictions on voluntary exchanges and, in the process, secure rents for their members while reducing both the liberties and the economic well being of other members of the economic nexus, both domestically and internationally.

A protectionist-mercantilist regime described by particularized and quite arbitrary politicized interventions into the workings of markets, both domestic and international, seems to represent a much greater threat to the achievement of the social order outlined above than any regime embodying socialist inspired direction, planning, and control. In two centuries, we have apparently come full circle. The selfsame institutional barriers that Adam Smith sought to demolish are everywhere resurging, as if from the depths of history. And the same arguments are heard in the land, both in support and in opposition. It must seem, therefore, to those of you outside economics that any scientific impact of the discipline matters little, if at all, on how we order our affairs, how we construct the rules within which we carry on our lives, one with another, in social interaction.

That this experience could repeat itself demonstrates the *public artifactuality* of the structure of social interaction, the feature that I noted to be that which distinguished the human and the nonhuman sciences. And, as this experience indicates, this feature has implications for the didactic role of the scientist. For the physicist, there is no requirement to repeat the arguments that long ago convinced his or her peers concerning the validity of a particular theorem. For the political economist, the arguments that Adam Smith once advanced were compelling, but we have allowed the artifactual structure to be shifted. Our task begins anew.

Adam Smith occupies the place that he does among our intellectual heroes because he was the first to demonstrate that politicized interferences with voluntary market exchanges reduce both economic well being and individual liberties. But Smith himself remained naïve in that he felt that, once the generalized harm of protectionist-mercantilist measures came to be understood, governments would act, as if on principle, to eliminate all such restrictions. We now know that governments, as they operate, will do no such thing. They will act only in response to constituency interests, a response that is, in itself, desirable. But in the dynamics induced by the particular constraints that exist, the interplay of interests insures that the patterns of protectionist restriction will emerge.

There will be no escape from the protectionist-mercantilist regime that now threatens to be characteristic of the approaching turn of the century so long as we allow the ordinary politics of majoritarian democracy to operate in the absence of adequate constitutional constraints. We have learned to understand interest-group politics. What is required is that we look to *principles* that can be incorporated in constitutional structure, principles that dictate the imposition of constraints that will prevent the intrusions of ordinary politics into market exchange. Acceptance of the arguments for, and active support for, the constitutional-structural reforms implementing these principles may, but need not, require some conversion to a new morality of public interest, as such. Individuals and representatives of specialized producer groups can be led to support generalized constitutional constraints *in their own interest*. So long as a person, as a specialized producer, knows that a constitutional prohibition against protection for his or her own industry will also be extended to all industries, he or she will recognize that his or her own interests will be served, not harmed, by such constraints. The protectionist-mercantilist thrust is necessarily fueled by the expectations that *some* interest groups can secure discriminatory advantage at the expense of others. If this expectation is re-moved, the protectionist-mercantilist regime must collapse.

The twenty-first century need not be ushered in by a cacophony of voices shouting for agricultural subsidies, textile tariffs, voluntary agreement on automobile imports, taxicab licensing, rent control laws, minimum wage regulations, retaliatory antidumping measures, and the myriad other all-too-familiar modern variants of the mercantilist economic order. Depoliticized economic order is within the realm of the politically-constitutionally possible, whether accomplished within one nation-state or within and among the whole community of nation-states.

5. The Potential and the Limits

In concluding this chapter, I return to its somewhat grandiose title, "The Potential and the Limits of Socially Organized Humankind." And let us clear the intellectual air by an early acknowledgement that without the benefits of social-legal-political organization, very few of us could be here today. We could not exist; the physical world would support only a tiny fraction of its population if we were forced to live in the almost unimaginable state of Hobbesian anarchy, or even under the tribal organization that described most of human history. We live now by the graces of those persons and forces that designed, constructed, maintained, and secured the institutions of order within which we live, work, and play.

A threshold was crossed in the eighteenth century when we learned how the rule of law, stability of private property, and the withdrawal of political interference with private choices could unleash the entrepreneurial energies that are latent within each of us. The modern age was born. Humankind seemed near to the realization of its socially organized potentiality only to have this future threatened, and in part forestalled, by the emergence of the socialist vision, a vision that has now been shown to be grounded in romance rather than scientific understanding. The central flaw in the socialist vision is its failure to recognize the *limits* of socialized organization. There can be no escape from the feasibility space that is defined by natural and human con-straints. And if these constraints are ignored in well-intentioned but mis-guided efforts to realize more than we can socially achieve, irrevocable harm may be imposed on all persons in the international social nexus.

Recognizing the limits in order to avoid such harm is as important as recognizing the potential that may be achieved within those limits. The orga-nized polities of the nation-states, and the association of these states, one with another, must be kept within the boundaries of the potential and the possible. As we enter soon into the twenty-first century, the prevention of politicized overreaching is perhaps our most obvious priority. The state-as-Leviathan described much of this century; we shall destroy all of our dreams if this "monster's" growth is not limited and its productive potential marshaled to guarantee the framework of order within which individuals can, indeed, pursue that which their own potential make them capable of realizing.

Author Index

Subject Index